# The Political Economy of the SARS Epidemic

W0235001

This book discusses the political economy of the SARS epidemic and its impact on human resources in East Asia, as it occurred in 2003. The epidemic spread from the People's Republic of China, to Hong Kong, Singapore and Taiwan, amongst other countries in East Asia and as far away as North America, particularly Canada, the EU and elsewhere. This book looks first at earlier precedents, such as Black Death and the way in which the potential threats of the recent epidemic were diffused across the world in 'instant news' reports; examining why it was dubbed the first 'global epidemic' due to its media coverage and how far the threat started a psychological 'tsunami' of fear and panic. Next, it examines the anticipated economic consequences arising from this phenomenon and how it affected the business of everyday life, market behaviour and human resources in the cases of the PRC, Hong Kong, Singapore and Taiwan. It concludes with a discussion of the issues involved and lessons to be learnt, and draws conclusions both for theory and practice vis-à-vis future pandemics that may threaten the global economy in the coming decade and the public policy issues involved.

**Grace O. M. Lee** is Associate Professor, Department of Public and Social Administration, City University of Hong Kong. Her research interests focus on labour markets, employment policy and public management.

**Malcolm Warner** is Professor and Fellow Emeritus, Wolfson College and Judge Business School, University of Cambridge, UK. His current research interests include Asian management, human resource management and international business.

# Routledge Studies in the Growth Economies of Asia

# The Political Economy of the SARS Epidemic

The impact on human resources in East Asia

**Grace O. M. Lee and Malcolm Warner**

Routledge
Taylor & Francis Group

LONDON AND NEW YORK

First published 2008
by Routledge
2 Park Square, Milton Park, Abingdon, Oxon OX14 4RN

Simultaneously published in the USA and Canada
by Routledge
711 Third Avenue, New York, NY 10017

*Routledge is an imprint of the Taylor & Francis Group,
an informa business*
First issued in paperback 2012

© 2008 Grace O. M. Lee and Malcolm Warner

Typeset in Times New Roman by
Newgen Imaging Systems (P) Ltd, Chennai, India

*British Library Cataloguing in Publication Data*
A catalogue record for this book is available
from the British Library

*Library of Congress Cataloging in Publication Data*
   The political economy of the SARS epidemic : the impact on
human resources in East Asia / Grace O.M. Lee and Malcolm
Warner.
      p. cm. – (Routledge studies in the growth economies of Asia)
   Includes cases studies of Hong Kong, The People's Republic of
China, Singapore, and Taiwan.
   Includes bibliographical references and index.
   1. SARS (Disease) – Economic aspects – East Asia. 2. Human
services – East Asia. 3. East Asia–Economic conditions – 21st
century. 4. East Asia – Social policy. 5. Globalization – Economic
aspects – East Asia. I. Warner, Malcolm. II. Title.
   RA644.S17L44 2007
   362.196'20095–dc22                                    2007012394

ISBN13: 978–0–415–39498–7 (hbk)
ISBN13: 978–0–415–54192–3 (pbk)
ISBN13: 978–0–203–93481–4 (ebk)

This book is dedicated to all those who died from SARS may their souls 'Rest In Peace'

# Contents

# Figures

# Tables

# Preface

In this interdisciplinary monograph, we attempt to survey the impact of the SARS epidemic of 2003 on East Asia.

To start, we set out the broad background of the SARS phenomenon; then more broadly, the links between epidemics, catastrophes and history; next, the epidemic and its timeline; and after, the impact on economies, labour markets and human resources in East Asia. We follow this with a detailed set of 'national' case-studies, in Hong Kong, PRC, Singapore and Taiwan. Last, we set out a discussion section looking at 'lessons to be learnt' followed by our conclusions. The emphasis throughout will be on the 'people' implications of SARS in terms of human resources and their management, taking a broad-brush 'political economy' interpretive approach. The study is based on empirical field-work in East Asia around the time of the epidemic and particularly in its aftermath. We built up a data-base of sources and statistics for the quantitative perspective. The evidence is also based on extensive interviewing and in-depth qualitative research.

We would like to thank the numerous faculty colleagues and collaborators in Cambridge and Hong Kong for their advice and assistance, as well as the regulatory authorities in Hong Kong, the PRC, Singapore and Taiwan. Without the help of numerous governmental departments, businesses and academic institutions, this study would not have been possible. A word of gratitude is also extended to our numerous interviewees, over two hundred in number, who were gracious enough to see us and were so helpful in their interaction with us. Without their cooperation, our research would have been impossible to carry out.

Our respective universities, as well as faculties and departments, have been most positive in their support and for this we are most grateful. We must mention here the Judge Business School, University of Cambridge and the Department of Public and Social Administration, City University of Hong Kong. The President and Fellows of Wolfson College, Cambridge must also be thanked. We also acknowledge the numerous learned institutions that have invited us to present papers on this research topic over the last few years, including most recently the International Industrial

Relations Association. Professor Peter Nolan, economist and sinologist and close colleague at the Judge Business School, University of Cambridge, as usual, projected his enthusiasm and encouragement. In addition, the eminent virologist Professor John S. Oxford, Queen Mary's Medical School, University of London, was very forthcoming with his advice on epidemics in general and Influenza in particular. Special thanks also to Dr Daniel Yan for his help with figures and graphics.

We are particularly indebted to our Editor at Routledge, Peter Sowden, and his associates who have made the production of this book possible.

*Grace O. M. Lee, City University of Hong Kong*
*Malcolm Warner, University of Cambridge*
*December 2006*

# Acknowledgements

Permissions have been generously given by *Asia Pacific Business Review*, *International Journal of Human Resource Management* and *Issues and Studies* to cite the following articles:

Grace O. M. Lee and Malcolm Warner (2007) 'Human resources, labour-markets and unemployment: the impact of the SARS epidemic on the service sector in Singapore', *Asia Pacific Business Review*, 12: 4, 507–27.

Grace O. M. Lee and Malcolm Warner (2005) 'Epidemics, labour-markets and unemployment: the impact of SARS on human resources management in the Hong Kong service sector', *International Journal of Human Resource Management*, 16: 5, May, 752–71.

Grace O. M. Lee and Malcolm Warner (2006) 'The impact of SARS on China's economy, labour market and level of employment', *International Journal of Human Resource Management,* 17: 5, 860–80.

Grace O. M. Lee and Malcolm Warner (2005) 'The impact of the SARS epidemic in Taiwan: implications for human resources, labour markets and unemployment in the service sector', *Issues and Studies*, 41: 3, September, 81–111.

# Abbreviations

| | |
|---|---|
| ADB | Asian Development Bank |
| AIDS | Acquired Immunodeficiency Syndrome |
| ASEAN | Association of Southeast Asian Nations |
| CA | Air China |
| CDC | Centers for Disease Control and Prevention |
| CEO | Chief Executive Officer |
| CITS | China International Travel Service |
| CYTS | China Youth Travel Services |
| DRC | Development Research Centre |
| FAO | Food and Agriculture Organization |
| FDI | Foreign direct investment |
| GDP | Gross domestic product |
| GITS | *Guangdong* International Travel Services |
| HCW | Health-care workers |
| HDB | Housing Development Board |
| HIV | Human immunodeficiency virus |
| HKIHRM | Hong Kong Institute of Human Resource Management |
| HKSAR | Hong Kong Special Administrative Region |
| HR | Human resources |
| HRM | Human resource management |
| IATA | International Air Transport Association |
| IHR | International health regulations |
| ILO | International Labour Organization |
| IMF | International Monetary Fund |
| IT | Information Technology |
| *JAMA* | *Journal of the American Medical Association* |
| MOM | Ministry of Manpower |
| NBS | National Bureau of Statistics |
| NPC | National People's Congress |
| NTUC | National Trades Union Congress |
| OIE | Organisation for Animal Health |
| PLA | People's Liberation Army |
| PRC | People's Republic of China |

| PWH | Prince of Wales Hospital |
| SAR | Special Administrative Region |
| SARS | Severe Acute Respiratory Syndrome |
| SARS-CoV | SARS-associated Coronavirus |
| SDRC | State Development and Reform Commission |
| SIA | Singapore Airlines |
| SME | Small and medium-sized enterprises |
| SNEF | Singapore National Employers' Federation |
| SOE | State owned enterprise |
| STAC | Shanghai Tourism Administrative Commission |
| TB | Tuberculosis |
| TTSH | Tan Tock Seng Hospital |
| UN | United Nations |
| UNESCO | United Nations Educational, Scientific and Cultural Organization |
| US | United States |
| USA | United States of America |
| WDA | Workforce Development Agency |
| WHO | World Health Organization |
| WTO | World Trade Organization |
| WTTC | World Travel and Tourism Council |

# Part I

# Background

The word 'plague' had just been spoken for the first time

Albert Camus ([1947]2002: 30)

# 1 Introduction

## 1.1 Introduction

Since ancient times, epidemics have repeatedly blighted the course of world history, necessarily involving widespread economic distress and always leaving a wake of human misery in their trail (see, for example, Cipolla, 1976).

The most common form of this form of catastrophe has been 'the Plague', referred to several times in the Bible; it was called *shechin* in classical Hebrew (see Hoenig, 1985 for the earliest known account of such diseases). In the Old as well as the New Testament, plagues appear, whether in the Book of Exodus, or the Book of Revelation. In *Exodus* [8:1] the threat of plague is used as a weapon of persuasion against the ancient Egyptians: 'And the Lord spake unto Moses, Go unto Pharaoh, and say unto him, Thus saith the Lord, Let my people go, that they may serve me.' As the Pharaoh desists, the 'Ten Plagues' ensue – with the ultimate desired effect.

Later, in the Book of Revelation, (6:1–8) the 'First Horseman of the Apocalypse' is called 'Plague', the other three being 'War', 'Famine' and 'Death'. The four named horsemen are highly symbolic descriptions of different events that will take place in the 'end-times' but the only one the Bible names is 'Death'; the others derive from the Bible's descriptions. We also find them today featured in 'modern myth-time' in the older movie version of 'The Four Horsemen of the Apocalypse' in 1921 and the more recent one, *The Matrix* in 1999.

The Plague was also noted in ancient Greek literary works, for example, by Homer in *The Iliad* and later by Thucydides in his *History of the Peloponnesian War*. This term in classical Greek can refer to any kind of illness; in Latin, the terms used are *plaga* and *pestis*. In antiquity, the two most devastating examples were the Athenian plague of 430 BC and the Justinianic plague of 542 AD. Plagues have also recurrently afflicted Imperial China for centuries, with fatalities running into millions (Benedict, 1988, 1993, 1996a,b).

The 'Black Death' that engulfed Europe from the fourteenth century onwards, was one of best-known examples closer to home, devastating both societies and economies, which Karl Marx interestingly drew attention to in *Das Kapital* (Marx, [1867]1977: Ch. XXV). Hunger and famine stalked the land and went hand in hand with the resultant decline in trade in the late medieval period and the Renaissance in the West (Herlihy and Cohn, 1997;

Cohn, 2002). Rising mortality rates negatively affected both the demand for, and supply of, goods, services and the labour that went into them, then as now. 'The Great Plague' of 1665 killed one in five inhabitants of London: 'Great fears of the sickness here in the City' wrote the chronicler, Samuel Pepys, in his *Diary,* written from 1660 to 1669, this being his entry for 30 May 1665 (see Pepys, [1660–1669]1937: 486). During the Great Plague, John Milton was forced to retire to Chalfont St Giles (his home), where he was able to finish his epic poem *Paradise Lost.* The English classical economist Thomas Malthus ([1798]1999) had studied the major impact of plagues on populations and economies, as checks on demographic growth (Pressman, 1999: 29ff.). 'Crises' such as plagues had led to peaks of mortality that linked negative population changes and labour supply with key economic variables (Floud and McCloskey, 1994: 60). However, Malthusian gloom was challenged on a number of counts; some economists saw technology as the 'engine of growth' in both agriculture and industry (Cipolla, 1976: 136). The most recent severe health catastrophe of the last century was the global influenza epidemic that spread after the First World War; the so-called Spanish Flu allegedly killed more people than all those who died in armed combat (see Beveridge, 1977). It had a global reach and it wreaked a devastating path across all continents, not least in Asia. Such epidemics – as subspecies of 'catastrophes' in general – represent distinct *exogenous,* as well as *endogenous,* 'shocks' that have had far-reaching impacts on economic activity, as we shall see spelled out in the next chapter.

Not long into the millennium, in 2003, a new threat to humankind appeared in East Asia and was feared by some observers to be another replay of the 1918–1919 'flu' disaster, namely what became known as the Severe Acute Respiratory Syndrome (SARS) epidemic of recent time. Although to date this tragic episode seemed to have ended in July 2003, any complacency was to be misplaced, as it soon killed 916 people worldwide (see Figure 1.1 for the key countries involved), mainly in the People's Republic of China (PRC) and the Hong Kong Special Administrative Region (HKSAR), and infected 8,422 others (World Health Organization, 2003a) as can be seen in Table 1.1.[1] There have been few cases of the virus reported since but the outbreak left a legacy of fear in the countries that had been directly affected. Interest in SARS has now been displaced by the new threats of what is popularly known as 'Avian Flu', new and deadly varieties of which have hit the headlines in the last two years, of which more will be discussed later.

Let us now turn to what we hope to cover in this monograph. We intend to explore the 'political economy' of the SARS epidemic of 2003 in Asia, looking at its broadest dimensions, as policy and economy were inextricably entwined. Within this overall approach, we shall specifically deal with its impact on human resources, labour markets and unemployment.

Part I of this book first discusses the background of the SARS epidemic in terms of its historical, epidemiological, macro- as well as microeconomic

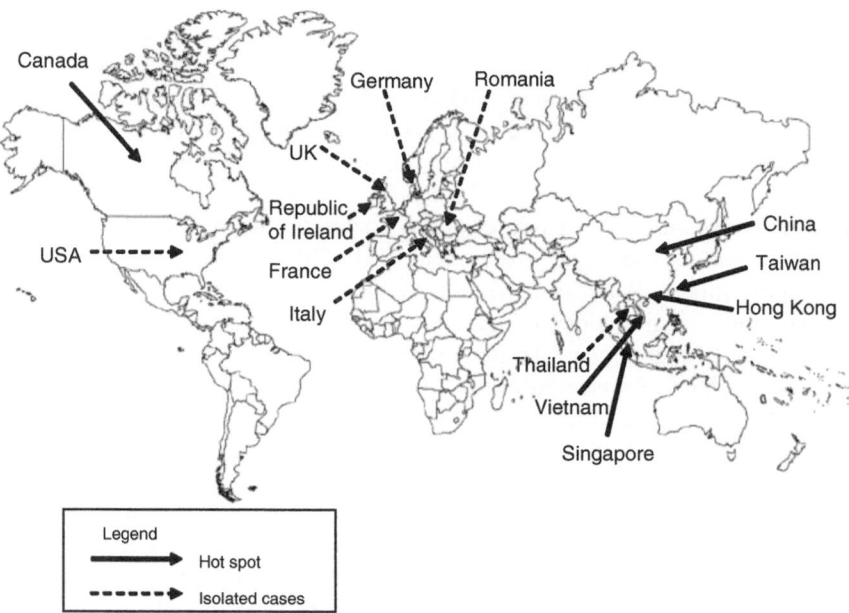

Canada

Germany  Romania

UK

Republic
of Ireland

USA

France

Italy

China

Taiwan

Hong Kong

Thailand

Vietnam

Singapore

Legend

━━━━▶  Hot spot

- - - - -▶  Isolated cases

*Figure 1.1* The spread of SARS.

Source: Adapted from BBC News; <http://bbc.co.uk/1/shared/spl/hi/pop_ups/03/health_
spread_of_severe_acute_respiratory_syndrome/html/1.stm - 8k->

aspects and so on. Within it, Chapter 1 offers an overview, followed by
Chapter 2 which sketches out an analytic framework of catastrophes,
epidemics and political economy. The onset and spread of the SARS epidemic
across the region will be spelled out in greater detail in Chapter 3. The
wider economic impact of SARS, the consequence for labour markets
and for human resources (HR) and human resource management (HRM)
across Asia, will be set out in Chapter 4.

Part II considers the specific consequences in a number of key locations
across Asia; for Hong Kong in Chapter 5; Mainland China in Chapter 6;
Singapore in Chapter 7; and Taiwan in Chapter 8; followed by Part III, with
Chapter 9 which looks at the broader implications, and Chapter 10 setting
out our conclusions.

This specific chapter begins with an overview of the onset of the 2003
epidemic and then moves on to briefly discuss – in broad-brush strokes –
the short-term economic impact of SARS on the Asian economies, labour
markets and the particularly vulnerable service sector vis-à-vis its human
resources. As we shall shortly see, epidemics, mortality and economics are
now perhaps integrally linked, as mass air travel has become a potentially
worldwide transmission-belt in the contemporary, globalized world.

## 1.2   Origin of SARS

The first fatal cases of 'atypical pneumonia', as it was initially called, probably occurred in Foshan, Guangdong Province in southern China, just next to Hong Kong, in mid-November 2002. A middle-aged village-committee official was sent to hospital with a suspected case of this apparently atypical pneumonia (Abraham, 2004); no one at the time had any notion that it would prove to be a major landmark in modern Asian history. Many hundreds of suspected cases were soon reported on the mainland, in Beijing and other major cities. The government of the PRC at first denied the news (see Kleinman and Watson, 2006), but eventually was shamed into adopting a more robust, nationwide and transparent public health policy.[2]

The term SARS appears to have been used for a patient in Hanoi who was visiting Vietnam (see Adams, 2003), then became ill on 26 February 2003, and was evacuated to Hong Kong where he died on 12 March. This first case in Hanoi, had stayed at a hotel in Kowloon, Hong Kong, at the same time as a 65-year-old who had himself been treating pneumonia cases in southern China. This doctor from Guangdong Province had stayed at the Metropole Hotel and was admitted to hospital on 22 February. He died from 'respiratory failure' soon afterwards (Tomlinson and Cockram, 2003). He was the first known case of SARS in Hong Kong, as we shall see in greater detail later in Chapter 3, and appears to have been the source of infection for most, if not all, cases in Hong Kong, as well as the cohorts in Canada, Vietnam, Singapore, United States, Ireland and subsequently Germany and Thailand and possibly elsewhere. The second major epicentre in Hong Kong, accounting for over 300 cases, was an apartment complex called 'Amoy Gardens' (see Chapter 5 for further details). Hong Kong was inevitably thrown into panic by the SARS outbreak as more and more mortalities were reported. Many medical staff were infected and a number of others died. Isolation of suspected cases became *de rigueur*.

The cosmopolitan setting of the infectivity presaged the global spread of the disease through international air travel (Kleinman and Watson, 2006: 12). Subsequently, in the first few months of 2003, SARS was indeed to spread across Asia (Abraham, 2004) and beyond; the World Health Organization (WHO) in its turn announced a travel alert advisory for Hong Kong and pointed East in early Spring. Business travellers and tourists in general cancelled their trips accordingly; if planes flew at all, they had a mere handful of passengers.

## 1.3   Economic impact of SARS

Whilst SARS did pose significant medical risks for local populations, it presaged far greater economic implications for the regional and perhaps ultimately, it was feared, for the global economy, because of the threat of a potentially devastating, worldwide epidemic, a prospect the global media were not slow to reinforce. Given the widespread anxiety generated by the events of '9/11', there was fertile ground for chronic anxiety to take root.

However, given its ultimately relatively low morbidity and mortality, we must ask the question – why had the economic impact of SARS appeared to be so potentially devastating? In the circumstances neither a lay observer nor a professional economist would *a priori* have predicted such a catastrophe in the making. There had been several incidences of new flu viruses in Hong Kong in recent years, as well as infections affecting chickens and the like, that had ultimately been contained (Huque and Lee, 2000). Much of the economic impact, it seemed, stemmed from the high degree of uncertainty and fear generated by SARS, more on which will be outlined in later chapters. The Asian Financial Crisis of 1997 was fresh in public memory; this set of events had been traumatic for economies from Bangkok to Jakarta, with the PRC allegedly less affected, although some (see Rawski, 2006) remain sceptical about this. Regional economies were more or less beginning to recover from this last travail however, as well as from the more recent global impact of 'Twin Towers' destruction. It is no exaggeration that panic gripped the region – the co-authors of this study are happily 'living witnesses' of this phenomenon (one of us lived in Hong Kong throughout the epidemic; the other flew around the region during the alert). Large numbers of people in the region wore masks and stocked up on masks; used disposable tissue paper to press lift buttons; frequently cleaned their homes and public utilities with 1:99 diluted bleach: vinegar sales in China and its diaspora surged, as it was regarded as a 'remedy' by some, mere disinfectant by others. Schools and universities had been closed for weeks. Offices were thinly attended and shopping malls were deserted. People across Asia opted to stay at home to reduce the probability of infection and kept out of each other's way. Not only the indigenous population was affected, but also visitor numbers just dried up. Service exports, in particular tourism-related exports, were to be very hard-hit. Airports were strangely silent, except for limited arrivals and departures. There were dire predictions that Asian economic growth would, as a consequence, be drastically reduced (see Koo and Fu, 2003), some predicting meltdown as stock market reactions were immediate and sharp, others more cautiously pointing to a fall of around 0.5 per cent of Gross Domestic Product (GDP), according to one World Bank estimate to which we will return to in Chapter 4, with large numbers unemployed in its wake and so on.[3]

How would this fall in the region's GDP, economic hardship and consequent loss of jobs across the variety of nation-states and cities have come about in such an event? There were a number of channels by which the SARS outbreak could affect economies. We have admittedly simplified the *causal* links in our model which we will highlight in Chapter 4, but briefly mention it at this point to exemplify the main variables ultimately affecting employment we have chosen to highlight in order to present the human resources consequences. One channel was seen as operating through *supply shocks*. If the outbreak could not be effectively contained, the work force would be reduced because of illness or precautionary measures to prevent the spread of SARS, thereby disrupting labour markets, business operations and production. There was also the risk of a major *demand shock* as people just stopped shopping, paralysed into economic indecision, with private consumption plummeting, as we shall amplify in greater detail later in the 'country' chapters.

Whilst SARS did pose significant medical risks and had major economic implications, it had also exerted a disproportionately large *psychological* impact on people, as we shall see later in more detail. In the short run, economic consequences appeared to arise from public fear, whether rational or irrational, of a major pandemic. This psychopathology underlies mass panics that occur on a major scale from time to time and which have major consequences for economic, political and social behaviour. Clinical depression as a specific result of the SARS climate was reported (see Lee and Yun, 2006), as suspected patients could not have family visits; those who lost their jobs plunged into despair, particularly given the very thin welfare cover available in the so-called Dragon Economies of the region.[4]

The pronounced impact of SARS may possibly be attributed to the combination of two aspects of information about the illness: the almost costless and rapid transmission of information due to the development of modern mass media and communication technologies in the so-called global village; and perhaps more importantly, to the lack of sufficient medical information on SARS at the time (Fan, 2003). This stimulus may be conceptualized as inducing a 'demand shock', particularly on consumption. In locations with a high incidence of SARS, physical movement of people was restricted, either voluntarily or involuntarily, thus potentially reducing consumer spending, as we have noted above. Thus we surmised that SARS affected economic growth here by sharply reducing demand, mainly in the conurbations of the region and beyond, whether in Beijing, Hong Kong, Singapore or Taipei, as we shall see in later chapters. The impact on service sector was noticeable very quickly, particularly in the often labour-intensive industries within it, such as hospitality, hotels, travel and so on. One

*Table 1.1* Aggregate number of SARS cases and deaths: key countries involved

|  | China | Hong Kong | Taiwan | Singapore | Vietnam | Canada |
|---|---|---|---|---|---|---|
| Cumulative SARS cases | 5,327 | 1,755 | 665 | 238 | 63 | 251 |
| Number of deaths related to SARS | 349 | 300 | 180 | 33 | 5 | 41 |

Source: World Health Organization (2003) summary table of SARS cases by country, 1 November 2002–7 August 2003, WHO: Geneva. Available online http://www.who.int/csr/sars/country/en/country/2003_08_15.pdf

estimate feared five million jobs would be lost in the immediate impact of the epidemic (International Labour Organization (ILO) press release, 14 May 2003).

## 1.4  Conclusions

The SARS epidemic appeared to be a distinctly new threat to global society emanating from the Asian continent, perhaps more dangerous than previous post-war epidemics, such as the previous flu panics of the recent past, and perhaps even presaging a major pandemic. From the above, we can also see how significant the potential threat to the prosperity of Asia appeared at the initial onset of the SARS epidemic. A decline in economic growth, a constrained labour market and a rise in unemployment now loomed on the horizon. In the next chapter, we attempt to place the SARS outbreak into a wider framework, vis-à-vis catastrophes, epidemics and their historical context.

# 2 Catastrophes, epidemics and history

## 2.1 Introduction

In Greek tragedy, *catastrophe* joins together human activity with the divine, as in plays like *Antigone* or *Oedipus Rex*. Literally, it was the 'turning downward' of the plot in a classical tragedy; traditionally, it occurs in the fourth act of the play after the climax. There is perhaps nothing as profoundly 'Greek' and as 'tragic' as these Sophoclean tragedies: indeed, as we find in *Antigone*: 'Great words of boasting bring great punishments.'

Catastrophes are still acknowledged as traumatic events in peoples' lives. They continue to overawe us and overwhelm us. But they are less well-covered in economic history literature than one might expect. Among the *exogenous* shocks that shape macroeconomic factors, we may find major ones that may have significant impacts on both labour demand as well as supply. Clearly, movements in the business cycle are the 'normal' critical events that do affect labour markets, as in the classic boom and bust situations. Some of these have had devastating effects on employment, such as the Wall Street Crash of 1929 (see Galbraith, 1992).[1] But there are also 'abnormal' occurrences, such as those relating to catastrophes, 'natural' or 'man-made' and these may also significantly affect the political economy of the environment in which they take place. We intend to look at these more closely in this chapter and see how they relate to the focus of this book, the SARS epidemic of 2003.

## 2.2 Catastrophes

A 'catastrophe' is defined by Webster's *Dictionary* as 'a momentous tragic usually sudden event marked by effects ranging from extreme misfortune to utter overthrow or ruin' (see Posner, 2004: 6). The 'natural' events concern earthquakes, tsunamis and the like, or epidemics like the Black Death in medieval times, the Spanish Flu epidemic of 1918–1919 (see Hoehling, 1961; Collier, 1974; Crosby, 1989; Hildreth, 1991) and more recently SARS; the 'man-made' relates to disasters like Bhopal, Chernobyl, Three Mile Island, Piper Alpha, Texas City and so on. Some would include the threat of Climate Change among the latter.[2] Epidemics, few would deny, have had immense impacts on world history (see Collins and Lehman, 1953); they have even been cited as a possible cause of the rise and fall of empires (see McNeill, 1976). Not only the past but the present may carry the seeds of disaster. Right now, we are imagining the worst-case scenarios of a possible Avian Flu outbreak on a major scale.

## 2.3   Epidemics and pandemics

Epidemics and pandemics have indeed often made their mark on history, generally with dire economic consequences (Cipolla, 1976). According to the *Encyclopaedia Britannica*, a pandemic is 'an occurrence of disease that is temporarily of high prevalence. An epidemic occurring over a wide geographical area is called a *pandemic*. The rise and decline in epidemic prevalence of an infectious disease is a probability phenomenon dependent upon transfer of an effective dose of the infectious agent from an infected individual to a susceptible one' (cited in *Encyclopaedia Britannica*, 2003). From the Biblical 'Ten Plagues' in Ancient Egypt to the present time, we have deeply etched folk-memories of these devastating events. Indeed, 'cholera, smallpox, measles, malaria and TB have been part of mankind's history.' Malaria afflicted both primates and the first humans, and numbered among its known victims are Roman emperors, St Augustine and Oliver Cromwell. Smallpox lesions and evidence of tuberculosis have been found on Egyptian mummies, although the populations of those kingdoms of the Nile are thought to have been too small to sustain major epidemics. Elsewhere in the ancient world, there is evidence of epidemics among the Hittites (1346 BC) and Athenians (490 BC), whose populations were larger. India, China, Korea and Japan suffered epidemics of smallpox in the first six centuries AD (Bell and Lewis, 2005: 6). All these phenomena had dire consequences for their economies and societies, some greater than others. One could learn a great deal from these. 'Infectious disease is one of the few genuine adventures left in the world. The dragons are all dead and the lance grows rusty in the chimney corner' (see Zinsser, 1935: 1).

The 'Black Death', it is generally acknowledged, was a major 'event' in the history of catastrophes (see Cipolla, 1976). This pestilence was supposedly derived from 'bubonic plague' from Asia, but some historians now doubt this (see Cohn, 2002); even so, it left a scar across Europe, more than once, from the fourteenth century onwards, with widespread consequences for both economies and societies. Whether the plague was diffused by rats still remains a moot point (Cohn, 2002).

The Italian writer Giovanni Bocaccio survived the plague in Florence in 1348. In his tale *The Decameron*, he tells us how the Black Death got its name.

> In men and women alike it first betrayed itself by the emergency of certain tumours in the groin or the armpits, some of which grew as large as a common apple.... The form of the malady began to change,

black spots or livid making their appearance in many cases on the arm
or the thigh or elsewhere, now few and large, then minute and numerous.
These spots were an infallible token of approaching death.

(1921: 112)

It possibly annihilated as many as one in three of the population of
Europe between the years 1346–1350; for instance, in some villages, more
than half the people who lived there died. Hunger and famine stalked the
land and accompanied a decline in trade (see Cohn, 2002). With massive
scale mortality came a fall in the demand for, and the supply of, goods as
well as services and the labour that went into them, then as now. Labour
shortages were endemic; workers enjoyed a sellers' market; real wages
initially rose but the return on capital declined. Adam Smith noted
that 'servants which were idle…(were)…not willing to serve after the
pestilence without taking excessive wages,' (see Smith, [1776]1904: 146).
Inheritance and land-tenure patterns were also substantially affected. But
it had wider systemic effects in its turn. It is said that in its wake it dealt
a fatal blow to the feudal system from which it allegedly never recovered
(Bell and Lewis, 2005: 14).

Economists have tried to link such catastrophes with their wider material
consequences. As we noted earlier, the English classical economist Thomas
Malthus ([1798]1999), for example, who was one of the first to systematically
focus on the impact of plagues on populations and economies, saw them,
amongst other things, not only as constraints on wealth creation but also
as checks on demographic growth (Pressman, 1999: 29ff.). 'Crises' such as
plagues, economic historians tell us, may have led to peaks of mortality that
connected negative population changes and labour supply with key economic
variables (Floud and McCloskey, 1994: 60). However, 'Malthusian gloom'
was challenged on a number of counts, discounting the effect of death rates
(Cipolla, 1976: 136). Populations, whether in Europe or Asia, continued to
grow in spite of plagues and pestilence.

There was also a further dark *behavioural*, dimension, as epidemics like
the Black Death led to the persecution of vulnerable minorities, such as the
local Jewish population, who were blamed by their Christian neighbours for
spreading the disease (see Singer, 1998). One of the 'lessons of history' from
past epidemics, such as the outbreaks of cholera and the numerous plagues
that blighted medieval Europe (see Watts, 1997), was the frequent pattern
of 'victimizing and stigmatizing of helpless members of such minority
groups and the indifference of public officials callous to human suffering'
(Briggs, 1961). Not understanding the catastrophe that unfolded, sufferers
looked around for someone to blame. Such 'demonization' as a phenomenon
took root in most parts of Europe around this time, as simplistic explana-
tions were sought by the afflicted. The 'other' was an easy target. Zealous
campaigns against 'witchcraft', blaming both males and females, also
characterized the subsequent period. It was a perverse psychology that had

profound implications. Fear of the unknown in its course led many to chiliastic and millennarian beliefs – and worse!

In Elizabethan London, William Shakespeare knew the Plague first hand – as his theatres were closed down in 1593 for two years, and then again in 1610. His 11-year-old son Hamnet may have died from it in 1596, and it was used metaphorically by him in many plays; for example, in *Romeo and Juliet* (III. i. 94), where we find the now widely used phrase 'a plague o' both your houses'.

The sense of the horror of living with an epidemic is well-conveyed by the English eighteenth century novelist Daniel Defoe in his invented account, *Journal of a Plague Year* (see Defoe, [1720]2003) which refers to the 'Great Plague' in the previous century, cited by Samuel Pepys in his *Diaries* ([1660–1669]1993), as noted earlier. Defoe's narrator brings into vivid detail the psychological as well as organizational impact of the *malaise*.

> The face of London was – now indeed strangely altered: I mean the whole mass of buildings, city, liberties, suburbs, Westminster, Southwark, and altogether; for as to the particular part called the city, or within the walls, that was not yet much infected. But in the whole the face of things, I say, was much altered; sorrow and sadness sat upon every face; and though some parts were not yet overwhelmed, yet all looked deeply concerned; and, as we saw it apparently coming on, so every one looked on himself and his family as in the utmost danger.
>
> ([1720]2003: 22)

In 1911, the German novelist Thomas Mann presciently (given the war clouds on the horizon) wrote of the insidious nature of plague, in this case cholera, in his novella *Death in Venice* (Mann, [1911]1971). His hero, Professor Aschenbach, found the city in a state of trauma but not wanting to scare off the tourists, its livelihood – but 'death unseen and unacknowledged was devouring and laying waste in the streets .... And the fears of the people supported the persistent official policy of silence and denial' (1971: 68).

Later, the French writer, Albert Camus, in his classic novel *The Plague/ La Peste* ([1947]2002) used the epidemic as an allegory for the 'Occupation' in the Second World War or indeed even the malaise of the twentieth century. He saw how fear, isolation and claustrophobia came in its wake. He wrote: 'There have been as many plagues in the world as there have been wars, yet plagues and wars always find people equally unprepared' (2002: 30).

## 2.4   Three major pandemics

In the twentieth century, the emergence of a number of new influenza A virus subtypes resulted in three major pandemics; all of these spread globally within a year of being detected (see Box 2.1) as follows (according to the US Center for Disease Control):

*Box 2.1* Three major pandemics of influenza in the twentieth century

> - **'1918–1919, "Spanish flu," [A (H1N1)],** caused the highest number
>   of known influenza deaths. (However, the actual influenza virus
>   subtype was not detected in the 1918–1919 pandemic). More than
>   500,000 people died in the United States, and up to 50 million
>   people may have died worldwide. Many people died within
>   the first few days after infection, and others died of secondary
>   complications. Nearly half of those who died were young, healthy
>   adults. Influenza A (H1N1) viruses still circulate today after
>   being introduced again into the human population in 1977.'
> - **'1957–1958, "Asian flu," [A (H2N2)],** caused about 70,000 deaths
>   in the United States. First identified in China in late February
>   1957, the Asian flu spread to the United States by June 1957.'
> - **'1968–1969, "Hong Kong flu," [A (H3N2)],** caused about 34,000
>   deaths in the United States. This virus was first detected in Hong
>   Kong in early 1968 and spread to the United States later that year.
>   Influenza A (H3N2) viruses still circulate today.'
>
> Source: CDC Report, Atlanta, GA, 17 January 2006: 1.

The most recent severe health disaster last century was the global
influenza pandemic after the First World War, the so-called Spanish Flu
of 1918–1919 as noted above, that may even be seen as a precursor of the
Great Depression of the inter-war years, as it was thought to have killed
many more people than all those who died in armed combat, and in its
turn severely undermined both demand and supply (see Beveridge, 1977;
Katz, 1977; Gilbert, 1994; Johnson and Mueller, 2002).

Why was the 1918–1919 influenza outbreak called the 'Spanish' variety – when
it may have originated, by historic accounts, in East Asia in 1917? Spanish
newspapers, it is said, were the only ones to report the new plague because
they were 'neutral' in the first World War and the combatant countries' press
were censored. Estimates of fatalities from this outbreak – which were earlier
rated as much lower – now exceed 50 million deaths. It had been preceded
by a number of influenza pandemics at the end of the nineteenth century,
such as the one that started in 1889 in Russia and spread westwards, that
had been serious but not as devastating as that of 1918–1919.

The 1889 flu pandemic appeared in Russia in October of that year, first
in Siberia and then later spread to St Petersburg, the capital, by November.
It then infected large numbers on both sides of the Atlantic within two
months. It featured high attack rates and high morbidity. At the time, the
diagnosis and classification of flu was in its infancy, so there were keen
debates about its significance. No one knew if there was a single disease

called 'influenza'. But the 'fingerprint' left on immune systems prepared the way for future vulnerability (see Beveridge, 1977).

The Spanish flu virus infected a fifth of the global population and was most deadly for those infected aged 20–40, different from normal influenza, which is principally a killer of the elderly and the young. The mortality rate was 2.5 per cent compared with 0.1 per cent in normal cases. The 'killer' was not the flu itself but the pneumonia that accompanied the infection. *La Grippe*, as it was known, killed both civilians and soldiers and was no respecter of race, class or gender in conditions of overcrowding (see Howard, 2005). It is likely that this pandemic, like the Black Death long before, pushed up real wages as there were 'black holes' in the labour force due to the high level of fatalities in the working population or those who were either serving in the armed forces or were demobilized. There would then have been a change in the capital–labour ratio and the return on capital would have fallen.

No one really knows how the 1918–1919 pandemic originated.[3] It was initially found in northeast France in and around the battlelines of the First World War; it infected both Allied and German troops. The virus may possibly have incubated in the mud and squalor of the trenches, together with very intense military population density found there. The proximity of animals and fowl reared to feed the troops (see Oxford *et al.*, 2005a) may have been a consideration.[4] The location was also on the route of the seasonal bird migration that year. Additionally, there was the presence of over 100,000 Chinese labourers who had been recruited to build the fortifications. Some say the virus resulted from a mutation that occurred in East Asia, possibly on the Chinese mainland in the first place (Beveridge, 1977). It is conceivable that these labourers brought the infection with them but hard evidence is not available on this point.

The 1918–1919 Spanish Flu was one of the worst pandemics to hit the modern world (see US Census Bureau, 1920). It wreaked a devastating path through the British population (see Loeb, 2005). Since the Industrial Revolution and the Age of Empire had laid the groundwork for what we now call 'globalization', there was already a greater degree of interconnectivity in communications and trade across the world. The scene was set for rapid transmission of disease than ever before. For example, the Royal Navy, as well as the US fleet, spanned the globe and indeed helped spread the Spanish Flu virus to most corners of the world. The virus may well be the likely ancestor of both the human and classical swine H1N1 lineages that link then and now, connecting to the current H5N1 problem.

As noted in the *Journal of the American Medical Association* final edition of 1918

> The year 1918 has gone: a year momentous as the termination of the most cruel war in the annals of the human race; a year which marked, the end at least for a time, of man's destruction of man; unfortunately

a year in which developed a most fatal infectious disease causing the death of hundreds of thousands of human beings. Medical science for four and one-half years devoted itself to putting men on the firing line and keeping them there. Now, it must turn with its whole might to combating the greatest enemy of all-infectious disease.

(*JAMA*, 28 December, 1918: 71)

Such epidemics may represent major *exogenous* (as well as *endogenous*) 'shocks' that had massive impacts on economic activity, as well as producing human tragedy on an often epic scale. Clearly, we must distinguish here between shocks that were 'megaeconomic' and those which were merely 'macroeconomic'. The Black Death and the 1918–1919 Spanish Flu probably belong to the former; the many lesser ones that have afflicted society may be subsumed under the latter, such as the relatively serious 1957 and 1968 flu epidemics.

Not long into the new millennium, a new threat appeared in Asia and was feared to be another replay of the 1918–1919 Flu disaster, namely, what became known as the SARS epidemic of recent time (see Oxford *et al.*, 2003; Abraham, 2004). Although to date this seemed to have ended in July 2003, any complacency would be misplaced as it killed almost a thousand people worldwide, mainly in the PRC and the HKSAR, and infected almost nine times as many (World Health Organization, 2003a) as we shall shortly see. But it was nowhere near the scale of the 1918–1919 outbreak in its morbidity. The latter hit a society weakened by the first World War in terms of its readiness and its resources to handle a pandemic. There were no available vaccines or antibiotic drugs to treat the sick. The subsequent pandemics we have noted have met with a far better-equipped medical response and this may be seen as a good reason why fatalities have been that much less.[5]

In the SARS 'catastrophe', however, we are observing a major but relatively short-term phenomenon, compared with what economists and economic historians have in the past analysed during the Braudelian *longue durée* (see Braudel, [1979]1981–1984). But it is still early days, although we hope we have seen the last of this specific epidemic, as Cipolla (1976: 130) reminds us, speaking of the aftermath of the plagues: 'The fact is that until the end of the seventeenth century not a year passed without particular cities or entire regions of Europe suffering badly from some epidemic.' As populations expanded around the world and became more concentrated in cities, the threat of potential mass infections became more threatening: we still live in such circumstances, however, with Hong Kong having possibly the world's highest population density. As Bell and Lewis point out: 'Urban crowding assists in efficient transmission, and geographic mobility enlarges the stock of "susceptibles", as was the case with influenza in 1918–1919 and SARS in 2003' (Bell and Lewis, 2005: 5). Today, the prospect of Avian Flu on a pandemic scale looms large (see Oxford, 2005b).

As a recent World Bank estimate projected

> There is a dearth of detailed studies of what these costs of a flu pandemic might amount to at a global level. However, one 1999 study of the United States calculated that, based on past patterns, a flu pandemic could lead to between 100,000 and 200,000 deaths in the US, together with 700,000 or more hospitalizations, up to 40 million outpatient visits and 50 million additional illnesses. The present value of the economic losses associated with this level of death and sickness was estimated at between $100 and $200 billion for the US alone (in 2004 dollars). If we extrapolate from the United States to all high income countries, there could be a present value loss of $550 billion. The loss for the world would of course be significantly larger, because of the impact in the developing world. Note also that these estimates for the US arose from a projected mortality rate of less than 0.1% of the US population, much lower than the 0.5% mortality rate in the US in the 1918–19 pandemic, or the 2.5% mortality rate for the world as a whole at that time.
>
> (Brahmbatt, 2005: 1)

## 2.5 Exogenous shocks

The variance in the strength of the 'catastrophic' forces impinging on the 'environment' of economies and organizations within them, taking into account a 'systems' view of these phenomena, is the principal focus of this section. It may take the form of an *exogenous shock*, which can be seen as coming from an external source and working directly on the economy or via intervening variables. We can model these shocks in a number of ways (see Figure 2.1).

The simple model may be specified or unspecified and depend on two variables, say (x, y) only. The multivariate model may involve these two main variables, plus intervening ones, say (a, b, c...). The intervening variables between the exogenous shock and the dependent variable (the economy, including demand and supply for human resources) might be demographic such as population size, population density and so on. Any number of intervening variables might be included but it would be sensible to keep them to the critical ones.

The disturbance caused by the exogenous shock may be *actual* or even merely *potential*, as just the threat of disruption may destabilize economies relatively quickly. The rise and fall of the stock-market index is good evidence of the preceding proposition. An anticipated event, if a natural disaster such as an earthquake prediction for downtown Tokyo, may in turn undermine stock markets; the 'real' event even more so. If the event is an epidemic, it is often hard to know whether the impact will be localized or spread further in its own terms. Physical catastrophes are mostly bounded by geography, whereas biological analogues such as pandemics may not be so, as infectious diseases do not normally respect frontiers. The

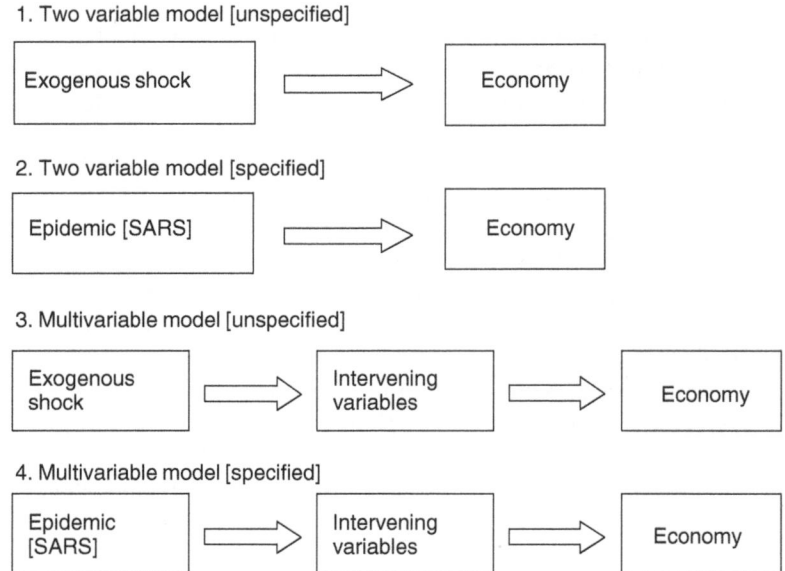

*Figure 2.1* Modelling exogenous shocks.

threat of SARS clearly destabilized Asian stock-markets at the time[6] (see Brown, 2004).

Plagues, like the Black Death, are a good example of potentially transnational contagion. The Spanish Flu epidemic, in 1918–1919 and after, was international in its impact; the latest, major virus-based threat, SARS, was seen as a 'global' emergency by UN agencies like WHO, although it only spread in terms of substantial fatalities (just under 1,000 in all) to a finite subset of countries, mostly in East and South East Asia in late 2002 and early 2003. We already have at hand HIV/AIDS that has killed huge numbers of people over the years[7] and accounted for over three million deaths in recent years; malaria claimed over one million lives at the lowest official estimate and possibly many times more, across a wide range of countries. Avian flu has killed in the low hundreds only at the time of writing.

## 2.6  A multidimensional approach

We next present a multidimensional taxonomy of catastrophic events and epidemics. We present three dimensions here, *length* (temporal), *breadth* (geographic) and *depth* (human impact). Initially, we set out a schema for both catastrophes and epidemics (see Figures 2.2 and 2.3) respectively; this has not been drawn exactly to scale however, but to what we thought was proportionate for the purposes of illustration. Against these arranged *vertically*, we then look at four categories across the *horizontal* span, namely natural catastrophes,

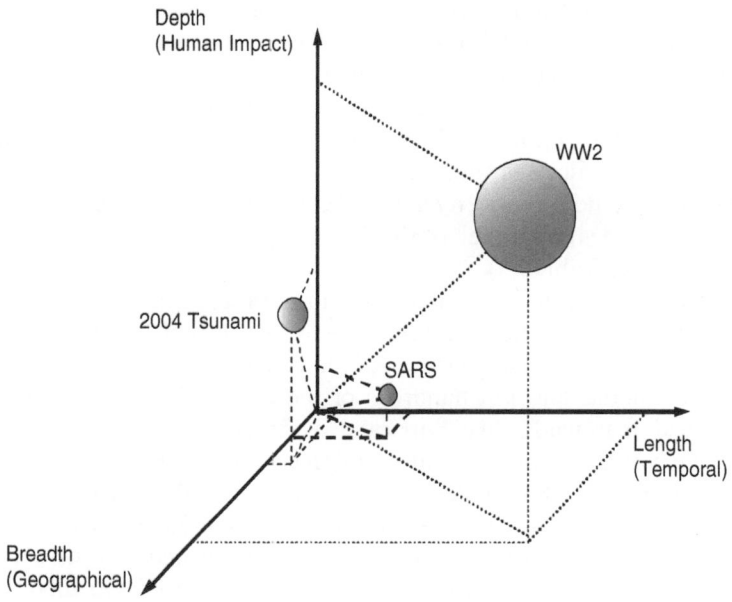

*Figure 2.2* A taxonomy of catastrophic events.

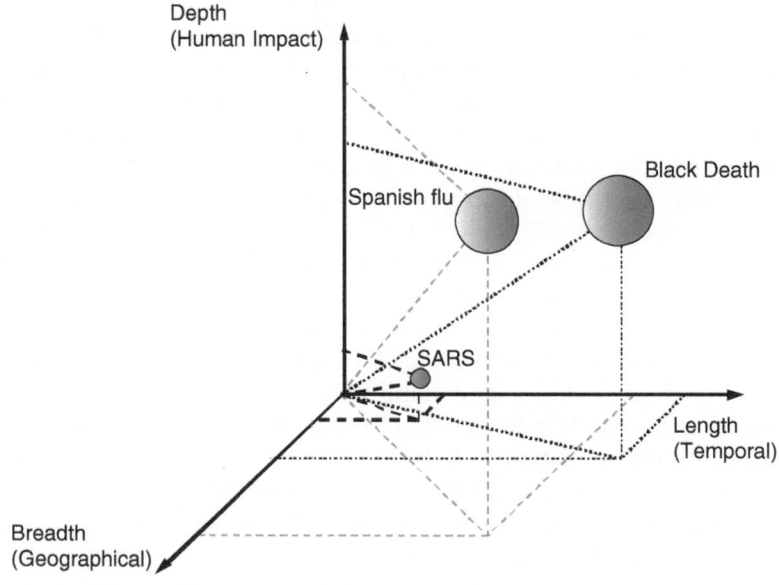

*Figure 2.3* A taxonomy of epidemics.

epidemics, wars and slumps (see Table 2.1). The first two are often said to be 'Acts of God'; the second pair are most likely to be 'man-made'. We specify the main variation in each and give some examples.

As for epidemics (see Figure 2.3), we may see SARS as for example, *short* in duration rather than lengthy, *regional* rather than global and *minimal* (vis-à-vis pandemics) in human impact *post facto*. Under pandemics, Spanish Flu would have been *long*, *global* and *maximal*, by comparison.

We will now deal with each of the four categories chosen on the *horizontal* axis in turn (see Table 2.1).

First, natural disasters are often short in duration, like the Asian Tsunami in late 2005; they are often local/regional in their extent but can be maximal in their impact. They may occur over the course of a day like the Tsunami but affect millions and kill hundreds of thousands. A disaster can be both natural and man-made, like hurricane 'Katrina' in New Orleans in mid-2005, where weather and human negligence are combined (see Steinberg, 2003; Quarantelli, 2006; United Nations International Strategy for Disaster Reduction, 2007). The earthquake in Taiwan in late 2006 nearly brought IT communication in Asia to a standstill. The relationship between costs of natural and man-made disasters in terms of insured losses from 1970 to 2006 is set out in Figure 2.4. We can see from this that natural cases were a much more expensive proposition than man-made ones except for a short peak in recent years. A much longer time-horizon may be involved in the case of Climate Change, whether man-made or otherwise. But as the noted economist, John Maynard Keynes (1924: 12) once pointed out, 'in the long-run, we're all dead' anyway!

Second, epi- and pandemics vary a great deal in their dimensions, but pandemics are, of course, by definition, epidemics writ large. They may be short or long; local or wider in scope; minimal or maximal in effect. An epidemic may be short in duration like the SARS outbreak or last for years like the Black Death. The impact may range from a thousand to tens of millions of deaths, as in the former and latter examples.

Third, wars vary in length, short like the Six-Day War or Gulf Wars, or longer; they may be local or wider; minimal or maximal. The Thirty Years War was an exception; the First and Second World Wars lasted four and six years respectively. But the impact of wars may be many more deaths than those killed in active combat alone; civilian casualties may be high and many become enfeebled from the lack of adequate nutrition and shelter, worse still if disease ensues on a major scale.

Last, slumps are often longer than recessions; they may be regional or global; minimal or maximal. A local economic 'hiccup' like a business slowdown in say, Hong Kong, may not cause distress on a massive scale, but an 'upheaval' like the Wall Street Crash of 1929 may spell misery across the world for millions in the years to come.

If we have a coincidence of natural, biological, military and economic shocks, then we may have a multiple explosion of consequences. Even two catastrophes together may present great difficulties, for example, a natural

*Table 2.1* Taxonomy of exogenous shocks

| | Natural disasters | Epi- and pandemics | Wars | Slumps |
|---|---|---|---|---|
| Time (length of event – in terms of days) | SHORT, for example, 2004 tsunami LONG, for example, climate change | SHORT, for example, 2003 SARS LONG, for example, fourteenth century Black Death | SHORT, for example, 1991 Gulf War LONG, for example, 1939–1945 the Second World War | SHORT, for example, 1997 Asian crisis MEDIUM TERM, for example, 1929 Great depression |
| Space (geographical breadth of event – in terms of territory affected) | MOSTLY LOCAL, for example, 1995 Kobe earthquake REGIONAL, for example, 2004 tsunami | LOCAL, for example, hand, foot, and mouth disease in Taiwan 1998 REGIONAL, for example, SARS GLOBAL, for example, 1918–1919 Spanish flu | LOCAL, for example, 1937 Spanish Civil War REGIONAL, for example, Napoleonic Wars GLOBAL, for example, 1939–1945 the Second World War | REGIONAL, for example, 1997 Asian crisis GLOBAL, for example, 1929 Great depression |
| Depth (intensity of event – in terms of human impact) | MINIMUM, for example, 1951 East Anglian floods MAXIMUM, for example, 2004 tsunami | MINIMUM, for example, 2003 SARS MAXIMUM, for example, 1918–1919 Spanish flu | MINIMUM, for example, 1812 US–Canada war MAXIMUM, for example, 1939–1945 the Second World War | MINIMUM, for example, 2003 Hong Kong recession MAXIMUM, for example, 1929 Great depression |

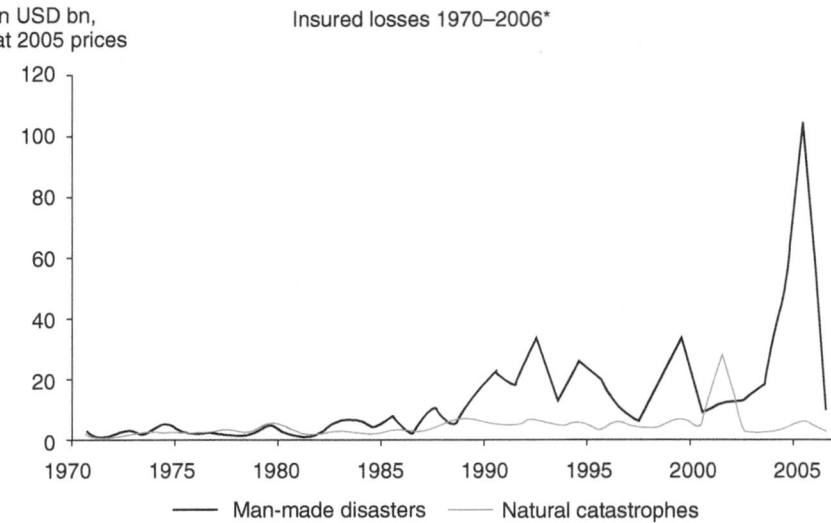

in USD bn,
at 2005 prices

Insured losses 1970–2006*

—— Man-made disasters   —— Natural catastrophes

*Figure 2.4* Preliminary sigma estimates of catastrophic losses 1970–2006.

Source: Swiss Re, Preliminary sigma estimates of catastrophe losses in 2006, sigma no. 2/2006.

Note
*2006 provisional figures.

disaster and an epidemic to follow. Again, as we have seen earlier, a military catastrophe such as a major war may bring an epidemic in its wake.

## 2.7   Conclusions

In the preceding sections, we have discussed the role of catastrophes in world history, focusing on the major pandemics of the twentieth century, in order to place the SARS outbreak of 2002–2003 in a wider perspective.

To date, the SARS corona virus epidemic may not only be seen as a 'media' phenomenon *par excellence* but also as one that fortunately had a relatively constrained impact vis-à-vis the major catastrophes of our time. It appears to have occurred in a time-defined frame and seems to have 'burnt' itself out but one can never be sure. In the next chapter, we will examine the life-cycle of the SARS epidemic in greater detail and ask where we go next. The advance of the ongoing Avian Flu epidemic has yet to make its mark, having caused only a small number of fatalities to date, at the time of writing, but has generated much anxiety.

In this chapter, then, we have seen how epidemics and pandemics have indeed often made their mark on history, generally with dire *economic* consequences, and we have looked at these in the context of the analysis of catastrophes. We are now faced with new 'Horsemen of the Apocalypse'; with the prospect of the aforementioned menacing Avian Flu pandemic (conceivably within the next decade) and beyond this; and the prospect of dramatic Climate Change (possibly within the half-century), whatever its shape and severity.

# 3   The SARS epidemic of 2003

## A timeline

## 3.1   Introduction

In late 2002 and early 2003, SARS, a newly emerging respiratory illness, dominated the headlines. As Albert Camus's narrator, Dr Rieux, points out in his novel *The Plague/La Peste*, concerning an affliction of an earlier genre, 'from that point on, it could be said the plague became the affair of us all' ([1947]2002: 53). The new epidemic Asia faced was associated with potentially significant morbidity and mortality, and presented an early major medical challenge to humankind, in the areas it most severely affected – namely, mainland China, Hong Kong, Taiwan, Singapore and Vietnam, as well as Canada and elsewhere. There was, and is still, no treatment to cure the disease or a vaccine to prevent it. Isolation and quarantine remain the best ways to control the disease (Chan-Yeung, 2004). The analogy of 'war' echoed throughout the SARS crisis – an 'attack' by an unknown microbe (Abraham, 2004). This war by microbes targeted the vital infrastructure of society; in this case, the public health system. The attack-rate for 'atypical pneumonia' in the Vietnam outbreak, the first documentation of what we now call SARS, varied from 30 per cent among hospital workers with patient-contact, 6.5 per cent among patients hospitalized for other diseases at one hospital, and 6.3 per cent among close contacts of one case; the overall case fatality was 10.9 per cent (Plant, 2003). The virus first hit doctors, nurses and health care workers, mowing them down like soldiers on a battlefield. One week after the SARS outbreak in Hong Kong, 33 people in the Prince of Wales (PWH) Hospital had fallen sick due to 'atypical pneumonia', including medical doctors and 17 medical students from the Chinese University of Hong Kong affiliated to PWH (Lee *et al.*, 2003). Professor Clive Cockram working at PWH lamented that 'it's been non-stop ... scary ... psychologically tough and harrowing.... We felt so helpless' (quoted in Seno and Reyes, 2004). Some health care workers, including doctors and nurses, were stigmatized and not allowed home; some did not want to go home because of the fear of infecting their families. In the areas hit hardest by SARS, people experienced a fear their forefathers had lived with constantly: the dread of death from disease.

The phenomenon of the 'super-spreader', someone who infects 10 or more people, was and remains a worrisome puzzle.[1]

## 3.2   International research collaboration

The war on SARS was a unique global campaign waged on many fronts. It was, says Dr Ebert of the Nocht Institute, 'the first time the WHO has coordinated such a large number of laboratories with scientists talking by phone, email or videoconference at least every second day to share information' (quoted in Seno and Reyes, 2004). Involved in the detection work were research facilities in North America, Britain, Europe, Japan and Hong Kong. The first mission of the laboratory teams around the world was to identify the virus causing SARS. Scientists from the University of Hong Kong, led by microbiologist Professor Malik Peiris, determined that the SARS virus was unique. On examining the virus under an electron microscope, they detected spikes on the cell surface that indicated what they were looking at was a *coronavirus*, the same type of virus that causes the common cold. This discovery generated considerable excitement within the international scientific community; while laboratories in Canada and the United States completed the genetic sequencing of the SARS virus first. By any measure, the global network mobilized by the WHO to combat SARS was incredibly successful and efficient.

SARS became an epidemic of 'firsts' for the global community, which helps explain why the outbreak is historic in many regards (Fidler, 2004). Scientifically, the SARS epidemic constituted the first time the causative agent behind SARS – a novel kind of coronavirus – was identified in human populations (Drosten *et al.*, 2003; Ksiazek *et al.*, 2003). As such, this SARS-associated coronavirus (SARS-CoV) and the disease it caused created many questions scientists had never confronted before, such as exactly how this pathogen caused morbidity and mortality in humans. The novelty of SARS-CoV generated new medical questions that the health care community struggled to understand during the outbreak. How does a clinician diagnose SARS? What was the incubation period of SARS? How should SARS patients be treated, and what were the best ways to protect medical personnel and other patients from contracting this new disease?

## 3.3   Infection, illness and fatalities

Scientists now know that the SARS virus is transmitted from person to person by inhalation of droplets. This typically occurs when a sick person sneezes or coughs. The microbe is carried in saliva sprayed into the air. Another person nearby who breathes in the saliva may become infected. Droplets can easily travel a metre or more. They may also land on a surface such as a table, doorknob or elevator button.[2] When somebody touches these surfaces with his hand, he may become infected if he then puts his hand to his eyes, mouth or nose. Other tests indicated that the virus was also present in human excrement (Chan-Yeung, 2004).[3] The SARS virus has a long incubation period that varies from two to ten days before symptoms begin to show. The average incubation period is about five days. The quarantine period for people suspected of SARS is 10 days, although during the outbreak WHO recommended two weeks.

Despite fears about transmission of SARS, the SARS-CoV has a relatively low infectivity. The concern is the virulence of the SARS-CoV, which can cause rapid and serious damage to human organs.[4] During the outbreak, between 10 and 25 per cent of patients required intensive care treatment, while 5–15 per cent died (Poutanen *et al.*, 2003), high by the standards of most common diseases (Abraham, 2004).[5] WHO estimated, on 7 May 2003, the case fatality ratio to be less than 1 per cent in persons up to 24 years old; 6 per cent in those aged 25–44; 15 per cent in those aged 45–64; and more than 50 per cent in those who are at least 65 years old (Whaley and Mansoor, 2006). Looking at the SARS epidemic statistics, we find that the incidence we may choose here to measure catastrophic 'depth', the death-rate per 100,000, varied between the nations concerned (see Table 3.1). We can see that Hong Kong had the most severe 'depth', with 0.0425 deaths per 100,000 of population, although China had the largest number of declared

*Table 3.1* Number of SARS cases and mortality in East and South East Asia (plus Canada)

|  | China | Hong Kong | Taiwan | Singapore | Vietnam | Canada |
|---|---|---|---|---|---|---|
| Cumulative SARS cases* | 5,327 | 1,755 | 665 | 238 | 63 | 251 |
| Number of deaths related to SARS | 349 | 300 | 180 | 33 | 5 | 41 |
| Death rate (%) | 6.55 | 17.09 | 27.06 | 13.86 | 7.93 | 16.33 |
| Total population in 2003# (thousands) | 1,304,196 | 7,049 | 22,605 | 4,253 | 81,377 | 31,510 |
| SARS deaths per 100,000 of population | 0.0267 | 0.0425 | 0.0079 | 0.0076 | 0.0061 | 0.0013 |

Sources:
* World Health Organization <http://www.who.int/csr/sars/country/2003_08_15/en/>;
# United Nations, *World Urbanization Prospects: The 2003 Revision Population Database*, <http://esa.un.org/unup/index.asp?panel=1>

cases, 5,327 in all. Taiwan had the greatest percentage of deaths of total cases but not of aggregate population, namely 27.06 in all.

## 3.4   Rapid international spread

The timeline in Table 3.2 show the sequence of major world events in the SARS epidemic.

*Table 3.2* SARS timeline (November 2002–July 2004)

---

*2002*

*November 16*
A 46-year-old village committee official, now recognized as the first known case of SARS, is admitted to hospital in Foshan, Guangdong province, with a mysterious respiratory ailment.

*December 10*
A 34-year-old restaurant chef is admitted to hospital in Heyuan with a respiratory illness that does not respond to ordinary treatment. Seven medical workers in Heyuan fall ill later in the month.

*December 21*
A 26-year-old male factory worker falls ill in Jiangmen, Guangdong Province, with a respiratory illness that does not respond to ordinary treatment.

*December 26*
A 30-year-old male who works as a chef in Zhongshan, Guangdong Province, is admitted to hospital. Two of his relatives and 10 health care workers are infected by him.

*2003*

*January 2*
As medical staff fall ill, people in Heyuan panic. Heyuan authorities inform the provincial centre for disease control in Guangzhou and appeal for public calm. The provincial centre for disease control sends investigators to Heyuan. A 49-year-old government official is admitted to the Guangdong Traditional Chinese Medicine Hospital in Guangzhou where he infects seven health care workers.

*January 18*
Health authorities in Zhongshan inform the provincial centre for disease control that 28 people including 13 health care workers have been infected with a respiratory illness. News of the illness causes public alarm in Zhongshan, and people queue for medicines and vinegar.

*January 21*
A team from the provincial centre for diseases control and the national centre for disease control in Beijing arrives in Zhongshan to investigate the epidemic.

*January 22*
A 49-year-old Hong Kong woman falls ill after visiting her mother in the mainland. She is admitted to hospital in Hong Kong and dies on February 3. Retrospective analysis of her serum samples shows she had been infected with SARS, making her one of the first cases in Hong Kong. A nurse who looked after her was also infected.

---

*Table 3.2* Continued

*January 23*
The investigating team in Zhongshan produces a five-page report describing the disease as 'atypical pneumonia' and releases the report and a letter warning major hospitals in the region about the disease.

*January 28*
Hospital workers begin to fall ill in Guangzhou. Seven hospital workers at the Guangdong Provincial Hospital for Traditional Chinese Medicine fall ill.

*January 30*
Zhou Zuofeng, the first SARS 'super spreader', is admitted to the Second Affiliated Hospital, Zhongshan Medical University, Guangzhou.

*January 31*
As the number of cases in Guangzhou increase, health authorities decide to centralize treatment by channelling all suspected SARS cases to seven hospitals in the city.

*February 10*
The WHO Regional Office in Manila asks the Chinese Ministry of Health for more information about reports of the illness in Guangdong. Hong Kong media reports a mysterious disease in Guangdong Province that causes panic. The Department of Health in Hong Kong tries to contact the authorities in Guangdong, but receives no reply.

*February 11*
The Chinese Ministry of Health reports that there have been 300 cases including five deaths in Guangdong Province from an 'acute respiratory syndrome'. The health authorities said the epidemic was under control, and there was no need for panic. The WHO receives the same report from the Chinese Ministry of Health.

*February 12*
Two researchers from the University of Hong Kong travel unofficially to Guangzhou to get samples from mainland patients, to see whether this disease had been caused by a virulent new influenza virus. The WHO global influenza network awaits their results.

*February 14*
A small notice in the Weekly Epidemiological Record reports 305 cases and 5 deaths from an unknown acute respiratory syndrome which occurred between 16 November and 9 February 2003 in the Guangdong Province, China. The illness is spread to household members and healthcare workers. The Chinese Ministry of Health informs the WHO that the outbreak in Guangdong is clinically consistent with atypical pneumonia. Further investigations rule out anthrax, pulmonary plague, leptospirosis and haemorrhagic fever.

*February 20*
After human deaths from bird flu are reported in Hong Kong, the WHO becomes more anxious to investigate the outbreak in Guangdong. The WHO Regional Director in Manila, Shigeru Omi, writes to the Chinese authorities asking for permission to send an investigative team. In Washington, the US Health Secretary, Tommy Thompson, also urges the visiting Chinese Deputy Minister of Health to allow the WHO request. China gives permission.

*February 21*
Liu Jianlun, a 64-year-old professor of nephrology from Guangzhou, arrives in Hong Kong for his nephew's wedding. He had treated patients with atypical

(*Table 3.2 continued*)

*Table 3.2* Continued

pneumonia prior to departure and is symptomatic upon arrival in Hong Kong. He and his wife check into the 9th floor of the Metropole Hotel in Hong Kong, but the next day he feels unwell and admits himself to Kwong Wah Hospital.

At the Metropole Hotel, he infects a group of travellers from different countries, and triggers a global epidemic.

*February 23–25*
Guests from the Metropole Hotel who had been infected by Liu carry the SARS virus to different parts of the world. A 78-year-old Canadian woman, Kwan Sui Chu, takes it to Toronto: Johnny Chen, a Chinese American businessman, takes it to Hanoi; and three young women take the disease to Singapore.

*February 23*
A two-member WHO team arrives in Beijing but is not given permission to visit Guangdong. They leave China after two weeks in Beijing waiting for permission.

*February 28*
Dr Carlo Urbani, a WHO official based in Vietnam, is asked by the French Hospital in Hanoi for advice on how to treat Johnny Chen. Urbani is alarmed by the severity of the symptoms, and the way it spreads among doctors and health care workers. His reports put the WHO on alert.

The Chinese Ministry of Health reports that the infective agent causing the outbreak of the atypical pneumonia was probably Chlamydia Pneumoniae.

*March 1*
Esther Mok, a 26-year-old guest at the Metropole Hotel, becomes Singapore's index patient for SARS and is admitted to Tan Tock Seng Hospital.

*March 4*
A 26-year-old Hong Kong man, who had visited a friend at the Metropole Hotel in February, is admitted to Ward 8A at the Prince of Wales Hospital with a severe respiratory ailment. He triggers an epidemic in the hospital, which spreads to the community.

*March 5*
Beijing receives its first SARS case, when a businesswoman from Shanxi Province who fell ill after a trip to Guangdong is hospitalized at a People's Liberation Army hospital. The Chinese National People's Congress also begins a crucial session to appoint a new government.

*March 7*
New reports of outbreaks of a severe form of pneumonia come in from Hong Kong, and Vietnam. The outbreak in Vietnam traces back to a middle-aged man who was admitted to hospital in Hanoi with a high fever, dry cough, myalgia and mild sore throat. Following his admission, approximately 20 hospital staff become sick with similar symptoms. In some cases, this is followed by bilateral pneumonia and progression to acute respiratory distress.

*March 10*
Eighteen healthcare workers on a medical ward in the Prince of Wales Hospital in Hong Kong report that they are ill. Within hours, more than 50 of the hospital's healthcare workers are identified as having had a febrile illness over the previous few days. On March 11, 23 of them are admitted to the hospital for observation as a precautionary measure. Eight develop early X-ray signs of pneumonia. The outbreaks, both in Hanoi and Hong Kong, appear to be confined to the hospital environment. Hospital staff seem to be at highest risk. The hospital authorities inform the Hong Kong Department of Health.

The new syndrome is now designated 'severe acute respiratory syndrome', or SARS.

*Table 3.2* Continued

*March 12*
The WHO issues a global alert about cases of severe atypical pneumonia following mounting reports of cases among staff in the Hanoi and Hong Kong hospitals.

*March 14*
The Ministry of Health in Singapore reports 3 cases of atypical pneumonia, including a former flight attendant who had stayed at the Hong Kong hotel. Contact tracing will subsequently link her illness to more than 100 SARS cases in Singapore.

*March 15*
The WHO confirms that Severe Acute Respiratory syndrome (SARS) is a 'worldwide health threat' and that possible cases have been identified in Canada, Indonesia, Philippines, Singapore, Thailand and Vietnam. The WHO issues a global health alert about SARS. The alert includes a rare emergency travel advisory to international travellers, healthcare professionals and health authorities, advising all individuals travelling to affected area to be watchful for the development of symptoms for a period of 10 days after returning.

*March 16*
Over 150 suspect and probable cases reported to the WHO from all around the world.

*March 17*
The WHO calls upon 11 leading laboratories in 9 countries to join a network for multicenter research into the etiology of SARS and to simultaneously develop a diagnostic test. The network takes advantage of modern communication technologies (e-mail; secure website) so that the outcomes of investigations on clinical samples from SARS cases can be shared in real time. On the secure WHO website, network members share electron microscope pictures of viruses, sequences of genetic material for virus identification and characterization, virus isolates, various samples from patients and post-mortem tissues. Samples from one patient can be analyzed in parallel by several laboratories and the results shared in real time. The goal: detection of the causative agent for SARS and the development of a diagnostic test.

A team from the University of Hong Kong isolates what it believes to be the causal agent for SARS, and begins tests to confirm this.

China provides a brief report to the WHO stating that the outbreak in Guangdong had tapered off.

*March 18–1 9*
Chinese University of Hong Kong and laboratories in Germany, Canada and Singapore announce the virus causing SARS might be a paramyxovirus. At the University of Hong Kong, this is ruled out, and tests continue on the virus they have isolated.

*March 19*
One week after the global alert, the WHO publishes an update on the situation, saying that the failure of all previous efforts to detect the presence of bacteria and viruses known to cause respiratory disease strongly suggests that the causative agent might be a novel pathogen.

SARS spreads to the US and Europe with the UK, Spain, Germany and Slovenia reporting cases.

*March 21*
Malik Peiris of the University of Hong Kong emails the WHO laboratory network to inform them that this team has isolated the SARS virus. The University of Hong Kong team also devises a basic diagnostic test based on the isolated virus.

(*Table 3.2 continued*)

*Table 3.2* Continued

Center for Disease Control (CDC) publishes a preliminary clinical description of SARS.

*March 23*
A WHO team arrives in Beijing and asks to travel to Guangdong province.

*March 24*
Scientists at the CDC and in Hong Kong announce that a new coronavirus has been isolated from patients with SARS. Within days, sequences of the coronavirus polymerase gene are compared with those of previously characterized strains and scientists are able to demonstrate that this virus is distinct from all known human pathogens. In addition, serum from patients with SARS is evaluated to detect antibodies to the new coronavirus, and seroconversion is documented in several patients with acute- and convalescent-phase specimens.

*March 26*
The first official acknowledgement of SARS in Beijing comes in a dispatch from Xinhua news agency which says the Chinese capital has a few 'imported' cases. The first global 'grand round' on the clinical features and treatment of SARS is held by the WHO. The electronic meeting unites 80 clinicians from 13 countries.

*March 27*
Various labs in the WHO network confirm the University of Hong Kong's findings and identify the SARS virus as a previously unknown coronavirus.
WHO recommends screening departing travellers from worst affected areas.

*March 28*
The CDC reports on the investigation into a cluster of 12 persons with suspected/probable SARS in Hong Kong which could be traced back to the medical doctor from southern China who arrived 21 February 2003 and stayed in the Metropole hotel.

*March 29*
Carlo Urbani, the WHO doctor who alerted the world to SARS, dies in Bangkok.

*March 30*
In Hong Kong, a steep rise in the number of SARS cases is detected in Amoy Garden, a large housing estate consisting of ten 35-storey blocks, which are homes to around 15,000 persons. The Hong Kong Department of Health issues an isolation order to prevent the further spread of SARS. The isolation order requires residents of Block E of Amoy Gardens to remain in their flats until midnight on 9 April. Residents of the building are subsequently moved to rural isolation camps for 10 days.

*March 31*
The New England Journal of Medicine publishes two articles about clusters of SARS patients in Hong Kong and in Toronto on its website.

*April 2*
The WHO issues an advisory recommending only essential travel to Hong Kong and Guangdong province. This is described as the most stringent travel advisory the WHO has ever issued, and follows evidence that travellers from Singapore, Beijing and Taiwan had caught SARS in Hong Kong and taken it back with them.
The WHO's Weekly Epidemiological Record publishes a new case definition, recommends measures to prevent the international spread of SARS, and proposes the implementation of global surveillance system. The WHO recommends that airport and port health authorities in affected areas undertake screening of passengers of presenting for international travel. In addition, the WHO

*Table 3.2* Continued

issues guidance on the management of possible cases on international flights, disinfection of aircraft carrying suspect cases and surveillance of persons who have been in contact with suspect cases while undertaking international travel. Although this guidance is primarily directed at air travel, the same procedures are recommended for international travel by road, rail or sea from affect areas.

*April 3*
A WHO team arrives in Guangdong. In Beijing, Health Minister Zhang Wenkang tells a televised press conference that the city had 12 cases of SARS, but the disease was under control.

*April 5*
China apologises for its slow response to the SARS outbreak amid allegations that officials have covered up the true extent of the spread of the disease.

*April 6*
A Finnish staff member of the International Labour Organization dies of SARS in Beijing, after catching the disease from a fellow passenger on a flight from Bangkok.

*April 8–10*
Three research groups publish results which suggest that a novel coronavirus might be the etiologic agent of SARS.

*April 9*
First SARS case reported in Africa.

*April 12*
Canadian researchers announce the first successful sequencing of the coronavirus genome believed to be responsible for the global epidemic of SARS. Scientists from the CDC confirm these reports. The new sequence has 29,727 nucleotides which fits well with the typical RNA boundaries of known coronaviruses. The results come just 12 days after a team of 10 scientists, supported by numerous technicians, began working around the clock to grow cells from a throat culture, taken from one of the SARS patients, in Vero cells (African green monkey kidney cells) in order to reproduce the ribonucleic acid (RNA) of the disease-causing coronavirus.

*April 16*
The WHO announces that a new pathogen, member of the coronavirus family never before seen in humans, is the cause of SARS. To prove the causal relationship between the virus and SARS, scientists had to meet Koch's postulates which stipulate that a pathogen must meet four conditions: it must be found in all cases of the disease, it must be isolated from the host and grown in pure culture, it must reproduce the original disease when introduced into a susceptible host and it must be found in the experimental host that was so infected.

To confirm whether the new virus was indeed the cause of the illness, scientists at Erasmus University in Rotterdam, the Netherlands, infected monkeys with the pathogen. They found out that the virus caused similar symptoms – cough, fever, breathing difficulty – in the monkeys to that seen in humans with SARS, therefore providing strong scientific evidence that the pathogen is indeed the causative agent.

The unprecedented speed with which the causative agent of SARS was identified – just over a month since the WHO first became aware of the new illness – was made possible by an unprecedented collaboration of 13 laboratories in 10 countries.

Chinese Premier Wen Jiabao acknowledges that the situation caused by SARS in China is 'extremely grave'. The next day President Hu Jintao calls a Politburo meeting to emphasize the gravity of the situation.

(*Table 3.2 continued*)

*Table 3.2* Continued

*April 17*
India confirms its first SARS case.

*April 20*
The Chinese government discloses that the number of SARS cases is many times higher than previously reported. Beijing now has 339 confirmed cases of SARS and an additional 402 suspected cases. Ten days earlier, Health Minister Zhang Wenkang had admitted to only 22 confirmed SARS cases in Beijing. Minister of Health Zhang Wenkang and the Mayor of Beijing are removed from their posts, apparently for having covered up the extent of the SARS outbreak. The city closes down schools and imposes strict quarantine measures. Most worrying is the evidence that the virus is spreading in the Chinese interior, where medical resources might be inadequate.
After the identification of a cluster of illness among employees of a crowded wholesale market in Singapore, the market is closed for 15 days and the vendors placed in home quarantine.

*April 23*
The WHO issues travel advisories and recommends postponement of non-essential travel to Toronto, Canada.

*April 25*
Outbreaks in Hanoi, Hong Kong, Singapore and Toronto show signs of peaking.

*April 26*
Health ministers from 13 east and south-east Asian countries – meeting in Malaysia – call for all international travellers to be screened for SARS.

*April 27*
Nearly 3,000 SARS cases have been identified in China. China closes theatres, internet cafes, discos and other recreational activities and suspends the approval of marriages in an effort to prevent gatherings where SARS can be spread.
A further 7,000 construction workers work around-the-clock to finish a new 1,000-bed hospital for SARS patients in Beijing.

*April 28*
After reporting no fresh outbreaks of SARS for two weeks, Vietnam becomes the first country to contain the disease.

*April 29*
The first report on SARS in children, published by the Lancet, suggests that young children develop a milder form of disease with a less-aggressive clinical course than that seen in teenagers and adults.

*May 1*
The complete SARS virus genome sequence is published by two groups in Science.

*May 2*
The Xiaotangshan Hospital opens its doors for 156 SARS patients from 15 hospitals in urban areas in Beijing. The Xiaotangshan Hospital was built by 7,000 builders in just eight days.
Taiwan, which has a rapidly evolving outbreak, reports a cumulative total of 100 probable cases, with 11 new cases in 24 hours. Eight SARS deaths have occurred in Taiwan.

*May 3*
The WHO sends team to Taiwan, as the number of cases begins to grow.

*Table 3.2* Continued

*May 4*
Scientists in the WHO network of collaborating laboratories report that the SARS virus can survive after drying on plastic surfaces for up to 48 hours; that it can survive in faeces for at least 2 days, and in urine for at least 24 hours; and that the virus could survive for 4 days in a faeces taken from patients suffering from diarrhoea.

*May 5*
The Chinese authorities quarantine 10,000 people in the eastern city of Nanjing.

*May 7*
The WHO revises its initial estimates of the case fatality ratio of SARS. It now estimates that the case fatality ratio of SARS ranges from 0% to 50% depending on the age group affected, with an overall estimate of case fatality of 14% to 15%. Based on new data, the case fatality ratio is estimated to be less than 1% in persons aged 24 years or younger, 6% in persons aged 25–44 years, 15% in persons aged 45–64 years, and greater than 50% in persons aged 65 years and older.

*May 8*
The WHO extends its SARS-related travel advice to the following areas of China: Tianjin, Inner Mongolia and Taipei in Taiwan province.

*May 9*
Publication of the first prospective study on SARS.

*May 11*
The southern Chinese city of Guangzhou bans spitting in public places to combat SARS.

*May 15*
China threatens to execute or jail for life anyone who breaks SARS quarantine orders.

*May 20*
In Taiwan, more than 150 doctors and nurses quit various hospitals in one week, because of their fear of contracting SARS. Nine major hospitals have been fully or partly shut down.

*May 22*
A fresh outbreak of SARS occurs in a Toronto hospital, a week after it was certified free of the disease by the WHO.
The infection rate reaches its apex in Taiwan, with 65 new cases in one day.

*May 23*
The World Health Organization removes its recommendation that people should postpone all but essential travel to Hong Kong Special Administrative Region and the Guangdong province, China.
   Research teams in Hong Kong and Shenzhen announce that they have detected several coronaviruses closely related to the SARS coronavirus in animal species taken from a market in southern China. Masked palm civets, raccoon-dogs and Chinese ferret badgers are wild animals that are traditionally considered delicacies and are sold for human consumption in markets throughout southern China.
   Two studies assess the epidemic potential of SARS, and the effectiveness of control measures. Their main message is that the SARS virus is sufficiently transmissible to be able to cause a very large epidemic if unchecked, but not so contagious as to be uncontrollable with good, basic public health measures.

*May 31*
Singapore is declared free of SARS.

(*Table 3.2 continued*)

*Table 3.2* Continued

Toronto is back on the WHO list of areas with local transmission after Canada reported new clusters of 26 suspected and eight probable cases of the disease linked to four Toronto hospitals.

*June 5*
The outbreak has peaked around the world – including China – the WHO says.

*June 6*
82 cases are now being reported in the second outbreak of SARS in Ontario, Canada.

*June 13*
The WHO withdraws its travel warnings for the Chinese provinces of Hebei, Inner Mongolia, Shanxi and Tianjin – but maintains the warning for Beijing.

In addition, the WHO removes Guangdong, Hebei, Hubei, Inner Mongolia, Jilin, Jiangsu, Shaanxi, Shanxi and Tianjin from the list of areas with recent local transmission.

*June 17*
WHO lifts its travel warning for Taiwan.

*June 21*
A study by Rainer, suggests that the current WHO guidelines for diagnosing suspected SARS may not be sufficiently sensitive in assessing patients before admission to hospital. Daily follow-up, evaluation of non-respiratory, systemic symptoms and chest radiography would be better screening tools.

*June 23*
China and Hong Kong are removed from the WHO's list of SARS-infected areas.

*June 24*
Beijing is declared free of SARS, and the WHO removes its recommendation against travel to the city.

*July 2*
Toronto is declared free of SARS after its second outbreak.

*July 5*
Taiwan is declared SARS free, and the WHO declares the epidemic has been contained worldwide. Taiwan is the last country to be removed from the WHO's list of infected areas.

*September 9*
Singapore announces that a patient has SARS, making him the first person to contract the disease in five months.

*September 24*
The Singapore Ministry of Health releases the report of an investigation of the recent SARS cases. The investigation concludes that the patient most likely acquired the infection in a laboratory as the result of accidental contamination. The patient was conducting research on the West Nile virus in a laboratory that was also conducting research using active SARS coronavirus.

*December 17*
Taiwan health officials say a medical researcher at a Taipei military hospital has contracted the virus.

*2004*

*January 5*
Chinese health officials confirm a 32-year-old man in southern Guangdong province has SARS, the country's first case in months, and announce plans to slaughter thousands of civet cats to curb the spread of the disease.

*Table 3.2* Continued

---

*January 16*
The WHO says it has found evidence suggesting that civets do carry SARS.

*January 17*
China confirms two new SARS cases in Guangdong province.

*April 26*
The Chinese health ministry says it is investigating at least four new suspected cases. Officials say all the new cases are connected to a confirmed patient who worked at a SARS research lab.

*May 19*
The WHO says China has contained the latest outbreak of SARS.

*July 1*
The director of China's main disease control centre, Li Liming, resigns over the April outbreak, which happened at one of his laboratories.

*July 7*
Hong Kong Health Secretary Yeoh Eng-kiong resigns after being criticized in a report on the handling of the 2003 SARS crisis. The report accused him of paying too little attention to SARS when it appeared in mainland China, and issuing misleading statements to the Hong Kong public.

---

Sources: Abraham, T. (2004) *Twenty-first Century Plague: the Story of SARS.* Hong Kong: Hong Kong University Press; Floyd, W. and Mansoor, O.D. (2006) 'SARS Chronology', in Kleinman, A. and Watson, J., (eds) *SARS in China: Prelude to Pandemic?*, California: Stanford University Press; SARS Expert Committee (2003) *SARS in Hong Kong: From Experience to Action*, Hong Kong: Government Logistics Department.

The outbreaks beyond the mainland PRC, namely in the HKSAR, Singapore and Vietnam, as well as in Toronto and elsewhere, were initiated by cases that were mostly imported from Guangdong Province, the southernmost one in China, before the virus had been identified and before appropriate measures had been put in place to prevent its transmission.[6] International travel appeared to be responsible for the rapid intercontinental spread of this disease. As SARS demonstrated, the speed of modern travel ensures that a virus that is in Hong Kong today can be carried by a sick traveller to any point in Southeast Asia within 3–4 hours, to Europe in 12 hours and to North America in 18 hours. Nearly 1.5 billion passengers travel by air every year, creating countless opportunities for diseases to spread rapidly across the globe.

The rapid international transmission of the disease can best be illustrated by the 'super-spreader' in Hong Kong. A doctor who stayed at the Metropole Hotel and died from 'respiratory failure' soon afterwards (Tomlinson and Cockram, 2003) was the first known case of SARS in Hong Kong (as we noted earlier in Chapter 1) and appears to have been the source of infection, spread through the contaminated elevator buttons, for most, if not all cases in Hong Kong, as well as the cohorts in Canada, Vietnam, Singapore, the United States and Ireland, and subsequently Thailand and Germany. On

1 March, a 26-year-old, Esther Mok, a former flight attendant who had been on a shopping spree in Hong Kong in late February, was admitted to Tan Tock Seng Hospital in Singapore with respiratory problems (Seno and Reyes, 2004). Four days later, a 78-year-old Kwan Sui-chu died in Toronto's Scarborough Grace Hospital. She too had been in Hong Kong during the past two weeks and, along with Mok and Johnny Chen, had stayed at the Metropole Hotel on the same floor as Liu Jianlun, the doctor from Guangzhou. Chen was airlifted to Hong Kong from Hanoi and brought to the Princess Margaret Hospital on 6 March. He died a week later. On 11 March, as healthcare workers at hospitals in Hong Kong were beginning to become sick, Dr Carlo Urbani, a 46-year-old Italian epidemiologist at the Hanoi French Hospital in Vietnam, who attended to Johnny Chen, fell ill and was hospitalized in Bangkok. Dr Urbani one of the first to identify the SARS virus as a new disease (see Oxford *et al.*, 2003) died less than three weeks later.

By this time, alarm bells were ringing. On 12 March, WHO issued the first 'global alert' warning of an outbreak of 'a severe form of pneumonia', later known as SARS, in Hong Kong, Vietnam and China's Guangdong Province (WHO, 2003b). When the first alert was sounded, there were 55 cases from Hong Kong and Hanoi. Within a month, there were 3,000 cases and more than 100 deaths in 20 countries and on every continent. By the end of the first week of May, there were 7,000 cases being reported in 30 countries. The beginning of May was the peak of the worldwide outbreak, with 200 new cases being reported a day, mainly from China (Abraham, 2004). By 7 August 2003, SARS had affected 32 countries (see Table 3.1) with a total number of 8,422 cases (916 proving fatal overall) (World Health Organization, 2003a). Table 3.3 shows the mortality rates of SARS in places most affected by the virus.

## 3.5  On one's guard

Trying to stop the disease from spreading to new areas was crucial to WHO's strategy for containing SARS. The only way to do this was to ensure that the risk of spreading SARS through airline travel was minimized. The ability of a single sick patient on an airplane to spread the disease was illustrated by the case of an Air China (CA) flight from Hong Kong to Beijing. A 72-year-old man boarded CA flight 112 after a visit to a sick niece at the PWH in Hong Kong, where he had been infected with the SARS virus. Not only was he sick, he happened to be a super-spreader of the disease. From his seat, 14E, he infected 21 other passengers and crew members, some sitting as far as seven seats from him. Two flight attendants caught the virus and took it back to their homes in Mongolia, setting off a chain of nearly 300 infections in the province: four Taiwanese employees of a Taipei-based engineering firm also on the flight fell sick in Taiwan. One Singaporean woman added to the number of cases in Singapore. Also on board were a group of 35 tourists from Hong Kong who were going to spend a week in Beijing. On their return to Hong Kong, at least 10 of them fell ill with SARS, setting off a frantic attempt by the Hong Kong Department of Health to contact all the other passengers and crew on the fateful flight to warn them of the danger (Abraham, 2004).

For WHO in Geneva, incidents like flight CA112 were proof that more needed to be done to ensure that people with SARS were not boarding international flights. The only way to do this was to ask airports and airline staff to check passengers for any of the outward symptoms of SARS: fever, a cough or recent close contact with a SARS patient. On 27 March, WHO put out a recommendation that airline passengers from the five areas that were known to be SARS-affected: Hong Kong, Singapore, Hanoi, China's Guangdong province and Taiwan, be screened at airports before departure using a simple questionnaire asking whether they had any of the symptoms of SARS. In the weeks that followed, Singapore and Hong Kong found high-tech solutions to the problem of screening passengers, and installed sophisticated temperature scanners that would check passengers for fever. Soon other airports around the world began doing the same. Despite the array of modern technology available to fight disease, it became apparent that the real key to containing the epidemic was to use one of the oldest weapons against disease: isolating and quarantining sick people to prevent them from spreading disease to others (see Cipolla, 1981). In the case of a new disease like SARS, there were neither vaccines nor drugs to rely on.

## 3.6 Will SARS return?

With international cooperation, controlling SARS became a matter of making sure that a few basic principles were followed: suspected SARS cases had to be detected and placed in isolation; anyone they had been in contact with needed to be traced and monitored for signs of the disease; doctors, nurses and hospital workers needed to stick to the highest standards of infection control. As national health systems in the worst SARS-affected areas put together the machinery to do this, the number of cases gradually began to decline. By 5 July, less than four months after the world was alerted to the presence of a new disease, WHO was able to declare that the current epidemic had been contained. But at WHO, beneath the exhaustion and nervous tension, there was little feeling of triumph (Abraham, 2004). The battle had been long and weary, but everyone knew the enemy had only been vanquished temporarily. The SARS virus was still present in nature, and it would probably be a matter of time before it reappeared among humans.[7] Other pathogens that have crossed over from animals to infect humans, such as the Ebola virus, periodically re-surface and then fade away (Chan-Yeung and Loh, 2004). SARS may return when conditions are ripe for it to spread to humans from some animal or environmental source.

Table 3.3 Summary table of SARS cases by country, 1 November 2002–7 August 2003

| Areas | Cumulative number of cases | | | | Status | | | | | | Date onset first probable case | Date onset last probable case |
|---|---|---|---|---|---|---|---|---|---|---|---|---|
| | Female | Male | Total | Median age (range) | Number of cases currently hospitalised | Number of cases recovered | Number of deaths | CFR (%)[a] | Number of imported cases (%) | Number of HCW affected (%) | | |
| Australia | 4 | 2 | 6 | 15(1–45) | 0 | 6 | 0 | 0 | 6(100) | 0(0) | 24-Mar-03 | 1-Apr-03 |
| Brazil | 1 | | 1 | 4 | 0 | 1 | 0 | 0 | 1(100) | 0(0) | 3-Apr-03 | 3-Apr-03 |
| Canada | 151 | 100 | 251 | 49(1–98) | 10 | 200 | 41 | 17 | 5(2) | 108(43) | 23-Feb-03 | 12-Jun-03 |
| China | Pending | Pending | 5327 | Pending | 29 | 4949 | 349 | 7 | NA | 1002(29) | 16-Nov-02 | 25-Jun-03 |
| China, Hong Kong Special Administrative Region | 977 | 778 | 1755 | 40(0–100) | 7 | 1448 | 300 | 17 | NA | 386(22) | 15-Feb-03 | 31-May-03 |
| China, Macao Special Administrative Region | 0 | 1 | 1 | 28 | 0 | 1 | 0 | 0 | 1(100) | 0(0) | 5-May-03 | 5-May-03 |
| China, Taiwan | 349 | 319 | 665 | 46(2–79) | 10 | 475 | 180 | 27 | 50(8) | 86(13) | 25-Feb-03 | 15-Jun-03 |
| Colombia | 1 | 0 | 1 | 28 | 0 | 1 | 0 | 0 | 1(100) | 0(0) | 2-Apr-03 | 2-Apr-03 |
| Finland | 0 | 1 | 1 | 24 | 0 | 1 | 0 | 0 | 1(100) | 0(0) | 30-Apr-03 | 30-Apr-03 |
| France | 1 | 6 | 7 | 49(26–61) | 0 | 6 | 1 | 14 | 7(100) | 22(29) | 21-Mar-03 | 3-May-03 |
| Germany | 4 | 5 | 9 | 44(4–73) | 0 | 9 | 0 | 0 | 9(100) | 1(11) | 9-Mar-03 | 6-May-03 |
| India | 0 | 3 | 3 | 25(25–30) | 0 | 3 | 0 | 0 | 3(100) | 0(0) | 25-Apr-03 | 6-May-03 |
| Indonesia | 0 | 2 | 2 | 56(47–65) | 0 | 2 | 0 | 0 | 2(100) | 0(0) | 6-Apr-03 | 17-Apr-03 |
| Italy | 1 | 3 | 4 | 30.5(25–54) | 0 | 4 | 0 | 0 | 4(100) | 0(0) | 12-Mar-03 | 20-Apr-03 |
| Kuwait | 1 | 0 | 1 | 50 | 0 | 1 | 0 | 0 | 1(100) | 0(0) | 9-Apr-03 | 9-Apr-03 |

| | | | | | | | | | | | | |
|---|---|---|---|---|---|---|---|---|---|---|---|---|
| Malaysia | 1 | 4 | 5 | 30(26–84) | 0 | 3 | 2 | 40 | 5(100) | 0(0) | 14-Mar-03 | 22-Apr-03 |
| Mongolia | 8 | 1 | 9 | 32(17–63) | 0 | 9 | 0 | 0 | 8(89) | 1(11) | 31-Mar-03 | 6-May-03 |
| New Zealand | 1 | 0 | 1 | 67 | 0 | 1 | 0 | 0 | 1(100) | | 20-Apr-03 | 20-Apr-03 |
| Philippines | 8 | 6 | 14 | 41(29–73) | 0 | 12 | 2 | 14 | 7(50) | 4(29) | 25-Feb-03 | 5-May-03 |
| Republic of Ireland | 0 | 1 | 1 | 56 | 0 | 1 | 0 | 0 | 1(100) | 0(0) | 27-Feb-03 | 27-Feb-03 |
| Republic of Korea | 0 | 3 | 3 | 40(20–80) | 0 | 3 | 0 | 0 | 3(100) | 0(0) | 25-Apr-03 | 10-May-03 |
| Romania | 0 | 1 | 1 | 52 | 0 | 1 | 0 | 0 | 1(100) | 0(0) | 19-Mar-03 | 19-Mar-03 |
| Russian Federation | 0 | 1 | 1 | 25 | 1 | 0 | 0 | | NA | 0(0) | 5-May-03 | 5-May-03 |
| Singapore | 161 | 77 | 238 | 35(1–90) | 0 | 205 | 33 | 14 | 8(3) | 97(41) | 25-Feb-03 | 5-May-03 |
| South Africa | 0 | 1 | 1 | 62 | 0 | 0 | 1 | 100 | 1(100) | 0(0) | 3-Apr-03 | 3-Apr-03 |
| Spain | 0 | 1 | 1 | 33 | 0 | 1 | 0 | 0 | 1(100) | 0(0) | 26-Mar-03 | 26-Mar-03 |
| Sweden | 1 | 2 | 3 | 33 | 0 | 3 | 0 | 0 | 3(100) | 0(0) | 9-Mar-03 | 9-Mar-03 |
| Switzerland | 0 | 1 | 1 | 35 | 0 | 1 | 0 | 0 | 1(100) | 0(0) | | |
| Thailand | 5 | 4 | 9 | 42(2–79) | 0 | 7 | 2 | 22 | 9(100) | 1b(11) | 11-Mar-03 | 27-May-03 |
| United Kingdom | 2 | 2 | 4 | 59(28–74) | 0 | 4 | 0 | 0 | 4(100) | 0(0) | 1-Mar-03 | 1-Apr-03 |
| United States | 16 | 17 | 33 | 36(0–83) | 7 | 26 | 0 | 0 | 31(94) | 1(3) | 9-Jan-03 | 13-Jul-03 |
| Viet Nam | 39 | 24 | 63 | 43(20–76) | 0 | 58 | 5 | 8 | 1(2) | 36(57) | 23-Feb-03 | 14-Apr-03 |
| Total | | | 8422 | | 64 | 7442 | 916 | 11 | | 1750(20) | | |

Source: World Health Organization (2003) *Summary Table of SARS Cases by Country, 1 November 2002–7 August 2003*, WHO: Geneva. Online. Available HTTP: <http://www.who.int/csr/sars/country/en/country/2003_08_15.pdf>

Notes
a Case fatality based on cases with known outcome and irrespective of immediate cause of death.
b Includes imported cases in Health Care Workers occupationally exposed.
c Following discarding of 3 cases, new breakdown by sex pending.

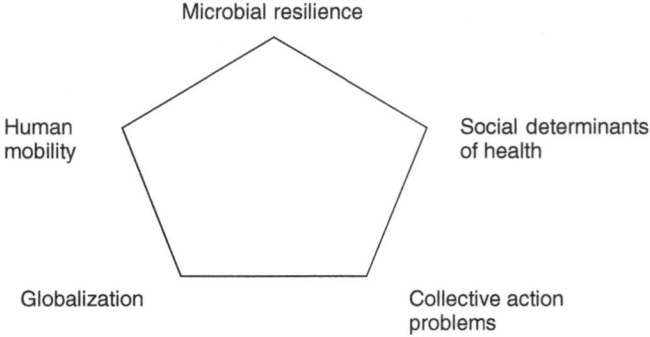

*Figure 3.1* Factors of emergence.

Source: Adapted from Fidler, D. (2004) *SARS, Governance and the Globalization of Disease*, Basingstoke, Hampshire, New York: Palgrave Macmillan.

Fidler's 'axis of illness' idea (see Figure 3.1) perhaps may provide 'a way to organize factors of infectious disease emergence to simplify this complex phenomenon by assigning the factors to five overarching categories':

> the category of microbial resilience captures the importance of microbial, genetic, and biological factors that power pathogenic evolution and its relationship to the human body. Human mobility emphasizes the role played by international trade, travel and migration in disease emergence, including the contributions technology has made in increasing the speed, scope, and impact of human mobility.... The category of social deter-minants of health focuses attention on the underlying societal problems that foster microbial penetration of populations.... Social determinants of health are under constant pressure from the other categories in the axis of illness and are undermined by factors, such as the breakdown in public health measures, that weaken the effort. Globalization refers to factors that accelerate economic development, technology, industry, and culture in ways that deterritorialize human behaviour.... The category of collective action problems refers to the governance challenges created by infectious disease emergence at national, international, and global levels.
>
> (Fidler, 2004: 181–2)

Fidler (2004) contemplates that the 'axis of illness' forms as these five categories interact to foster the emergence and spread of infectious diseases. The SARS outbreak underscores each element of the 'axis of illness' and the challenges it poses for states, international organizations and non-state sectors. The speed with which SARS-CoV apparently jumped from animals to human and then triggered a local, regional and global epidemic is evidence of 'the potent miasma the global village creates for the microbial world' (Fidler, 2004: 181–2). SARS reinforces the effectiveness of human mobility, in combination with the processes of globalization, as a means of spreading pathogenic microbes. The economic damage caused to SARS-affected countries from lost tourism and business-related travel, as we shall see in subsequent chapters, is a further indication of how dependent the globalized world is on air travel. The SARS outbreak also illustrated the importance of social determinants of health in disease emergence (the sale of exotic animals for food or medicine in southern China), and the role collective action problems can play in disease emergence (the epidemic revealed weaknesses and problems in the public health capabilities of many countries affected by SARS).

## 3.7 Conclusions

In this chapter, we have set out to show how SARS took root and then spread from southern China to most of Asia and beyond. We have taken pains to show the *timeline* involved in some detail and addressed the critical steps in the process of gestation, diffusion and resolution. In the next chapter, we turn to the economic impact of epidemics such as SARS, and the consequences for human resources. The question of where we go next, remains problematic and attention has been diverted in the direction of a potential Avian Flu pandemic.

Viewed from the perspectives of Fidler's 'axis of illness', SARS might be likely to re-emerge in one form or other where most of the factors including 'microbial resilience', 'globalization', 'human mobility' and 'social determinants of health' are prevalent, but we cannot be sure. The unique mix of rural–urban migration that would facilitate the rapid spread of any potential new viruses that have jumped from domesticated animals in the villages to humans; intensive animal husbandry (especially involving avian and other wild species, such as civet cats[8] which have been a suspect of carrier of the disease); slaughtering practices on village farms as well as in urban markets; and the lack of proper hygiene standards, have made Guangdong Province and most of southern China a likely epicentre of new emerging viruses (Leung *et al.*, 2003). At the time of writing, a high level of vigilance remains the order of the day!

# 4 Impact on economies, labour markets and human resources in East Asia

## 4.1 Introduction

In this chapter, we will look at the impact of the SARS epidemic of 2003 on economies, labour markets and human resources. This epidemic followed in the wake of the 1997 Asian Financial Crisis and the events of '9/11', two years earlier. Divine judgement might have come to mind to those of the local populations who knew their biblical scriptures: 'And I will bring a sword upon you, that shall avenge the quarrel of my covenant: and when ye are gathered together within your cities, I will send the pestilence among you; and ye shall be delivered into the hand of the enemy' (Leviticus, 26, 25).

It would be tempting to follow this up with: 'And it came to pass that the Asian economies concerned were just beginning to recover, when they were to be traumatized once more.' We have already, the reader may recall, hinted at the potential gravity of the SARS outbreak and its prospective costs not only in medical terms but also in economic and associated costs. We shall take each of these aspects of the political economy of SARS in turn and examine their broad implications. In the following Chapters, 5, 6, 7 and 8, we will see how these are exemplified in the economies of Hong Kong, the PRC, Singapore and Taiwan.

## 4.2 Impact on economies

The Chief Economist for World Bank East Asia at the time estimated that a direct impact effect of SARS would be to reduce East Asian growth by 0.4–0.5 per cent of GDP, bringing the estimated cost of SARS in the range of US$20 billion to US$25 billion, a huge amount in absolute terms.[1] The Asian Development Bank (ADB) calculated the likely effect of the disease under different epidemic scenarios, and forecast losses totalling up to US$20 billion in the four most potentially vulnerable economies, namely China, Hong Kong, South Korea and Taiwan. In the case of Hong Kong, the ADB predicted that SARS could knock four percentage points off economic growth in 2003, taking it down more or less to zero. The Asia Pacific Business Network produced estimates of GDP growth forecasts for the four economies on which we are focusing, before and after the epidemic, no less discouraging and mostly negative, apart from those for China (see Table 4.1).

There was a drastic decline in the GDP of the Hong Kong economy, for example, in the first and second quarter of 2003 when SARS was most severe in its impact. It was a bad time for any news of this kind to reach Hong Kong, as a downturn in economic activity had already occurred and deflation had begun to appear, with slow but relentless increases in unemployment.[2] The ultimate long-term economic impact of SARS on Hong Kong, let alone China, as well as on the region, has yet to be fully assessed.[3]

Asian economies are, as we have already noted, heavily dependent on tourism, which accounts for at least 10 per cent of GDP in most of the affected countries, perhaps more in some. We have here perhaps the 'Achilles' Heel' of the economies of many places. City-states such as Hong Kong and Singapore are heavily dependent on the sort of service-sector industries which demand regular and varied human contact – something that many in the region, fearing they were at risk from infection, were eager to avoid: these sectors are very labour intensive. Although analysts found it hard to estimate the economic cost, through travel disruption and lost output of goods and services, some authorities put the figure at a higher level – more than US$30 billion (*BBC News*, 25 August 2005; *Financial Times*, 30 July 2005).

Consumer confidence did in fact dramatically decline in a number of economies, as we shall see in greater detail later, leading to a significant reduction in private consumption spending. Services rather than manufacturing bore the brunt. Much of the impact stemmed from the fear of the unknown; people had opted to just stay at home to reduce the probability of infection. The extraordinary thing is that so many survived on a 'day-to-day' basis in the circumstances, but there was a price to pay. Already hit by negative equity, many tightened their belts and waited.

*Table 4.1* GDP forecast: before and after SARS

| Country | Previous GDP forecast (%) | New GDP forecast (%) |
| --- | --- | --- |
| China | 7.5 | 7.5 |
| Hong Kong | 2.5 | 1.5 |
| Indonesia | 4.0 | 3.7 |
| Malaysia | 5.0 | 4.0 |
| Singapore | 3.5 | 2.0 |
| Taiwan | 3.5 | 3.3 |
| Thailand | 4.5 | 4.3 |

Source: Asia Pacific Business Network, Vol. 7, No. 9, 2003.

Invisible earnings were immediately and negatively affected in the economies concerned. Service exports, in particular tourism-related exports, were to be hard-hit. Investment was affected by reduced overall demand, heightened uncertainties and increased risks. Foreign investment inflow was delayed or reduced in reaction to SARS (see Fan, 2003). The resultant fall in the demand for labour, and for the goods and services that people would not be buying, which is a major specific focus of this book, was soon evident.

Although SARS had affected every component of aggregate demand, private consumption, as we have suggested, plummeted. Services involving face-to-face contact had been dealt a severe blow by the widespread fear of infection through such interactions. Tourism, transportation (particularly airlines) and retailing had been the hardest hit sectors – as consumers shunned shops, restaurants and entertainment venues, and travellers cancelled trips, leaving hotels almost deserted, as noted in an earlier chapter.

In such turbulent environments, economists have to estimate economic, as well as accounting, costs of shocks. Accounting costs only include *explicit* costs such as labour and other input costs changes in sales and profits, damage to capital and facilities and tax implications (see Adams, 2003). Economic costs also include *implicit* costs, including changes in business environment, changes in opportunities for formal and informal sectors and changes in supply and demand patterns (see Adams, 2003). The stages of estimation can be divided into three separate rounds, according to the International Monetary Fund (see IMF, 2003). The first round quantifiable channels of impact are assumed in the tourism, retail and external trade sectors. The second round quantifiable effects could also include manufacturing and financial services, as well as lower Foreign Direct Investment (FDI) flows. The third round relating to prolonged psychological and social impacts will only be observable or measurable much later.

Impacts on external trade included cutbacks in flights and ship arrivals, badly hitting supply chains; major 'dents' in tourism, which count as part of 'service exports' in the current account of the balance of payments; and possible related effects on foreign exchange earnings, which affected the reserves balance of the country (see IMF, 2003) were soon clearly seen. There were both negative and positive impacts on retail sales. The negative effect on retail sales entailed a bigger effect on restaurants and tourist-related sales than on consumer sales. But the positive impact would count in 'stocking-up' effects on medical supplies and food.

A number of questions of political economy remain to be answered. First, impacts on tourism can be temporary or permanent; will tourists return later in the same year or delay to the next year? Second, business tourists and leisure tourists may have different elasticity; does SARS have full-country impact on tourism or only in affected cities? Third, worse still, will there be regional psychological effects? We will return to these queries in the specific subsequent 'country' chapters and in our conclusions.

## 4.3 A model of supply and demand shocks

There were a number of channels by which an epidemic, such as the SARS outbreak, might affect an economy. We have admittedly simplified the causal links in our model but use it at this point to exemplify the main variables we have chosen to highlight in order to present the labour market and human resources consequences. One channel was seen as operating through 'supply shocks'. If the outbreak could not be effectively contained, the workforce would be reduced because of illness or precautionary measures to prevent the spread of SARS, thereby disrupting business activity (Asian Development Bank, 2003). There was also the risk of a major 'demand shock' as people just stopped shopping and were paralysed into economic indecision (see Figure 4.1).

Consumer confidence did in fact dramatically decline in a number of economies, as we shall see in greater detail later, leading to a significant reduction in private consumption spending. The possible fall in the demand for labour, and for the goods and services that people would not be buying, which is part of the specific focus of this book, will have to be taken into account. As it was difficult, even dangerous, to get to work and many were more than cautious about doing so, there was also a supply-side implication.

Although SARS had affected every component of aggregate demand, private consumption in particular had borne the brunt of the impact. Services involving face-to-face contact, as we have made clear, had been dealt a severe blow by the widespread fear of infection through such interactions. Avoidance of others was not necessarily an irrational reaction.

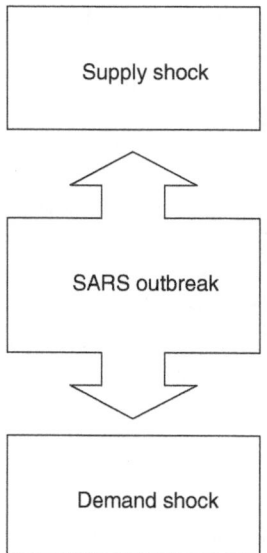

*Figure 4.1* The economic impact of SARS.

Whilst it is true to say that SARS did pose significant medical risks and had major economic implications, it had exerted a disproportionately large psychological impact on people's fears of the gravity of the epidemic, whether rational or irrational. In the short run, economic consequences arose almost wholly from public perceptions and fear of the disease, which was greater than in recent flu epidemics, harking back perhaps to accounts of the worst that may have occurred in Imperial China, or in medieval Europe. New virus, no known cure: result – chronic anxiety and even panic.

As we suggested in Chapter 1, the pronounced anxieties regarding SARS may possibly be attributed to the combination of two aspects of information about the illness: the almost costless and rapid transmission of information due to the development of global 24/7 media-coverage and communication technologies; and perhaps more importantly the lack of sufficient medical information on SARS (see Fan, 2003). For new infectious diseases, the cost of infection of SARS is not normally known with certainty, especially in the initial period. The mortal dangers of the epidemic only revealed themselves as the death-count rose but something touched a deeper *angst*. The cost of postponing services and social activities was relatively small to individuals and collectives, when compared to its possible costs; higher prevalence of disease increased the risk of infection and therefore further reduced interactions. This was nonetheless a rational reaction, although side by side with other even more irrational responses.

This stimulus of the epidemic may be conceptualized as inducing a 'demand shock', particularly affecting consumption patterns. In locations with a high incidence of SARS, the mobility of people was to be highly restricted, either voluntarily or involuntarily, thus potentially reducing consumer spending. Thus, we surmised, SARS mainly affected economic growth by reducing demand. Consumer confidence did in fact dramatically decline in a number of economies, leading to a significant reduction in private consumption spending, very noticeably in Chinese cities like Beijing, Shanghai and Guangzhou, but even more markedly in Hong Kong, Singapore and Taipei, as we shall see in the chapters to come.

To sum up thus far, people had opted to stay at home, literally within the four walls of the apartments or houses, to hopefully reduce the probability of infection. Businesses went into a tailspin and the main streets and shopping malls were empty. The possible fall in the demand for labour for the goods and services that people would not be buying had therefore to be taken into account.

## 4.4   Distorted behaviour of individuals

Given its relatively low morbidity and mortality, why had the economic impact of SARS appeared to be so devastating? Neither an outside observer nor even an economics expert, would have *a priori* predicted such catastrophe in the making in the circumstances. Much of the economic impact, it seemed, stemmed from the many factors we have adumbrated above, both rational and irrational. In addition to inflicting direct costs such as the human loss and the expenditure on prevention and treatment, infectious diseases also distort the behaviour of individuals (Kantarevic *et al.*, 2005). Research in psychology highlights three factors that increase the level of perceived risk: how dreaded, uncontrollable and fatal the risk is; how observable, unfamiliar and unknown it is; and the level of personal and social exposure to the risk (Slovic, 1987). Prospect theory (Kahneman and Tversky, 1979) predicts that rare events tend to be overweighed, in the absence of the risk-learning process through repeated experience.

It is no exaggeration to say that panic had gripped the region. The role of the media was critical but also mobile phones and text messages, as well as emails, played their part in diffusing both fact and rumour. As we have noted in earlier chapters, the SARS virus is transmitted from person to person by inhalation of droplets, and this typically occurs when a sick person sneezes or coughs, so people in the affected cities wore masks and stocked up on masks. When one of the authors arrived in Hong Kong airport at the peak of the epidemic, it seemed as if one was entering a science fiction movie. As people across Asia, as well as foreign business executives or visiting tourists had opted to stay at home to reduce the probability of infection, schools and universities, and indeed many enterprises and offices, had been closed for weeks. Tourism and transportation (particularly airlines) ground to a halt, and the hospitality industries were closed down. It was therefore very likely that there would be immediate implications in terms of labour markets and human resources, to which we now turn.

## 4.5  Impact on labour markets and human resources

Unemployment rates across Hong Kong, Taiwan and Singapore, for example, as we shall later see in greater detail in the subsequent chapters, had significantly increased by May 2003, and the underemployment rate also increased over the same period, mostly reflecting the adverse impact of the spread of SARS since mid-March 2003, although less in the case of the PRC. While decreases in employment were seen in many major economic sectors, including construction, restaurants and hotels, and manufacturing, there were also increased incidents of employees being temporarily suspended from work or asked to take 'no-pay' (i.e. unpaid) leave, thereby leading to an increase in underemployment. The difficulties were compounded by the growing economic slow-down in Asia and indeed worldwide, that had already been taking root even before the SARS virus first appeared (see Table 4.1). Disentangling these multiple macro-economic and labour-market trends, is of course, very difficult, but is clear that SARS seriously aggravated the ongoing cyclical factors.

One or two examples of how the epidemic hit businesses and employment in the region follow: The chairman of the Hong Kong Federation of Restaurants and Catering Services, for instance, noted that 25 restaurants had been closed within the first two weeks of April 2003, leading to unemployment of over 1,600 restaurant staff, and over 16,000 of their members were either on 'no-pay' leave or were forced to accept pay cuts ranging from 10 to 30 per cent. Government statistics indicated that the restaurant trade suffered a drop of 9 per cent in revenue in the first quarter of 2003 when compared to the same period in 2002. A publicly listed Chinese restaurant that had 18 outlets closed down seven of its outlets in May 2003, causing around 500 redundancies. As a result of the drastic 70 per cent plunge in the number of visitors in April and May when compared to the same months in 2002, the Ocean Park theme-park in Hong Kong suffered a monthly loss of HK$15 million to HK$20 million. It was the first time in its 26 years' operation that the Ocean Park authorities declared that the Park would be closed every Monday starting from June 2003, until further notice. Furthermore, all of the 600 staff had to take four days' 'no-pay' leave a month (Interviews, June 2003). It was thus very likely that there would be major implications in terms of labour markets and human resources flowing from the epidemic.

Asian economies are heavily dependent on tourism, which accounts for at least 10 per cent of GDP in most of the affected countries. City-states such as Hong Kong and Singapore are heavily dependent on the sort of service industries that demand regular and varied human contact – something many in the region are eager to avoid: these sectors are very labour-intensive. According to the analysis of the ILO, reduced travel due to new concerns over SARS, combined with the ongoing economic downturn, was set to cut another 5 million jobs in the battered world tourism sector in 2003 (ILO press release, 14 May 2003). The situation was exacerbated by the travel advice issued by the WHO recommending that 'persons travelling to Hong Kong Special Administrative Region and [adjacent] Guangdong Province, China consider postponing all but essential travel' (WHO press release, 12 March, 2003b: 1).

In attempting to study the impact of SARS on the Asian economies, labour markets and human resources, as adumbrated above, we adopted a two-pronged methodology. First, we generated an information database of information about the SARS epidemic, its economic as well as its HRM implications, by using the internet, library resources and literature searches. Second, we carried out on-site empirical field research, involving interviewing over 200 decision-makers in the Asian economies and its service-sector industries, such as senior managers and union officials, as well as government officials and academics, over the period of the epidemic and its aftermath.

In order to apply our model to the four economies concerned, we formulated the following hypotheses:

1   The greater the adverse impact of SARS on the Asian economies, the greater will be the negative impact on the service sector and specifically on the hotel industry.
2   The greater the adverse impact of SARS on consumer demand in the Asian hotels and hospitality industry, the greater will be the negative impact on the related demand for labour in terms of hotel employees in specific hotel groups in the industry.
3   The greater the adverse impact on the demand for labour in the Asian hotel industry, the greater will be the negative impact on the labour-market in terms of lay-offs and redundancy among hotel employees in specific hotel groups in the industry.

We shall return to each of these hypotheses in the next four chapters that follow.

## 4.6   Conclusions

In this chapter, we have pointed to the ways in which the SARS epidemic of 2003 had a significant impact on the economies, labour markets and human resources in Asia that were affected. We have suggested that there was serious concern regarding a disastrous downturn in economic activity, there and elsewhere in the global economy. We also set out a set of hypotheses relating the most vulnerable sector and industries within it that would bear the brunt of the downturn. We now turn to the specific economies, labour markets and human resources in the region in which we conducted empirical field research, just after the epidemic had waned. In Chapters 5, 6, 7 and 8, we will look at Hong Kong, the PRC, Singapore and Taiwan, to investigate in greater detail the effects of these developments.

# Part II

# Impact on East Asia

The telegram read: 'DECLARE A STATE OF PLAGUE STOP CLOSE TOWN'

Albert Camus ([1947]2002: 50)

# 5  Hong Kong

## A case study

## 5.1  Introduction

Catastrophes often come in twos, even threes; so it was with Hong Kong's woes. The Asia financial crisis, '9/11' and then SARS. As Defoe ([1720]2003: 4) notes 'The People shewed great Concern at this, and began to be allarm'd all over the Town.' The 1997 Asian financial crisis had started just as Tung Chee-hwa took office as the Chief Executive of the newly constituted HKSAR.[1] The crisis occurred after a frantic 12 months of speculative activity in an exuberant property market. Unfortunately, the external conditions did change – liquidity drained out of Asia. How would the very open Hong Kong economy accommodate this 'shock'? While many of the detrimental influences on Hong Kong's economy were not of its own making, the Hong Kong government did inadvertently emphasize these negative influences by greatly increasing the supply of residential property with the explicit intent of lowering prices (Brown, 2004). Subsequent to the US dollar weakening, a move which infers an easier monetary regime for Hong Kong because of its 'peg' to that currency, and with the impact of the 2003 Iraq war fading, there were signs that a recovery in the domestic economy could slowly pick up. Just prior to the outbreak of SARS, the Hong Kong economy grew by 4.5 per cent in real terms in the first quarter of 2003 (Brown, 2004). One sector that helped to offset the very depressed domestic demand picture was tourism (see Fan, 2003).

In many ways, SARS could not have hit Hong Kong at a worse time (see Wong et al., 2004). All of a sudden, the hint of optimism was shattered. Domestic economic activity ground to a near halt as restaurants and shops were deserted. This was bad enough but it was then followed by the final straw. 'It quickly became apparent that the mainland SARS outbreak could be worse than had previously been imagined – and this was followed by the revelation that Taiwan was also similarly affected ... As more and more flights were cancelled, the lifeblood seemed to be draining out of the virtuous economic triangle that ties together Hong Kong, Taiwan and mainland China' (Brown, 2004: 190). Passenger arrivals by land and air collapsed and tourism dried up. Cathay Pacific cut its scheduled passenger flights by over 80 per cent and throughput at the Hong Kong airport fell by

80 per cent. Some hotels had less than ten rooms occupied at the height of the crisis (Brown, 2004). How would its hotel industry survive in face of the drastic plunge of average hotel occupancy rates which fell from 83 per cent to 18 per cent, when compared to the same months in 2002? We shall shortly see that – *ex post facto* – the industry did survive, but only because it took drastic steps to tighten its belt.

Now we move on to the background of the start of the epidemic in Hong Kong, and we will then examine the consequences for Hong Kong, its labour-market and one particularly vulnerable sub-sector of its service-sector industries, namely hotels and hospitality (see Belau, 2003). We deal with Hong Kong first, (before we turn to mainland China in the next chapter), because the former had more dramatically hit the world's headlines and excited the 24/7 global media, due to the greater transparency in the Special Administrative Region's governance, as well as the mechanism of diffusion to the outside world, to which we now turn.

## 5.2    SARS in Hong Kong: origins

To recapitulate, the first fatal cases of SARS probably occurred in Guangdong Province in southern China in November 2002, as noted earlier in Chapter 3. A patient in Hanoi who was visiting Vietnam, became ill on 26 February 2003 and was evacuated to Hong Kong where he died on 12 March. This first case in Hanoi had stayed at a hotel in Kowloon, Hong Kong, at the same time as a 64-year-old doctor who had been treating pneumonia cases in southern China, as we have seen (see Chapter 1).

The second major epicentre of the SARS crisis in Hong Kong, accounting for over 300 cases, had been an apartment complex called 'Amoy Gardens', as already noted. It was to prove to be a traumatic event, with grave implications and at first a source of medical mystery.

The source has been attributed to a patient with renal failure receiving haemodialysis at the Prince of Wales Hospital who stayed with his brother at Amoy Gardens (see Ng, 2004). He had diarrhoea, and infection may have spread to other residents by a leaking sewage-drain, allowing an aerosol of virus-containing material to escape into the narrow light-well between the buildings and spread in rising air-currents (Tomlinson and Cockram, 2003). Sewage had back-flowed into bathroom floor drains in some of the apartments. It also spread to people in nearby buildings probably by person-to-person contact and by contamination of public installations (Ng, 2004). But it took some time to solve the mystery, to see how the infection had spread and how far, as in the case of the Metropole Hotel.

## 5.3    Economic impact of SARS

Figure 5.1 shows the drastic decline in the GDP of the HKSAR in the first and second quarter of 2003 when SARS hit Hong Kong. It was a bad time

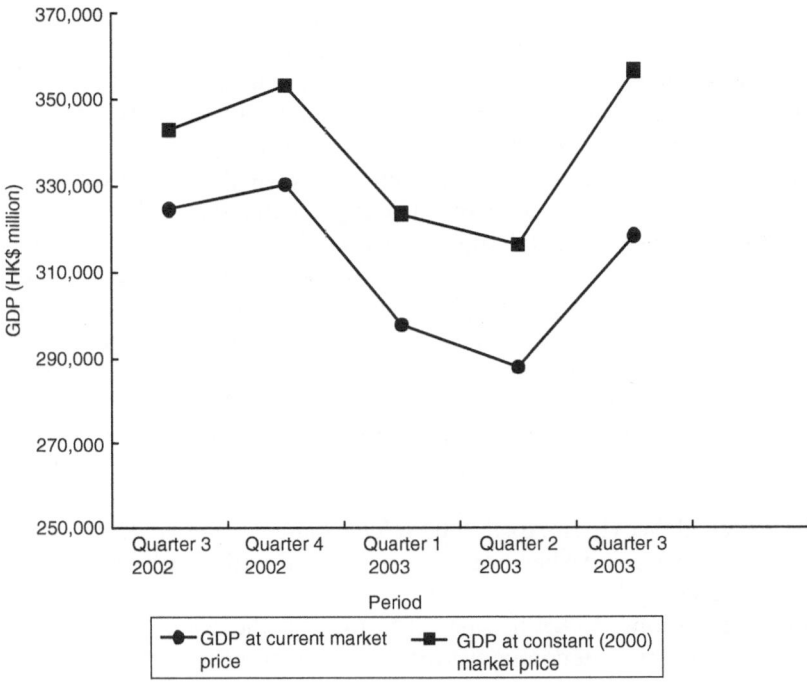

*Figure 5.1*  Gross domestic product (GDP) of the Hong Kong special administrative
region.

Source: Census and Statistics Department, HKSAR government <http://www.info.gov.hk/
censtated/eng/hkstat/fas/nat_account/gdp/gdp1_index.html>

for any news of this kind to reach Hong Kong, as a downturn in economic
activity had already occurred and deflation had begun to appear, with slow
but relentless increases in unemployment[2] (see Wong *et al.*, 2004).

Services involving face-to-face contact had been dealt a severe blow
by the widespread fear of infection through such close interactions (see
Gerberding, 2003). Tourism, transportation (particularly airlines) and
retailing had been the hardest-hit sectors, as consumers shunned shops,
restaurants and entertainment venues, and travellers cancelled trips. An
International Air Transport Association (IATA) director commented that
the Hong Kong airline industry was the hardest hit. According to statistics
in April 2003, passenger rates had fallen by 60 per cent in Hong Kong,
compared to 40 per cent in Seoul and Singapore; 37 per cent in Bangkok;
and 36 per cent in Kuala Lumpur. Prior to 2 April 2003, the Hong Kong
International Airport received 90,000–100,000 inbound passengers every
day and was one of the world's busiest air hubs. In the month of April,
passenger numbers fell 68 per cent. While the normal number of passengers
for the month would have been around 2.9 million, the actual number was

only 909,000. Hong Kong tour operators reported an 80 per cent plunge in bookings while retail sales had plummeted by about 50 per cent (*Hong Kong Standard*, 15 April 2003). Matters worsened in May with only 565,000 arrivals, down nearly 80 per cent from the same time a year earlier. During the height of the crisis, the airport had a mere 15,000 arrivals a day (Loh and Welker, 2004). Even the number of visitors from mainland China fell by 40 per cent as China, too, was caught up in its own efforts to fight SARS.[3] Findings from an impact-assessment study commissioned by the World Travel and Tourism Council suggested that SARS would cost a loss of 41,720 jobs in the Hong Kong tourism and travel-related industries, 'chopping HK$280 billion off the economy' (*Ming Pao*, 17 May 2003). The deputy president of the Council remarked that the impact of SARS on the travel industry was five times more detrimental than the loss caused by 11 September 2001 terrorist attack on the United States (*Ming Pao*, 17 May 2003).

The impact on aviation was very quickly felt and it had grave effects on the sector. As visitor arrivals had dropped, airlines such as Cathay Pacific had cancelled a large number of flights; over 45 per cent of the flights had been cancelled weekly in April 2003 (*Hong Kong Economic Times*, 1 May 2003) during the period when one of the present co-authors was entering and later exiting Hong Kong airport. The information screens were a mass of red-lit cancellations. Ticketing sales of Cathay Pacific, which accounted for 40 per cent or more of the company's total revenue, plunged by over 70 per cent in the first two weeks of April from HK$120 million to HK$4 million (*Hong Kong Economic Times*, 1 May 2003). The monthly passenger rate had fallen by 80 per cent, from 1 million to a little more than 200,000 compared to the same time the previous year; Cathay Pacific made a daily loss of HK$23 million in May. It was in a serious crisis; its cash reserve could only last for 40 days (*Ming Pao, South China Morning Post, Hong Kong Economic Journal*, 7 May 2003). The business of the airline's caterer was so badly affected that all of its 600 staff had to take 15 days' 'no-pay' leave in the consecutive months of May and June 2003, meaning a 50 per cent pay cut (*Ming Pao, South China Morning Post, Hong Kong Economic Journal*, 10 May 2003).

The human consequences were soon to register with the public – as well as with officialdom. Hong Kong's seasonally adjusted unemployment rate had increased to 8.7 per cent by May 2003, and the underemployment rate also increased to 4.2 per cent over the same period, mostly reflecting the adverse impact of the spread of SARS since mid-March 2003, compounded by the growing economic slow-down in Asia, and indeed worldwide (see ADB, 2003), that had been taking root even before the SARS virus first appeared (see Table 5.1). Disentangling these multiple economic trends, is of course, very difficult, but it is clear that SARS seriously aggravated the cyclical factors.

Whilst a decrease in employment was seen in many major economic sectors, including construction, restaurants and hotels, and manufacturing,

*Table 5.1* Statistics on labour force, unemployment and underemployment

| Period | Unemployed ('000) | Unemployment rate (Seasonally adjust) (%) | Underemployed ('000) | Underemployment rate (%) |
|---|---|---|---|---|
| 1/2003–3/2003 | 259.8 | 7.5 | 100.7 | 2.9 |
| 2/2003–4/2003 | 273.7 | 7.8 | 112.7 | 3.2 |
| 3/2003–5/2003 | 287.3 | 8.3 | 135.0 | 3.8 |
| 4/2003–6/2003 | 300.0 | 8.6 | 151.0 | 4.3 |
| 5/2003–7/2003 | 309.2 | 8.7 | 148.7 | 4.2 |
| 6/2003–8/2003 | 309.4 | 8.6 | 141.0 | 4.0 |
| 7/2003–9/2003 | 297.8 | 8.3 | 126.6 | 3.6 |
| 8/2003–10/2003 | 282.7 | 8.0 | 120.7 | 3.5 |
| 9/2003–11/2003 | 265.3 | 7.6 | 117.3 | 3.4 |
| 10/2003–12/2003 | 254.2 | 7.4 | 116.1 | 3.3 |

Source: Census and Statistics Department, HKSAR government <http://www.censtatd.gov.hk>

there were also increased incidents of employees being temporarily suspended from work or asked to take 'no-pay' (i.e. unpaid) leave, thereby leading to an increase in underemployment (Census and Statistics Department, 2003). The human resources consequences would prove to be very extensive as hotel group after hotel group was forced to 'downsize' (Belau, 2003; Lee and Warner, 2005a).

## 5.4 Human resources consequences

The economic impact of SARS on the Hong Kong hotel industry will now be examined first in terms of the *labour demand* of hotel services as well as their *labour supply*. We will discuss these in terms of the model we described earlier, in Chapter 4.

Between March and June 2003, many business sectors in Hong Kong had been adversely affected. Starting from the outbreak of SARS and the issue of global advisory warning by the WHO on Hong Kong, businesses related to tourism – including retail, travel agents, restaurants, airlines and hotels – had dropped dramatically. The HKSAR government announced that the number of passenger aircraft had been reduced by no less than 59 per cent in May 2003 (*Information Services Department*, 13 June 2003). Tourists from all over the world had postponed or cancelled their trips to Hong Kong. The number of visitor arrivals from March 2003 to May 2003 dropped significantly from 1,347,386 to 427,254 (see Table 5.2).

The average hotel occupancy rates plunged from 79 per cent in March 2003 to 18 per cent in May 2003, a dramatic fall to say the least (see Table 5.3).

The Hong Kong Hotels Association announced in April that the hotel occupancy rates of all five-star hotels dropped to single digits, compared

*Table 5.2* Tourism performance

| Month | Visitor arrivals | Average hotel occupancy (%) |
|---|---|---|
| June 2002 | 1,174,202 | 79 |
| July 2002 | 1,368,693 | 82 |
| August 2002 | 1,501,078 | 86 |
| September 2002 | 1,370,279 | 82 |
| October 2002 | 1,584,563 | 85 |
| November 2002 | 1,570,192 | 92 |
| December 2002 | 1,668,474 | 89 |
| January 2003 | 1,545,978 | 82 |
| February 2003 | 1,408,139 | 81 |
| March 2003 | 1,347,386 | 79 |
| April 2003 | 493,666 | 22 |
| May 2003 | 427,254 | 18 |
| June 2003 | 725,236 | 34 |
| July 2003 | 1,291,828 | 71 |
| August 2003 | 1,644,878 | 88 |
| September 2003 | 1,478,699 | 82 |

Source: *Tourism Commission, Tourism Performance* <http://www.info.gov.hk/tc/tourism_per/index.htm>

*Table 5.3* Hotel room occupancy rate from January–May (2002 and 2003 compared)

| Month | All categories | |
|---|---|---|
| | 2002 (%) | 2003 (%) |
| January | 81 | 82 |
| February | 75 | 81 |
| March | 86 | 79 |
| April | 87 | 22 |
| May | 83 | 18 |

Source: Hong Kong Tourism Board (26 June 2003) *May Arrival Figures Hit New Low, But Signs of Recovery Now Starting to Show. Annex II.* Hong Kong: Hong Kong Tourism Board.

Note
All categories include the High Tariff A Hotels, High Tariff B Hotels, Medium Tariff Hotels, Tourist Guesthouses.

to an average of around 80 per cent for the same time the previous year, and suffered an average daily loss of half a million dollars (*Sing Tao Daily*, 13 April 2003). To survive in such a turbulent environment, hotels in Hong Kong had to resort to various measures to cut costs, as no-one knew if or when the epidemic would peak and decline. Figure 5.2 shows that the unemployment and underemployment rates of the hotel sector climbed

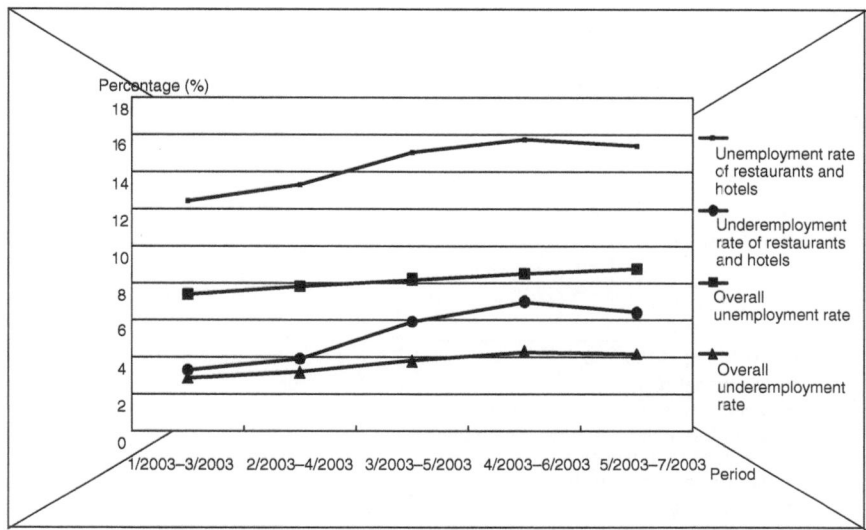

*Figure 5.2* Unemployment rate and underemployment rate of the Hong Kong special administrative region (1 March 2003–5 July 2003).

Source: Census and Statistics Department, HKSAR government <http://www.info.gov.hk/censtatd/eng/hkstat/fas/labour/ghs/labour1_index.html>

steeply, when compared to the overall unemployment and underemployment rates in Hong Kong.

We now go on to discuss the HRM implications of the changing labour demand and labour supply consequences, as noted above (see Figure 5.3). The 'devil is in the detail' as we shall. We look in turn at each of the hypotheses we suggested in Chapter 4.

In one prominent example, the five-star Hyatt Regency Hotel dismissed 130 staff – 22 per cent of its total establishment – positions ranging from front line staff to managerial level. The principle of 'last in, first out' was adopted in making redundancy decisions. Most of the dismissed staff were not eligible for redundancy compensation, as they had worked in the hotel for less than two years. The rest of 470 staff had to take 10 days' 'no-pay' leave per month (*Ming Pao, South China Morning Post, Hong Kong Economic Journal*, 15 May 2003). Hotels throughout the region took tough human resource decisions, with many introducing 'no-pay' leave that ranged from 20 per cent to 48 per cent of the working month (Keith, 2003). But senior staff were still expected to continue to work the 'hours required', which effectively made the unpaid leave an ill-disguised pay cut. The *Report of Weekly Consultations on Effect of SARS* on Business revealed that employment in the hotel industry dropped by 2.4 per cent in late April 2003, and the percentage rose to 7.1 per cent in early August 2003. The average

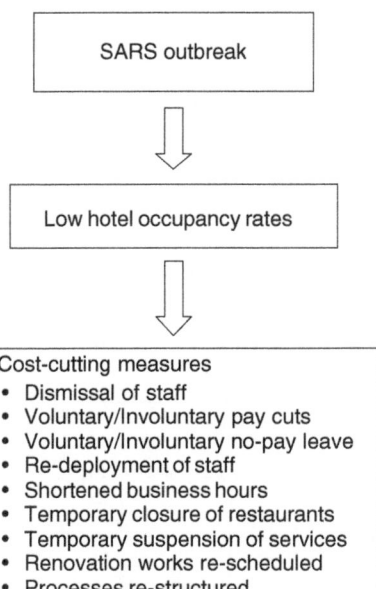

*Figure 5.3* Cost-cutting measures adopted by the Hong Kong hotel industry.

percentage of hotel employees who had to take 'no-pay' leave also rose from 79.3 per cent to 88.9 per cent from early to late June 2003 (see Table 5.4).

Table 5.5 shows the human resources emergency arrangements of major hotels in Hong Kong.

Other cost-cutting measures adopted by hotels in Hong Kong included: temporary closure of restaurants, shortened business hours, redeployment of staff, rescheduling of renovations and restructuring of kitchens. The Grand Hyatt temporarily closed three of its restaurants and bars, and staff who were affected were redeployed (*Sing Tao Daily*, 13 April 2003). The prestigious Mandarin Oriental temporarily suspended its breakfast buffet, and shortened the business hours of the café by two hours, to close an hour before midnight.

Although no staff had been laid off in the equally famous Peninsula Hotel, employees were told to clear annual leave almost immediately, while some were deployed to other departments – including engineering to paint guest rooms (Shellum, 2003). According to the executive chef of the Peninsula who had worked in the hotel for 16 years, the staff did not mind 'as long as they keep their jobs'. The eight kitchens were combined into 'one big unit' where everyone did everything. The chef was quoted to inform that 'previously, each kitchen needed a certain amount of people just to switch on the lights in the morning' (Shellum, 2003). Planned renovations of a

*Table 5.4* Weekly average percentage change in current employment of hotels as compared with the normal situation and no-pay leave arrangements of hotel staff

| Week ended | Change in current employment | Current no-pay leave arrangements | | |
| --- | --- | --- | --- | --- |
| | | *Proportion in the sector (%)* | *% of staff involved in hotel groups concerned* | *Average % of staff with no-pay leave in the sector* |
| 26/4/2003 | −2.4 | Not avaliable | | |
| 3/5/2003 | −2.6 | | | |
| 10/5/2003 | −2.8 | | | |
| 17/5/2003 | −2.7 | | | |
| 24/5/2003 | −5.6 | | | |
| 31/5/2003 | −4.3 | | | |
| 7/6/2003 | −6.9 | 100.0 | 79.3 | 79.3 |
| 14/6/2003 | −6.6 | 100.0 | 85.0 | 85.0 |
| 21/6/2003 | −6.8 | 100.0 | 89.0 | 89.0 |
| 28/6/2003 | −5.9 | 100.0 | 88.9 | 88.9 |
| 5/7/2003 | −6.6 | 91.7 | 90.2 | 82.7 |
| 12/7/2003 | −6.0 | 90.5 | 88.6 | 80.1 |
| 19/7/2003 | −7.0 | 80.0 | 89.2 | 71.3 |
| 26/7/2003 | −7.2 | 70.8 | 87.2 | 61.8 |
| 2/8/2003 | −7.1 | 62.5 | 85.8 | 53.6 |
| 16/8/2003 | −5.8 | 30.4 | 78.6 | 23.9 |
| 30/8/2003 | −4.6 | 12.5 | 80.0 | 10.0 |

Source: Census and Statistics Department, *Report of Weekly Consultations on Effect of SARS on Business.* <http://www.info.gov.hk/censtatd/eng/interest/sars/sars_index.html>

*Table 5.5* Human resources arrangements of major hotels in Hong Kong

| | |
| --- | --- |
| Hyatt Regency | Sacked 130 staff. Other 470 staff took 10 days no-pay leave per month. |
| Grand Hyatt | Closed some floors. All staff on no-pay leave. |
| Regal Hotel Group | All employees of its 5 hotels took 8 days no-pay leave per month. |
| Marriott | Voluntary no-pay leave. CEO took one month off as a showcase. |
| Excelsior | All staff on no-pay leave (days not disclosed). |
| Peninsula | No-pay leave of 2 days per month since April 2003. |
| Island Shangri La | Voluntary no-pay leave of 2–8 days per month since April 2003. |
| Great Eagle | All of 800 staff took no-pay leave of 1–5 days in April and May 2003. |

Source: *Ming Pao*, 15 May 2003.

Swiss restaurant were brought forward. The Verandah kitchen was closed and certain menus combined. The room-service kitchen was moved to the lobby, which allowed 24-hour operation with minimum manning. Because of the drastic cut in demand, contracts with food suppliers had to be renegotiated to cut down supplies immediately. With the introduction of unprecedented discounts and local packages, the Peninsula's restaurants are starting to fill again. According to the executive chef, the positive aspects of the SARS crisis are twofold: that hygiene awareness has been put into the forefront of people's minds, and the crisis has brought his whole team together (Shellum, 2003).

With the SARS epidemic over, tourists, especially from mainland China, began to return to Hong Kong in mid-2003. There has been a significant increase in hotel occupancy rates since tourists from key cities in Guangdong Province were allowed to apply for individual tourist visas in July. However, hotel occupancy rates in Hong Kong are still below levels seen before the SARS outbreak that devastated business in the second quarter of 2003. The chairman of the Hong Kong Hotels Association expected the average hotel occupancy rate to reach around 70 per cent, compared with 81 per cent the previous year 2002, and hotel room rates to fall about 10–15 per cent in 2003 compared to the previous year (*Dow Jones Business News*, 9 September 2003). Beijing and Shanghai were added to the list subsequently in September. The main reason for launching the Individual Visit Scheme was to boost the economies of both Hong Kong and Macau (Lee and Warner, 2007a). The scheme was extended to all 21 other cities of Guangdong Province in May 2004 and to nine other cities in Jiangsu, Zhejiang and Fujian provinces in July 2004.

## 5.5 Discussion

We now turn to a discussion and evaluation of the economic and HRM impact of SARS on Hong Kong and its hotel sector.

We will discuss the evidence we have collected in terms of the set of hypotheses we adumbrated earlier. Taking each hypothesis in turn, we can see

1    The greater the adverse impact of SARS on the Asian economies, the greater will be the negative impact on the service sector and specifically on the hotel industry.

Figure 5.4 shows the negative relationship between the number of SARS cases and the number of tourist arrivals in Hong Kong. The higher the number of confirmed SARS cases in Hong Kong, the steeper the drop in the number of tourists.

As seen in Table 5.2, the number of tourist arrivals drastically declined after the travel advice issued by the WHO (WHO press release, 12 March, 2003b). The number of visitors had plunged from 1,347,386 in March 2003

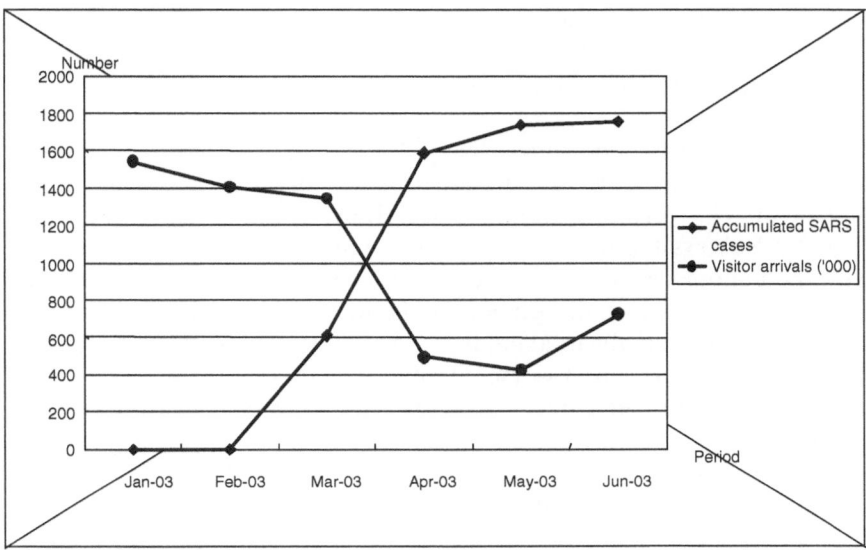

*Figure 5.4* SARS and visitor arrivals.

Source: Tourism commission, *Tourism Performance* <http://www.info.gov.hk/tc/toursim_per/index.htm>; Health, Welfare and Food Bureau, HKSAR Government, *SARS Bulletin*, 23 June 2003. <http://www.info.gov.hk/dh/diseases/ap/eng/bulletin0623e.pdf>

to 493,666 in April 2003, and the hotel occupancy rate plummeted from 79 per cent to 22 per cent within a month. The Personnel Manager of a five-star hotel that targeted at the 'MICE' market (business travellers who visited Hong Kong for [m]eetings, on [i]ncentive tours, for the purpose of [c]onventions and [e]xhibitions) informed us during the interviews that their room occupancy rate fell from over 90 per cent in March to 13 per cent in April 2003, resulting in a loss of around 20 million in expected revenue. The situation deteriorated in May and June 2003. Single digit room occupancy rates of 2–3 per cent led to a loss of HK$50 million. Group cancellations of rooms, ranging from 250 room nights per booking to 2,200 room nights per booking, became the norm for the three months of March, April and May 2003. For example, the cancellation of a concert performance by the rock band 'The Rolling Stones' incurred a business loss of 360 room nights. As a result of the infrequent visitors, food and beverage businesses also dropped to very low levels. Some restaurant outlets that had very few customers were shut down in that period. The Personnel Manager lamented that 'the situation had never been worse. It was even worse than the 1989 June Fourth incidents in Beijing, the 1997 Asian Financial Crisis and the September 11 terrorist attack on the US in 2001' (Interviews, November 2003).

Next, we look at the second hypothesis.

2   The greater the adverse impact of SARS on consumer demand in the Asian hotels and hospitality industry, the greater will be the negative impact on the related demand for labour in terms of hotel employees in specific hotel groups in the industry.

As business was poor across the sector, hotels resorted to temporary closures of business or restaurant outlets, and shortening of business hours in general. This certainly impacted negatively on the demand for labour. Figure 5.5 shows the drastic drop in the number of vacancies registered with the Labour Department for the SARS period, when compared to the figures in 2002. While the general economy of Hong Kong suffered, as reflected by a drop in the total number of vacancies, the 'hotel and boarding house' industry fared even worse. Despite the fact that there were various channels of recruitment, statistics of the Labour Department did to some extent serve as a barometer of the demand for labour in Hong Kong (see also Belau, 2003).

We now turn to the third hypothesis.

3   The greater the adverse impact on the demand for labour in the Asian hotel industry, the greater will be the negative impact on the labour-market in terms of layoffs and redundancy among hotel employees in specific hotel groups in the industry.

The number of layoffs and redundancies in the hotel industry was relatively low despite the crisis situation. Only one in the eight hotels

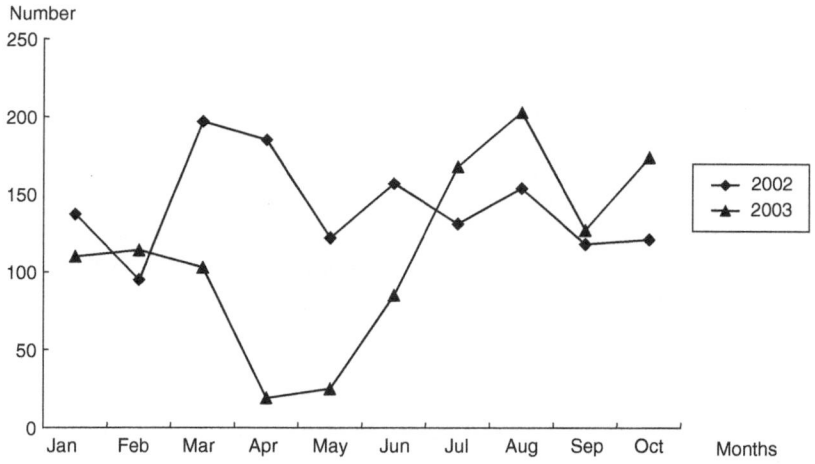

*Figure 5.5* Hotel and boarding house vacancies registered with the labour department (January–October 2002 and 2003 compared).

Source: HKSAR government Press Releases.

covered in Table 5.5 had actually dismissed staff. Most hotels squeezed their savings from the payroll by compulsory requirement of employees to clear their accumulated leave and take 'no-pay' leave. Human resources released from closure of restaurants were redeployed to take up the duties of staff that were on leave. The amount of 'no-pay' leave taken varied from one hotel to another, as shown in Table 5.5.

In one of the five-star hotels, employees could go on leave for weeks as they had to clear all their accumulated leave, (in that particular hotel, employees with less than 10 years' service were entitled to 12 days' per year, while employees with more than 10 years' service could have 24 days per year); and take 'no-pay' leave. To meet the lessened demand for labour, supply was reduced by encouraging staff to take unpaid leave. All employees had to take 'no-pay' leave from the months of April to August 2003 across the board. Three days' 'no-pay' leave were taken in April 2003. This accounted to a salary reduction of 9.9 per cent; this helped the hotel save an average of 1 million dollars per person in that month. Impact on business was reviewed every month. As business deteriorated in the months that followed, all employees across the board had to take nine days' leave in the respective months of May and June 2003, resulting in a substantial salary reduction of 30 per cent, per person. The decision of taking 'no-pay' leave across the board was made by the General Manager in consultation with their US-based headquarters and the local hotel owner. The situation became relatively more promising in July; the number of 'no-pay' leave to be taken was reduced to six days, and then to three days in August 2003. Altogether, all such savings amounted to about 10 per cent of the total business loss of more than HK$50 million over the period. As such measures involved a change in the terms and conditions of employment, each employee was required to sign a letter of consent to that effect every time the number of days of 'no-pay' leave changed. Yet employees were said to be 'very understanding', and that 'sacrifices were made to keep the jobs' (Interviews, November 2003). One interviewee confided that senior staff often conduct 'business as usual', despite being on 'no-pay' leave (Interviews, November 2003). With the end of SARS and the central government's boost of tourism by allowing travellers from Guangdong Province, as well as Beijing and Shanghai to arrange self-visits, room occupancy rates returned to normal (over 80 per cent and 90 per cent) in the months of September to November 2003. Since then, the 'no-pay' leave policy has been suspended.

Human resources practices adopted by hotels appear to have been relatively low-key in their operation – for example, in the form of effecting pay-cuts by encouraging the taking of 'no-pay' leave, for the most part. The apparent compliance of hotel employees in this 'sharing the pain' policy *was prima facie* facilitated by the ostensibly 'paternalist' HR practices of 'good communication' and 'caring organizational culture' (according to several HR managers interviewed).

Most major hotels were fairly transparent with their employees about the bad business situation. In one of the hotel manager interviews, we were told that business losses due to room cancellations, expected revenue losses and the low occupancy rates were shared with staff during their quarterly employees' meeting, amongst other information about SARS, such as signs and symptoms of SARS; health advice, and preventive mechanisms such as taking body-temperature daily before going to work; compulsory wearing of masks; proper disposal of masks; and cleaning of lift-buttons every two hours with diluted bleach. Repeated emails and notices were sent and posted to employees reminding them of the importance of adequate rest, good personal hygiene and staying away from work if they felt unwell (Interviews, November 2003). Pregnant employees in one hotel were given 'special leave' with full pay when their annual leave was exhausted, as fatality among pregnant SARS victims was the highest.

The so-called caring organizational culture of one hotel could best be illustrated by an Employee Loan scheme initiated by one major hotel owner (Interviews, September 2003). Each employee could apply for a HK$10,000 interest-free loan, payable in four equal payments in the four months when 'no-pay' leave was in place, to be repaid in 10 monthly instalments in 2004 by monthly auto-pay deductions. Furthermore, the Personnel Manager of a hotel that exercised the across the board 'no-pay' leave system confided that a one month discretionary bonus would be paid to staff before the Lunar New Year in gratitude to employees for helping out in the difficult months.

Coincidentally, Cathay Pacific airline had also announced that it would pay staff a year-end bonus equal to the greater of half a month's salary or HK$7,000; and employees who took the special leave (three weeks' unpaid leave between June and September 2003) would be entitled to reimbursement of foregone salaries (*South China Morning Post*, 26 November 2003). Cathay Pacific's trade unions were said to be pleased with the reinstatement of bonuses, as it would 'highlight the recovery in air traffic since SARS, and was an effort to reward staff that had helped the airline get through the crisis' (*South China Morning Post*, 26 November 2003).

Investment in employee training and development also helps to foster a 'people-oriented' and 'caring' culture. Most of the top hotels began to conduct workshops on topics like 'service excellence', 'leadership' and 'languages'. For example, with the growing market of the mainland 'big spenders', Mandarin Chinese (*putonghua*) language training became an allegedly 'trendy' training programme for front-line staff (Interviews, November 2003). Special interests courses, such as 'flower arrangement' and 'Chinese Opera', taught and organized by staff were supported by one hotel with the provision of a training venue (Interviews, November 2003).

The so-called employee-focused philosophy may be demonstrated in the case of one specific hotel by an annual Employee Opinion Survey to measure employee satisfaction and opinion towards management (Interviews, November 2003). The Personnel Manager informed us that more than 10 sessions of 'Powerpoint' presentations explaining the survey had been held in 2003. Staff then returned an anonymously completed questionnaire in a glued envelope to be sent to a consultancy firm in the United States for data-analysis. Results were to be shared with employees in January 2004, followed by action plans for improvements (Interviews, November 2003).

Apart from the formal mechanisms, social activities such as an employee mahjong competition and a soccer competition also serve to encourage team spirit. One hotel sponsored employee-outings on a departmental basis at a modest HK$100 per head per year (Interviews, November 2003). Others included visits to the Ocean Park, annual staff parties, hotel anniversary celebrations crowned by senior management cutting cakes, live bands and lucky draws (all videotaped and replayed in the employee common room for a 're-experience of the good memories').

## 5.6 Conclusions

In this chapter, we have looked at the effect of the SARS epidemic on Hong Kong. We examined the impact on the economy, labour-market and human resources, in general and in the hotel industry, in particular.

It is clear that the impact of SARS on the Hong Kong economy and specifically the hotel sector was on the whole significantly negative. Both the quantitative, as well as the qualitative, data we have gathered points in this direction. The HRM implications were dire, if apparently benignly administered; yet mass layoffs and redundancies were not rife. The impact of labour-displacement and cost-cutting appear to have been mitigated by the paternalist HR practices adopted.

On the other hand, employee compliance may be seen both negatively as well as positively. It is well-known that unionization in Hong Kong is relatively low but not negligible (approximately 22.15 per cent in 2002), even by urban Asian standards. As at the end of 2002, there were across the Special Administrative Region an accumulated total of three registered trade union federations and 666 registered trade unions (comprising 622 employee unions, 23 employer unions and 21 mixed organizations of employees and employers). The declared membership of the 622 employee unions was 676,534 (Commissioner for Labour, 2002). Unionization in the hotel industry worldwide is generally weak, but in Hong Kong it is probably worse. The number of employees joining employees' unions of the hotel industry was 3,493 in 2002. Hotel-workers had little option but to comply with the stopgap HRM measures put forward by management.[4]

In the absence of collective bargaining, tripartite collaboration at the industry level with a view to fostering harmonious labour relations was promoted by the Labour Department. Nine industry-based tripartite committees have been set up over the years, including the catering, hotel and tourism industries (Commissioner for Labour, 2002). These committees provide forums for the representatives of employers, employees and the government to discuss issues of common concern relevant to the industries.[5] The Tripartite Committee on the Catering Trade that comprises nine employers' associations and nine trade unions have at least drawn up a *Code of Labour Relations Practice* and a sample employment contract for the catering industry, and produced a reference guide on employment-related issues relevant to the hotel and tourism industry in 2003[6] (*Labour Focus*, 16 June 2003 to 1 July 2003).

The Hong Kong experience of 'de-industrialization' in the later half of the 1980s and early 1990s had earlier led to a labour surplus of almost half a million factory workers. These were, however, mostly drawn into the booming economy and the growth in tertiary industries, hence the low unemployment rates (as low as 1.4 per cent in 1989) before Hong Kong was exposed to 1997 Asian crisis. Trade and tourism were then badly hit as in the recent SARS epidemic, although the earlier crisis's effects lasted longer, with Hong Kong's trading partners suffering from even more severe setbacks. The crisis of business confidence in 1997 had led to a wave of business collapses and closures that inevitably led to more widespread layoffs and retrenchment.

As the economy recovered by the early 2000s, it was thought that service-sector jobs above all, in sectors like the hotel sector, both in low as well as high-valued added products and services, would compensate for job losses. The SARS epidemic of early and mid-2003 has probably been a grim reminder of the Special Administrative Region's economic vulnerability (see Brown, 2004).

To sum up, if it was thought that the expansion of service-employment, such as in the hotel industry or any other, would create a positive and stable employment equilibrium and compensate for the loss of manufacturing jobs, the Hong Kong authorities may have to reconsider their strategy and continually be on their guard against unforeseen circumstances.

# 6  People's Republic of China (PRC)

## A case study

## 6.1  Introduction

Long ago, Mao Zedong hearing of an epidemic in the distant provinces in the late 1950s, penned this poem:

> We ask the God of Plague: 'Where are you bound?' Paper barges aflame and candle-light illuminate the sky,
>
> (Mao Zedong, 1976)

The 'God of Plague' was on its long march again 50 or so years later in the form of SARS. The diffusion of this deadly virus from the People's Republic of China to the outside world seemed to a helpless public to be a global 'catastrophe' in the making (see Chapter 2), if, in the final analysis, only on a limited scale; WHO figures show that the virus had appeared in 32 countries, affected 8,422 people and led to 916 deaths. China (including the mainland, the HKSAR and Taiwan) was the worst hit, accounting for 92 per cent of the accumulated cases and 90.5 per cent of total deaths as Table 3.1 in Chapter 3 reveals. It had an immediate impact, as we suggest in Chapter 4, on economic growth, employment levels and human resources and more broadly, day-to-day social activities.

## 6.2  SARS in mainland China: origins

In November and December 2002, doctors in Guangdong Province, the most populated in southern China, began to see cases involving a mysterious and contagious 'flu-like' virus they referred to as 'atypical pneumonia', as noted earlier in Chapter 3. Provincial officials took emergency measures and the PRC government sent medical teams to Guangdong Province to investigate the outbreak. Still, for months, official Chinese sources downplayed the seriousness and extent of the mysterious illness (see Kleinman and Watson, 2006). The Guangdong Provincial Health Bureau made the first official PRC announcement about the new illness on 11 February 2003, reporting that five had died and more than 300 had become sick (*Renmin Ribao* (*People's Daily*), 12 February 2003).

Soon, it was hinted that there was 'good news' in sight. On 12 February 2003, the official Xinhua News Agency announced that the mysterious illness had been 'brought under control' and no new cases had been reported in China (*People's Daily*, 13 February 2003). This remained the official story from the Chinese government through mid-March 2003, even as the WHO issued a global alert on 12 March 2003, following new outbreaks of an 'atypical pneumonia' in Hong Kong (see Lee and McKibbin, 2003; Wilder-Smith *et al.*, 2003), and Vietnam (see Adams, 2003).

In keeping with past history, official PRC reluctance to be forthcoming continued throughout March (see Davis and Siu, 2007). Since the new leadership was about to gain formal power, the issue was sidelined since it might raise a fuss at the impending Party Congress. On 15 March 2003, WHO issued a rare 'emergency travel advisory' warning, for the first time referring to the illness as Severe Acute Respiratory Syndrome, abbreviated to SARS, and saying that its further spread to Canada (Poutanen *et al.*, 2003), Singapore (Tambyah, 2002; Hsu *et al.*, 2003) and Europe now made it a 'global health threat'. According to WHO officials, it was only at this point that the Chinese government began providing WHO with information about the February atypical pneumonia outbreak in Guangdong Province, although WHO reported that the PRC still declined to provide biological samples, test results, or even details about courses of treatment. On 18 March 2003, PRC officials admitted that the SARS outbreak was continuing in this same province, but had not expanded elsewhere in China (*Wen Wei Po*, 19 March 2003). This was contradicted by reports from Chinese doctors that two people in Beijing had died from the disease earlier in the month.

The outside world was very unhappy and diplomatic pressure began to be applied; with SARS cases continuing to multiply and expand to other countries, including the United States, in April 2003 the PRC began to react to growing criticism over their handling of the SARS crisis. A team of WHO investigators were permitted to go to Guangdong Province on 2 April. Two days later, the head of the PRC's Centre for Disease Control issued an unprecedented public apology for the government's mishandling of the health crisis (*Wen Wei Po*, 5 April 2003). Greater impetus for fuller disclosure appeared to come from within China's medical community itself. On 9 April, a prominent Beijing surgeon publicly disclosed that the government was seriously under-reporting cases of SARS in Beijing, and that the number was far more than 22 cases the government indicated.[1] WHO officials also bluntly told PRC officials on 17 April that the SARS figures Beijing was reporting were unreliable.

New government, new faces, it would seem (see Saich, 2006); the next day, China's newly chosen Premier, Wen Jiabao, threatened dire consequences for any official that did not make full and timely disclosure about SARS cases (*People's Daily*, 19 April 2003). The real official turnaround in the crisis came on 20 April, when PRC leaders fired two senior officials for covering up the extent of the crisis[2] – the first in a series of such firings. PRC leaders also promptly announced that a national week-long May holiday would be reduced to one day to deter travel. Officials also held a nationally televised press conference to announce that 339 cases of SARS had been confirmed and another 402 were suspected in Beijing alone, not the 37 confirmed cases as previously reported. As of 27 April 2003, the number of confirmed cases in Beijing alone had passed 1,100 and SARS outbreaks had been reported in 26 of the PRC's 31 provinces, very likely an under-estimate. That same day, the PRC government ordered the emergency closure of movie theatres, discos, churches and other public places in Beijing (*People's Daily*, 28 April 2003). Although daily PRC announcements showed that confirmed SARS cases were now increasing on a daily basis, on 29 April WHO officials criticized the government as continuing to be unforthcoming with further details about the Beijing cases.

The US Government had issued several travel warnings encouraging Americans to defer non-essential travel to the PRC. In addition, on 1 April 2003, the Department of State authorized the departure of non-essential personnel and family members from the US Consulate General in Guangdong Province and Hong Kong, and similarly on 3 April 2003 from the US Embassy in Beijing and from US Consulates General in Chengdu, Shenyang and Shanghai.

The threat was perceived as very grave by the international community. Whilst SARS did pose significant medical risks for local populations, it was feared, mistakenly as we now know, that it would have far greater lasting economic implications for the world economy, mainly because of the threat of a potentially devastating, worldwide epidemic, for which there was seemingly no medical protective vaccine or indeed cure available, as we have pointed out earlier in Chapters 3 and 4.

## 6.3 Economic impact of SARS

We fully recognize the fallible nature of official Chinese statistics (see Rawski, 2006) but do also offer estimates from non-Chinese experts. We are, additionally, aware of the complex, multi-causal and multi-variate nature of the possible causal links, but, given the limitations of space here, have tried to mainly make the explanation offered as compressed and intelligible as possible. Even the straightforward narrative of what happened seems complex in itself (see Chapter 3 for the 'timeline' we have adapted from various sources for the diffusion of SARS). We see our results as a tentative attempt to analyse the human resources implications, and will return to this point in our conclusions.

The Chief Economist of the World Bank Resident Mission in China described the SARS effect on China's economy as 'temporary' and said that the expected negative impact of SARS on the Chinese economy should not be 'over-exaggerated', as China would remain one of the fastest growing economies in the world in 2003 (*China Daily*, 29 April 2003). The Boao Forum's secretary-general for Asia noted that 'China still offers the most competitive labour market, and remains one of the biggest consumer markets and its size is growing rapidly' (*China Daily*, 29 April 2003). Many economists were equally of the opinion that the 'demand shock' was potentially severe and that the service sector industries, such as catering, hospitality, hotels, tourism, transportation and exposition industries, that had been the hardest hit by SARS, assumed only a small proportion of the country's GDP (*China Daily*, 29 April 2003; *People's Daily*, 28 April 2003).[3]

Furthermore, the growing demand to fight the SARS epidemic meant growth for industries producing medicine, medical apparatus and equipment, textiles such as gauze face-masks and protective suits, sanitation detergents and disinfectants, as well as for the telecom sector (*People's Daily*, 24 May 2003; *Xinhua News Agency*, 10 May 2003).[4] A Chinese economic evaluation, for instance, confidently acknowledged that SARS' adverse impact could be offset by a host of other factors which might also spur economic growth because China, with its huge market, has a strong capability of confronting

*Table 6.1* GDP and GDP growth in China, 1980–2003

| Year | Gross Domestic Product (billion yuan) | GDP growth rate (%) |
|------|------|------|
| 1980 | 451.78 | 7.8 |
| 1981 | 486.24 | 5.2 |
| 1982 | 529.47 | 9.1 |
| 1983 | 593.45 | 10.9 |
| 1984 | 717.10 | 15.2 |
| 1985 | 896.44 | 13.5 |
| 1986 | 1,020.22 | 8.8 |
| 1987 | 1,196.25 | 11.6 |
| 1988 | 1,492.83 | 11.3 |
| 1989 | 1,690.92 | 4.1 |
| 1990 | 1,854.79 | 3.8 |
| 1991 | 2,161.78 | 9.2 |
| 1992 | 2,663.81 | 14.2 |
| 1993 | 3,463.44 | 13.5 |
| 1994 | 4,675.94 | 12.6 |
| 1995 | 5,847.81 | 10.5 |
| 1996 | 6,788.46 | 9.6 |
| 1997 | 7,446.26 | 8.8 |
| 1998 | 7,834.52 | 7.8 |
| 1999 | 8,206.75 | 7.1 |
| 2000 | 8,946.81 | 8.0 |
| 2001 | 9,731.48 | 7.5 |
| 2002 | 10,479.06 | 8.0 |
| 2003 | 11,669.40 | 9.1 |

Sources: National Bureau of Statistics, *China Statistical Yearbook 2003* (Beijing: China Statistics Press, 2003), pp. 55–57 (figures for 1980–2002); *Statistical Communiqué of the People's Republic of China on the 2003 National Economic and Social Development*, National Bureau of Statistics website, <http://www.stats.gov.cn/english/newrelease/statisticalreports/t20040303_402133921.htm> (figure for 2003).

shock from the outside. The senior author, Professor Hu Angang, a leading economist, based at the prestigious Tsinghua University in Beijing, was convinced that the Chinese economy had shown an obvious self-propelling and self-increasing degree of inertia (*People's Daily*, 24 May 2003; *Xinhua News Agency*, 10 May 2003). Judging from the data published by China's State Statistical Bureau, one might argue that SARS had caused an adverse impact on China's economy but that it had not altered the basic situation or changed the general trend of rapid growth (see Table 6.1). It can therefore be surmised here that expert opinion in China blew both 'hot' and 'cold'.

Foreign opinion was still impressed with China's growth track-record. Although many international corporations had put off or cancelled business travel and conferences in China since the outbreak of SARS, and could cause the delay of an expected US$1 billion in China's total foreign investment in the second quarter of 2003, the official FDI figure for the year was in the end still to hit the US$53.5 billion level[5] (see Table 6.2).

*Table 6.2* Realized value of FDI in China, 1983–2003

| Year | Realized value of FDI (billion US$) |
| --- | --- |
| 1983 | 0.92 |
| 1984 | 1.42 |
| 1985 | 1.96 |
| 1986 | 2.24 |
| 1987 | 2.31 |
| 1988 | 3.19 |
| 1989 | 3.39 |
| 1990 | 3.49 |
| 1991 | 4.37 |
| 1992 | 11.01 |
| 1993 | 27.52 |
| 1994 | 33.77 |
| 1995 | 37.52 |
| 1996 | 41.73 |
| 1997 | 45.26 |
| 1998 | 45.46 |
| 1999 | 40.32 |
| 2000 | 40.72 |
| 2001 | 46.88 |
| 2002 | 52.74 |
| 2003 | 53.51 |

Sources: Ministry of Commerce, Invest in China website, <http://www.fdi.gov.cn/common/info.jsp?id=CENSOF T0000000008072> (figures for 1983–2002); *Statistical Communiqué of the People's Republic of China on the 2003 National Economic and Social Development*, National Bureau of Statistics website, <http://www.stats.gov.cn/ english/newrelease/statisticalreports/t20040303_402133921. htm> (figure for 2003).

In addition, financial bell-wethers, like the Shanghai and Shenzhen stock-markets (see Figures 6.1 and 6.2) displayed no inordinate downturn during the SARS period, that is, the second quarter of 2003, then rose sharply when the epidemic seemed to have abated, but for other reasons, and then dipped later in the third and fourth quarters of the year, mainly due to perceived problems of 'overheating' in the Chinese economy and so on.

We may therefore perhaps concede here that many of the fears regarding the economic impact for mainland China may have often been exaggerated, with less of a 'demand shock' perceived than, say, in Hong Kong, pointing more to a 'public health' crisis than an economic one, unlike the experience in the former colony where the overall economic implications were more extensive.

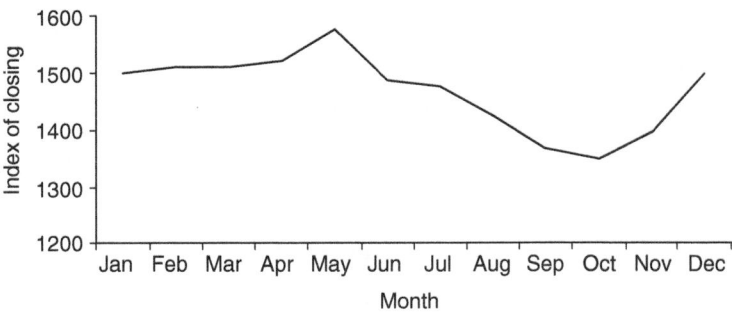

*Figure 6.1*  Composite index of Shanghai Stock Exchange, January 2003–December 2003.

Source: China Securities Regulatory Commission website, <http://www.csrc.org.cn/cn/tongjiku/ehtml/y2004/01/N200401.html>

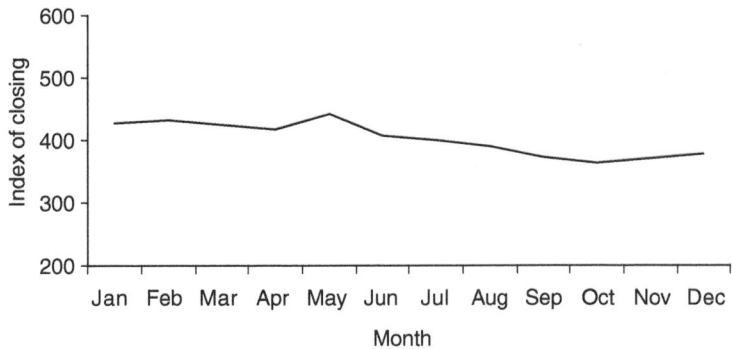

*Figure 6.2*  Composite index of Shenzhen Stock Exchange, January 2003–December 2003.

Source: China Securities Regulatory Commission website, <http://www.csrc.org.cn/cn/tongjiku/ehtml/y2004/01/O200401.html>

## 6.4   Human resources consequences

We now turn to a discussion and evaluation of the economic and human resources impact of SARS on China, its service sector and its hotel industry, taking into account both the 'demand' and 'supply' shocks. We will discuss the evidence we have collected in terms of the set of hypotheses we adumbrated earlier in Chapter 4. Taking each hypothesis in turn, we envisaged that

1   The greater the adverse impact of SARS on the Asian economies, the greater will be the negative impact on the service sector and specifically on the hotel industry.

Was this the case? Official economic data suggests that real GDP growth had indeed fallen back in the second quarter and was 6.7 per cent (see Table 6.3). Hu Angang, in turn, attributed the meagre growth of the tertiary industry figures in the second quarter by 0.8 per cent to SARS, as the impact of SARS was mainly concentrated in late April and in May 2003, and mainly in the tertiary sector, especially retail, tourism and transportation (Hu and Hu, 2003). We found that this reporting of this downturn was confirmed in our on-site field interviewing in the hotel industry (Interviews, mid-Summer 2003).

Given the many unknowns about SARS, it is clear that it had appeared to threaten the general health of the huge population of the PRC and, if not brought under full control, might potentially jeopardize the hard-won economic progress that China had achieved in recent years. Given the range of uncertainties, the World Bank's new update on East Asia projected that growth would fall by almost a percentage point in 2003, to 5 per cent, before rebounding in 2004. The expected negative impact of SARS on the Chinese and Asian economies was still a major fear (Lee and Warner, 2005a,b, 2006a,b, 2007b). Representatives or spokespersons of many influential policy institutes were of the opinion that SARS could well do more damage to economic growth in Asia than the war in Iraq.

In Beijing, the worst hit city in China, it was suggested that the deadly SARS virus caused a loss of 450 million yuan (US$54.4 million) during the

*Table 6.3* Growth of China's major economic indicators (Unit: percentage)

| Indicator | First quarter | Second quarter | Third quarter | Jan.–Sept. |
|---|---|---|---|---|
| GDP | 9.9 | 6.7 | 9.1 | 8.5 (10) |
| Service | 7.7 | 0.8 | 7.6 | not available |

Source: State Statistical Bureau, *China Economic Cycle Monthly Report*, September 2003, in Hu Angang and Hu Linlin, *A Review of China's Health and Development from the Perspective of SARS*, a paper presented at the celebrations of the 20th anniversary of the founding of the China Health Economics Society on November 6, 2003.

first four months of 2003 (*China Daily*, 14 May 2003). Table 6.4 shows that Beijing had seen a year-on-year increase in tourist arrivals and tourism receipts from 1978 to 2002, leaping from rank 18 of the world's tourist arrivals and rank 34 of the world's tourism receipts in 1980, to rank 5 in both categories in 2002, the majority being Overseas Chinese visitors (see Table 6.4).

The capital now saw a serious downturn in visitors; Beijing received 1.85 million overseas tourists in 2003, a drop of 40.4 per cent from 2002, according to official figures (*China Daily*, 13 April 2004). The 'devil', as ever, is 'in the detail'. According to a survey of 20 four- and five-star hotels in Beijing by the China Economic Monitoring Centre under the National

*Table 6.4* China's tourist arrivals and tourism receipts, 1978–2005

| Year | Tourist arrivals (10,000) | Rank | Tourism receipts (100 million US$) | Rank |
|------|---------------------------|------|------------------------------------|------|
| 1978* | 71.60 | 48 | 2.63 | 41 |
| 1979 | 152.90 | n.a. | 4.49 | n.a. |
| 1980 | 350.00 | 18 | 6.17 | 34 |
| 1981 | 376.70 | 17 | 7.85 | 34 |
| 1982 | 392.40 | 16 | 8.43 | 29 |
| 1983 | 379.10 | 16 | 9.41 | 26 |
| 1984 | 514.10 | 14 | 11.31 | 21 |
| 1985 | 713.30 | 13 | 12.50 | 21 |
| 1986 | 900.10 | 12 | 15.31 | 22 |
| 1987 | 1,076.00 | 12 | 18.62 | 26 |
| 1988 | 1,236.10 | 10 | 22.47 | 26 |
| 1989 | 936.10 | 12 | 18.60 | 27 |
| 1990 | 1,048.40 | 11 | 22.18 | 25 |
| 1991 | 1,246.40 | 12 | 28.45 | 21 |
| 1992 | 1,651.20 | 9 | 39.47 | 17 |
| 1993 | 1,898.20 | 7 | 46.83 | 15 |
| 1994 | 2,170.00 | 6 | 73.23 | 10 |
| 1995 | 2,003.40 | 8 | 87.33 | 10 |
| 1996 | 2,276.50 | 6 | 102.00 | 9 |
| 1997 | 2,377.00 | 6 | 120.74 | 8 |
| 1998 | 2,507.29 | 6 | 126.02 | 7 |
| 1999 | 2,704.66 | 5 | 140.99 | 7 |
| 2000 | 3,122.88 | 5 | 162.24 | 7 |
| 2001 | 3,316.67 | 5 | 177.92 | 5 |
| 2002 | 3,680.26 | 5 | 203.85 | 5 |
| 2003# | 3,297.05 | 5 | 174.06 | 7 |
| 2004 | 10,903.82 | n.a. | 257.38 | n.a. |
| 2005 | 12,029.23 | n.a. | 292.96 | n.a. |

Source: World Tourism Organization, *China Tourism Statistics*, http://www.cnto.org/chinastats.asp.

Notes
* *Report on Development of Chinese Tourism* (in Chinese) 《 中 国 旅 游 业 发 展 报 告 》 <http://www.usc.cuhk.edu.hk/wk_wzdetails.asp?id= 2160>; #China Tourism Bureau website <http://www.cnta.gov.cn/ tongjibanlan/2005/3.htm>
n.a.: not available.

Bureau of Statistics, their occupancy had fallen by 30 per cent in April 2003 compared to the same period the previous year. The occupancy of six five-star hotels surveyed had decreased by 50 per cent (*China Daily*, 29 April 2003). Occupancy rates had dipped to as low as 20 per cent at hotels catering for foreigners in the capital (Tang, 2003). The five-star Grand Hyatt Beijing in Chang'an Street had a usual occupancy rate of around 80 per cent in March. However, the rate was sharply slashed in April 2003 following the spread of SARS. In Beijing, more than 1,440 tour groups of 40 or more people had postponed tours since the outbreak of SARS. At the beginning of April, a total of over 10,000 people had cancelled their advanced bookings with China International Travel Service (CITS), as well as over 7,000 with China Youth Travel Service (CYTS). Guangdong International Travel Service (GITS) had almost stopped its cross-border travel service, according to our on-site investigation (Interviews, Summer 2003).

Many tourists simply gave up and took their money back. The Shanghai Tourism Administrative Commission (STAC) reported in late April that local travel agencies had refunded payments to 3,464 inbound groups involving 75,182 tourists, and 279 outbound groups with 8,901 tourists, after they cancelled their 2003 tours (Eastday.com, 2003). According to the Commission, travel agencies offering both domestic and overseas tour packages reported their income plummeted by 78 per cent in April compared to the same period the previous year, while agencies dealing in domestic travel said their income dropped 20 per cent year-on-year (Eastday.com, 2003). The occupancy rate at 398 local hotels was less than 20 per cent on average, while at five-star hotels it was only 13 per cent. Luxury hotels in Shanghai slashed room-rates to counter the effects of SARS (Interviews, Summer 2003). The five-star Westin Tai Ping Yang Hotel offered a standard room at 528 yuan (US$64) a day, compared with the previous record low of 756 yuan (US$91) plus a 15 per cent service charge. Another five-star venue, Shanghai JC Mandarin Hotel, offered up to 60 per cent discounts on rooms. An overnight stay in a standard room then cost 488 yuan (about US$59) plus a 15 per cent service charge, while the full rate used to be US$150 plus a 15 per cent service charge. The city government has announced to offer subsidies to hotels and travel agencies, while exempting all hotels of the social construction fees (*Wen Wei Po*, 9 May 2003). Interviews in the Shanghai hotel industry confirmed these reactions (Interviews, mid-Summer 2003).

At this juncture, we look further at our second hypothesis.

2    The greater the adverse impact of SARS on consumer demand in the Asian hotels and hospitality industry, the greater will be the negative impact on the related demand for labour in terms of hotel employees in specific hotel groups in the industry.

As people avoided hotels, restaurants and other places in fear of catching the disease, some establishments took the opportunity for renovation and HRM renewal (Interviews, Summer 2003). An executive with the hotel management company of Jinjiang Group, the largest group in east China's Shanghai, said that their group had decided to 'bring forward renovation and employee training programmes' in some of their hotels (*Xinhua News Agency*, 18 May 2003). In the Tibetan-Qiang Autonomous Prefecture of Aba, a tourist area in southwest China's Sichuan Province, brisk construction had replaced the swarms of tourists. A planning official of the prefecture, home to the world-renowned Jiuzhaigou Natural Scenic Reserve and the Yellow Dragon Resort[6] said tourist arrivals had increased at double-digit speed in recent years and pressure on transportation and accommodation facilities was enormous. Affected by SARS, tourist arrivals in May, June and July 2003 were predicted to drop by around 1 million compared with the same period the previous year. This shift would give a precious opportunity for the officials to accelerate the upgrading of 'accommodation facilities and projects under construction including tunnels, highways and the Jiuzhaigou-Yellow Dragon Airport (*Xinhua News Agency*, 18 May 2003). On the other hand, many hotels took measures to reduce costs; including stopping all overseas training programmes, halting advertisements and promotional activities, and encouraging staff to take leave without pay, as they did in Hong Kong – as we showed in Chapter 5 (Interviews, late Summer 2003; Lee and Warner, 2006a).

There was worse yet to come; the situation was deteriorated when the State Council promulgated a notice that shortened the seven-day Labour Day holiday to five days, and called for a ban on travel to avoid the fast spread of the epidemic (*People's Daily*, 21 April 2003). This holiday is one of the three 'Golden Weeks' in China, and has significantly boosted China's tourism over the past several years. As a result of the leaps in income per capita in the urban areas (see Table 6.5), the revenue from the Labour Day holiday usually accounts for over 40 per cent of the year's total.

More survey data shows a bleak picture as a result of SARS; telephone interviews with 48 trans-national corporations conducted by the China Economic Monitoring Centre – under the National Bureau of Statistics – revealed that they had banned their employees from travelling in China and that their businesses in the country had been affected to varying degrees. A survey of 50 enterprises in Beijing showed that 36 of them had cancelled or reduced domestic business travel. Another interview with 160 Beijing residents showed that 72 per cent of them had cancelled journeys and cut back on shopping trips and socializing, for fear of catching the disease.

A survey of Beijing, Guangzhou and Shanghai residents revealed that the fear of contracting SARS has drastically changed people's lifestyle and attitude (Eastday.com, 2003). In the random survey of 314 residents in the three cities, it was discovered that intimate contact, such as 'kissing' and 'hugging', became taboo. In Beijing, about one-fifth of those surveyed no longer shared a bed or even a meal with family members. About 40 per cent people surveyed in the three cities had changed their routine by working at

*Table 6.5* Income per capita in urban China, 1990–2003

| Year | Income per capita in urban areas (yuan) |
|------|------------------------------------------|
| 1990 | 1,510.2 |
| 1991 | 1,700.6 |
| 1992 | 2,026.6 |
| 1993 | 2,577.4 |
| 1994 | 3,496.2 |
| 1995 | 4,283.0 |
| 1996 | 4,838.9 |
| 1997 | 5,160.3 |
| 1998 | 5,425.1 |
| 1999 | 5,854.0 |
| 2000 | 6.280.0 |
| 2001 | 6,859.6 |
| 2002 | 7,702.8 |
| 2003 | 8,472.0 |

Sources: National Bureau of Statistics, *China Statistical Yearbook 2003* (Beijing: China Statistics Press, 2003) (figures for 1990–2002); *Statistical Communiqué of the People's Republic of China on the 2003 National Economic and Social Development*, National Bureau of Statistics website, <http://www. stats.gov.cn/english/newrelease/statisticalreports/ t20040303_402133921.htm> (figure for 2003).

home or reducing their working hours. More than one-third of them put off business trips. To stop the spread of SARS, an estimated 8,000 people were under quarantine in Beijing in late April 2003 (*BBC News* website, 27 April 2003; 28 April 2003). According to the Shanghai Statistics Bureau, 77 per cent of local residents did not shop downtown during the Labour Day holidays, while 90 per cent of them did not dine out. Less than 1 per cent of the people surveyed travelled to other provinces. Such fears had serious adverse impact on other service sectors, including civil aviation, railway and road passenger transport, restaurants and hotels. The findings of the above surveys were closely paralleled and confirmed by those of our own interviews (Interviews, late Summer 2003).

Chinese airlines had been among the first to feel the pain as the central government tightened control over trans-provincial passenger flows due to the spread of SARS. The airlines had experienced very low seat-occupancy rates since April 2003, and many of them had cut some of their regular flights to save costs, as did Cathay Pacific in Hong Kong. Wang Yongsheng, director of Air China's publicity department, said that the airline cut at least half of its regular flights during the May Day holidays, a traditional transport peak, because of the huge drop in the number of passengers (*China Daily*, 10 May 2003; *Wen Wei Po*, 3 May 2003). Based in Beijing, Air China then ran most of the international flights into and out of China. But, as more and more countries worldwide were restricting the issuing of visas to Chinese citizens because of the SARS panic, the formerly lucrative international transport business had now turned out to be a money-losing one. Since March, Air China had cut 2,100 flights and affected routes to 63 countries and regions; its losses were considerable. Outside Beijing, the Shanghai-based China Eastern Aviation Group has also failed to escape the impact of the industry setback. Nearly 70 per cent of seats in its planes were empty, while almost half of the traditional 'golden' routes to Europe, Japan and Southeast Asia were cut (*China Daily*, 10 May 2003; *Ta Kung Pao*, 22 March 2003). The airline had cut more than 2,900 flights since March. Its major domestic flights to SARS-affected cities, such as Beijing, Guangzhou and Taiyuan, were also severely cut.

China faces an ongoing employment crisis (see Lee and Warner, 2007b). Since the service sector, a major channel for absorbing the labour force in urban areas, was most affected by SARS, the employment situation still remains vulnerable from fears of epidemics and a further 'supply shock'. We return now to our third hypothesis.

3    The greater the adverse impact on the demand for labour in the Asian hotel industry, the greater will be the negative impact on the labour market in terms of layoffs and redundancy among hotel employees in specific hotel groups in the industry.

The State Council has admitted that the outbreak of SARS has worsened China's already 'grave' employment situation (see Lee and Warner, 2001a,b, 2002, 2004, 2007b). Zhang Xiaoqiang, secretary-general of China's State Development and Reform Commission (SDRC) acknowledged at a China-ASEAN Symposium on Economic and Social Impact of SARS immediately after the end of the epidemic crisis, that China started to feel growing employment pressure due to the impact of SARS (*Xinhua News Agency*, 16 July 2003). According to another report released by a special research team under the Ministry of Labour and Social Security on the post-SARS employment situation, gross employment, employment structure, job-seekers and employment services had all been affected by the SARS crisis. The report asserted that SARS exerted more expected negative influences on such employment than just generally affecting the economy. Those hardest-hit sectors, though accounting for a small part of GDP, provided a high proportion of the labour-intensive employment opportunities. The micro-economic consequences proved to be trenchant. These enterprises laid-off employees as a short-term measure to counter a sharp decline or suspension in business and revenue: many firms suffered substantially and it took time to recover (Interviews, Summer 2003).

The HRM implications are intriguing. In the SARS period that peaked from late April to July 2003, the tourism industry was seriously affected. Let us first look at small and medium-sized business (SMEs); here, for example, shops catering for tourists, such as those selling jade carvings and ornaments, were mostly closed. Retail workers in one of these shops, the Long Di Superior Jade Gallery, informed us that their shop was shut up for three months; employees were all on leave but they stayed in their dormitories and the main gate was closed to outsiders. Since the shop was state-operated, staff was paid a basic wage of 300 yuan (Interviews, April 2004). Another retail outlet that sells cloisonné to tourists was kept open during the SARS period, but it was manned by a minimum number of shop assistants because it was visited by not more than 10 tour groups per day. Staff who went on leave voluntarily would get 300 yuan (half of their basic salary), while staff who carry on working would be paid a full salary of 600 yuan (Interviews, April 2004). Many shop assistants had opted for taking leave; some went home and some stayed in the dormitories. Since all local tours were suspended, the tour guides were also paid basic wages. Drivers of the *hu-tung* (alleys) ride-on tricycles also informed us that their business was suspended and they were paid basic wages. Workers of state-operated enterprises were not the hardest hit as they could live on their basic wages, but part-time workers were the largest victim group (Interviews, mid-Summer 2003).

Bigger enterprises suffered as much; despite a slow recovery, the retail, catering, hotel and recreation industries were dealt the biggest blow from SARS. The manager of a large hotel that targeted the 'MICE' market (business travellers who visited Beijing for [m]eetings, on [i]ncentive tours, for the purpose of [c]onventions and [e]xhibitions) informed us during an interview session that their worst room occupancy during the SARS period was one single customer in one room. Although the hotel was not closed, the three restaurants were merged into one; the convention rooms were all closed; the retail shop was moved to the reception area and only one floor of rooms was open. All such measures were adopted to cut costs. Permanent workers took all their accumulated annual leave, statutory leave and even leave in advance on a rotating basis. State-operated hotel employees could get 70–80 per cent of their full salary, while employees of hotels with foreign investments could get only their basic wages. The manager informed us that there was little resistance from employees because they held a *gongdan* (sharing the burden) attitude. Temporary workers who were mostly non-Beijing residents working as sanitary workers and dish cleaners, left voluntarily as they were paid on a daily basis (Interviews, late Spring 2003).

About a quarter of the 210.9 million employees working in the tertiary industries were employed in these sectors (*China Daily*, 24 June 2003) (see Table 6.6). If their total business shrank by 10–20 per cent, 5–10 million jobs would be under threat.

*Table 6.6* Value added and number of employees by industries, 1980–2003

| Year | Primary industry | | Secondary industry | | Tertiary industry | |
|------|------------------|---|--------------------|---|-------------------|---|
| | Value added (billion yuan) | Number of employees (million persons) | Value added (billion yuan) | Number of employees (million persons) | Value added (billion yuan) | Number of employees (million persons) |
| 1980 | 135.94 | 291.22 | 219.20 | 77.07 | 96.64 | 55.32 |
| 1981 | 154.56 | 297.77 | 225.55 | 80.03 | 106.13 | 59.45 |
| 1982 | 176.16 | 308.59 | 238.30 | 83.46 | 115.01 | 60.90 |
| 1983 | 196.08 | 311.51 | 264.62 | 86.79 | 132.75 | 66.06 |
| 1984 | 229.55 | 308.68 | 310.57 | 95.90 | 176.98 | 77.39 |
| 1985 | 254.16 | 311.30 | 386.66 | 103.84 | 255.62 | 83.59 |
| 1986 | 276.39 | 312.54 | 449.27 | 112.16 | 294.56 | 88.11 |
| 1987 | 320.43 | 316.63 | 525.16 | 117.26 | 350.66 | 93.95 |
| 1988 | 383.10 | 322.49 | 658.72 | 121.52 | 451.01 | 99.33 |
| 1989 | 422.80 | 332.25 | 727.80 | 119.76 | 540.32 | 101.29 |
| 1990 | 501.70 | 389.14 | 771.74 | 138.56 | 581.35 | 119.79 |
| 1991 | 528.86 | 390.98 | 910.22 | 140.15 | 722.70 | 123.78 |
| 1992 | 580.00 | 386.99 | 1,169.95 | 143.55 | 913.86 | 130.98 |
| 1993 | 688.21 | 376.80 | 1,642.85 | 149.65 | 1,132.38 | 141.63 |
| 1994 | 945.72 | 366.28 | 2,237.22 | 153.12 | 1,493.00 | 155.15 |
| 1995 | 1,199.30 | 355.30 | 2,853.79 | 156.55 | 1,794.72 | 168.80 |
| 1996 | 1,384.42 | 348.20 | 3,361.29 | 162.03 | 2,042.75 | 179.27 |
| 1997 | 1,421.12 | 348.40 | 3,722.27 | 165.47 | 2,302.87 | 184.32 |
| 1998 | 1,455.24 | 351.77 | 3,861.93 | 166.00 | 2,517.35 | 188.60 |
| 1999 | 1,447.20 | 357.68 | 4,055.78 | 164.21 | 2,703.77 | 192.05 |
| 2000 | 1,462.82 | 360.43 | 4,493.53 | 162.19 | 2,990.46 | 198.23 |
| 2001 | 1,541.18 | 365.13 | 4,875.00 | 162.84 | 3,315.30 | 202.28 |
| 2002 | 1,611.73 | 368.70 | 5,354.07 | 157.80 | 3,513.26 | 210.90 |
| 2003 | 1,724.70 | 365.46 | 6,177.80 | 160.77 | 3,766.90 | 218.09 |

Sources: National Bureau of Statistics, *China Statistical Yearbook 2003* (Beijing: China Statistics Press, 2003), pp. 55, 124 (figures for 1980 to 2002); *Statistical Communiqué of the People's Republic of China on the 2003 National Economic and Social Development*, National Bureau of Statistics website, <http://www.stats.gov.cn/english/newrelease/statisticalreports/t20040303_402133921.htm> and <http://www.stats.gov.cn/tjsj/ndsj/2005/html/E0502e.htm> (figures for 2003).

Over 100 million workers are engaged in service sector jobs in construction, household services, real estate, tourism and the like. According to statistics from the National Tourism Administration, over 6 million people directly work for the tourism industry. Among them, part-time workers are the most vulnerable group to be laid-off. Employment in related industries will definitely be affected as a result of the multiplier effect. The epidemic also brought many challenges to employment in urban services, business and trade, catering, passenger and freight transport sectors. In hard-hit regions, the social service sectors were on 'shutout' or semi-'shutout'. Employees engaging in the trade business were either forced to go on vacations, or trickled back to their home towns. The aviation and railway industries cut flights and trains because demand for transport had dropped. Some major retail outlets laid-off part-time workers, while some privately owned family stores went out of business (Interviews, late Summer 2003).

The massive migrant worker (*mingong*) population was amongst the hardest-hit employment group. A sizeable number of migrant workers in small and medium-sized restaurants and entertainment venues were laid-off when the government ordered a closure of 'all entertainment business involving mass public gatherings' – cinemas, theatres, internet cafes and karaoke bars, until the outbreak of SARS was brought under control. According to estimates by the Ministry of Agriculture, around 8 million peasant workers of the over 100 million working in urban and prosperous areas had trickled back to rural areas, accounting for 8 per cent of the rural migrant working population.

The second hardest-hit group was the laid-off (*xiagang*) and unemployed (*shiye*) workers. According to the report on post-SARS employment situation, as many as 15 million laid-off workers were 're-employed' in flexible employment patterns (Interviews, late Summer 2003). College graduates had markedly tough employment prospects as well. Universities produced 2.12 million graduates in 2003, a number that had exploded because of the nation's campaign to expand college enrolment four years ago. These avid job hunters had the same gloomy prospects in the job market. Since late April 2003, almost all recruitment activities were delayed or cancelled. As a result, consultation, interviews and recruitment for college graduates were suspended. Enterprises had stopped their plan to recruit new blood from campuses.

A report from the Development Research Centre of the State Council (DRC) showed that China's labour supply had peaked in recent years (*China Daily*, 24 April 2003).[7] In 2003, there was an increase of over 2 million workers. A significant 70 per cent of the new workforce in the past five years found their jobs in the service sector. Over the past two decades, the tertiary industry has on the whole maintained a much greater capacity in bringing out jobs than the primary (natural resources-based economic sectors such as agriculture and mining) and secondary industries (mainly manufacturing and processing businesses) (*People's Daily*, 25 June 2002; *Xinhua News Agency*, 16 June 2003).[8] The service industry has become a major channel for surplus labour. Table 6.7 shows that its share of the 'employment pie' had increased from 13.1 per cent in 1980 to 28.6 per cent in 2002 (see Table 6.7).

The rapid development of individual and private businesses has also contributed greatly to the country's employment efforts. Statistics indicated that 30 million urban residents, representing 40 per cent of the total increase in urban employment, found jobs in the private sector from 1990 to 2001. However, since China's catering, commerce and social service-industries were worst hit by the SARS epidemic, and many small and medium-sized

*Table 6.7* Share of GDP and employment by industries, 1980–2003

| Year | Primary industry | | Secondary industry | | Tertiary industry | |
|---|---|---|---|---|---|---|
| | GDP (%) | Employment (%) | GDP (%) | Employment (%) | GDP (%) | Employment (%) |
| 1980 | 30.1 | 68.7 | 48.5 | 18.2 | 21.4 | 13.1 |
| 1981 | 31.8 | 68.1 | 46.4 | 18.3 | 21.8 | 13.6 |
| 1982 | 33.3 | 68.1 | 45.0 | 18.4 | 21.7 | 13.5 |
| 1983 | 33.0 | 67.1 | 44.6 | 18.7 | 22.4 | 14.2 |
| 1984 | 32.0 | 64.0 | 43.3 | 19.9 | 24.7 | 16.1 |
| 1985 | 28.4 | 62.4 | 43.1 | 20.8 | 28.5 | 16.8 |
| 1986 | 27.1 | 60.9 | 44.0 | 21.9 | 28.9 | 17.2 |
| 1987 | 26.8 | 60.0 | 43.9 | 22.2 | 29.3 | 17.8 |
| 1988 | 25.7 | 59.3 | 44.1 | 22.4 | 30.2 | 18.3 |
| 1989 | 25.0 | 60.1 | 43.0 | 21.6 | 32.0 | 18.3 |
| 1990 | 27.1 | 60.1 | 41.6 | 21.4 | 31.3 | 18.5 |
| 1991 | 24.5 | 59.7 | 42.1 | 21.4 | 33.4 | 18.9 |
| 1992 | 21.8 | 58.5 | 43.9 | 21.7 | 34.3 | 19.8 |
| 1993 | 19.9 | 56.4 | 47.4 | 22.4 | 32.7 | 21.2 |
| 1994 | 20.2 | 54.3 | 47.9 | 22.7 | 31.9 | 23.0 |
| 1995 | 20.5 | 52.2 | 48.8 | 23.0 | 30.7 | 24.8 |
| 1996 | 20.4 | 50.5 | 49.5 | 23.5 | 30.1 | 26.0 |
| 1997 | 19.1 | 49.9 | 50.0 | 23.7 | 30.9 | 26.4 |
| 1998 | 18.6 | 49.8 | 49.3 | 23.5 | 32.1 | 26.7 |
| 1999 | 17.6 | 50.1 | 49.4 | 23.0 | 33.0 | 26.9 |
| 2000 | 16.4 | 50.0 | 50.2 | 22.5 | 33.4 | 27.5 |
| 2001 | 15.8 | 50.0 | 50.1 | 22.3 | 34.1 | 27.7 |
| 2002 | 15.3 | 50.0 | 50.4 | 21.4 | 34.3 | 28.6 |
| 2003 | 14.4 | 49.1 | 52.2 | 21.6 | 33.4 | 29.3 |
| 2004 | 15.2 | 46.9 | 52.9 | 22.5 | 31.9 | 30.6 |

Sources: National Bureau of Statistics of China, *China Statistical Yearbook 2005*, <http://www.stats.gov.cn/tjsj/ndsj/2005/indexeh.htm>; <http://www.stats.gov.cn/tjsj/ndsj/2005/html/E0502e.htm> (figures for 2003 and 2004).

enterprises had to shut down their business which inevitably led to a sharp decrease in demand for labour, China had implemented a most extensive tax exemption system in a bid to support industries affected by SARS (*People's Daily*, 24 May 2003).[9] Airlines, the catering industry, hotels and taxi companies would benefit from the exemptions. The measures were meant to help medium- and small-sized enterprises that continue to absorb labour in China, as they provided jobs for 75 per cent of the urban population (Interviews, late Spring and mid-Summer 2003).

## 6.5   Discussion

Words like layoffs (*xiagang*) and unemployment (*shiye*) used to sound strange to the Chinese, as the Chinese government had for many years after 1949, adopted a 'cradle-to-grave' employment and welfare strategy that covered much of the urban population, through the 'iron rice bowl' (*tie fan wan*) policy. Meanwhile, Chinese enterprises also suffered from overstaffing and low efficiency in its State-owned Enterprises (SOEs), and lacked vitality and market competitiveness. In the previous two decades, China's market-oriented economic reform and industrial restructuring had sharply cut the redundant workforce of SOEs, while its oversized population, now standing at about 1.3 billion, had made the overall employment situation even worse. SARS only added to this huge burden if only marginally.

China's fledgling labour market, developed since a socialist market economy was introduced in the early 1990s to replace the old planned economy, is now under immense pressure from a huge army of job-seekers. According to official sources, a combination of nearly 14 million laid-off workers from the SOEs, 150 million rural surplus labourers coveting an urban life, and an annual increase of some 10 million urban youngsters who have reached the working age (*Ming Pao*, 9 March 2004)[10] were expected to boost the official urban unemployment rate to 4.7 per cent in 2004.[11] Wang Mengkui, director of the *Development and Research Centre under the State Council*, said in April 2003 that '[g]iven the huge population base of China, an average of 10 million people annually will arrive on the employment market before 2010, creating huge strain on a marketplace already affected by an eight per cent unemployment rate' (Solinger, 2003).[12] It is predicted that in the next three to five years, Chinese cities and towns will have to provide job opportunities for some 22–23 million people annually. Pessimists say that even if the Chinese economy maintains its current high growth of 7 or 8 per cent, the country will still face a shortage of more than 10 million jobs a year. Table 6.8 shows the rising urban unemployment rate since 1980 (see Table 6.8). SARS was an unwelcome, additional huge burden if only marginally.

The employment issue poses a serious challenge to China's economic development and social stability, as well as to the government's goal of building a 'harmonious society'. In his *Government Work Report* to the 2003 NPC session, the then Chinese Premier Zhu Rongji stressed that the Chinese government would adhere to the policy of 'the workers finding jobs on their own, the market regulating employment and the government promoting job creation', and should 'do everything possible' to expand employment (*Xinhua News Agency*, 7 March 2003).

China's entry into the World Trade Organization (WTO) has now brought more uncertain factors and could possibly cause a new wave of unemployment (see Warner, 2005). The greatest opportunity China's entry into the WTO brought to the Chinese people, we would argue, is to push forward the integration of Chinese industries with the globalized economy; to bring the Chinese economy onto a path of long and stable development; and hopefully to create conditions for a stable increase of job opportunities. Furthermore, it will further promote the establishment of a market mechanism for employment by stepping up the urbanization process. In the long run, it may mean an increase of 2–3 million job opportunities every year

*Table 6.8* Urban unemployment and unemployment
rate in China, 1980–2003

| Year | Urban unemployment (10,000 persons) | Unemployment rate (%) |
|------|-----|-----|
| 1980 | 541.5 | 4.9 |
| 1981 | 439.5 | 3.8 |
| 1982 | 379.4 | 3.2 |
| 1983 | 271.4 | 2.3 |
| 1984 | 235.7 | 1.9 |
| 1985 | 238.5 | 1.8 |
| 1986 | 264.4 | 2.0 |
| 1987 | 276.6 | 2.0 |
| 1988 | 296.2 | 2.0 |
| 1989 | 377.9 | 2.6 |
| 1990 | 383.2 | 2.5 |
| 1991 | 352.2 | 2.3 |
| 1992 | 363.9 | 2.3 |
| 1993 | 420.1 | 2.6 |
| 1994 | 476.4 | 2.8 |
| 1995 | 519.6 | 2.9 |
| 1996 | 552.8 | 3.0 |
| 1997 | 576.8 | 3.1 |
| 1998 | 571.0 | 3.1 |
| 1999 | 575.0 | 3.1 |
| 2000 | 595.0 | 3.1 |
| 2001 | 681.0 | 3.6 |
| 2002 | 770.0 | 4.0 |
| 2003 | 800.0 | 4.3 |

Sources: State Statistical Bureau, *China Labour Statistical Yearbook 2003* (Beijing: China Statistics Press, 2003), p. 128 (figures for 1980–2002); Press Release by the Ministry of Labour and Social Security, Ministry of Labour and Social Security website <http://www.molss.gov.cn/news/2004/0216. htm> (figure for 2003).

(*People's Daily*, 27 May 2003).[13] But the greatest risk is of structural contradictions, namely, the failure of the supply of surplus labour to meet the demand of available jobs. Although WTO accession may lead to employment growth in the long run (see Lee and Warner, 2007b), it could well cause pain in the initial stages. Some sectors with weak international competitiveness will suffer a heavy blow and have to lay off more workers. This is especially marked at the initial phase of the entry into the WTO. Surplus workers laid-off from the SOEs, coupled with industrial restructuring will exert great pressure on employment. Unemployment (*shiye*), once banished officially, is now a spectre haunting Chinese market socialism (see Lee and Warner, 2007b).

The sectors that have certain advantages in international competition, such as textile and garment industries, might be able to develop rapidly and create more jobs. Yet these sectors will face a structural unemployment problem, caused by a gap between the quality of available labour and the qualifications demanded by jobs. Old, poorly educated and unskilled laid-off workers will be put in an extremely disadvantaged position in the increasingly fierce competition of the job market, and face long-term unemployment. A recent estimate is an additional rise in unemployment of 3–4 million, boosting the official unemployment rate by another two percentage points (see Lee and Warner, 2007b).

According to the analysis of different trades by the '*Report on China's Population and Job Opportunity*', Chinese agriculture will receive the greatest blow, with employment opportunities reduced by 10 million (see Lee and Warner, 2007b). Most of this surplus workforce in the countryside will flow to the cities for employment. It had been hoped that the labour-intensive secondary industries, tertiary industries and small private enterprises would be further developed, thereby increasing elasticity of employment. Ironically, such elasticity for employment has proven to be vulnerable to crises like the SARS epidemic.

In January 2004, the UN Food and Agriculture Organization (FAO), the Organisation for Animal Health (OIE) and the WHO issued a joint statement to warn against the spread of a highly pathogenic avian influenza in several areas in Asia as a threat to human health and a disaster for agricultural production (World Health Organization, 2004a). The current 'bird flu' phenomenon, according to the pundits, carries the risk of evolving into an efficient and dangerous human pathogen. The epidemic of highly pathogenic avian influenza (World Health Organization, 2004b) caused by H5N1, which began in mid-December 2003 in the Republic of Korea, is now being seen in other Asian countries. H5N1 variants demonstrated a capacity to directly infect humans in 1997.[14] After a period of quiescence in Southeast Asia, outbreaks of highly pathogenic avian influenza (H5N1) are again being reported in chickens and ducks in China, Indonesia, Thailand and Vietnam. In Thailand, outbreaks have been reported in 21 of 76 provinces; and in Vietnam outbreaks were reported in the northern, central and southern parts of the country. These outbreaks, many without apparent epidemiological links to each other, suggest H5N1 is now widely prevalent and is very likely to have become endemic by the end of 2006 (Gibbs and Soares, 2005).

The outbreaks among birds pose a significant threat to human health as SARS had done. As WHO has stated, since the first H5N1 outbreaks were reported, this virus has the potential to ignite a global influenza pandemic in humans. In a number of these outbreaks since the beginning of 2004, the virus has jumped from infected chickens or ducks directly to humans. New variants were reported in 2005 and 2006. These direct human infections have produced severe and sometimes fatal outcomes (see note 14, Huque and Lee, 2000). WHO's continuing concern is that this virus may combine its genes with those from a human influenza virus, thereby acquiring the ability to move easily from human to human and thus triggering a pandemic.

## 6.6   Conclusions

It is clear that the overall impact of SARS on the Chinese economy, other things being equal, was and will remain problematic (see Rawski, 2006), given the lack of independent assessment; however, it is equally observable that the effect on employment in the service sector, specifically in the hotels industry was, as we have seen, relatively negative in the short-term, at least at the time. Both the quantitative, as well as the qualitative, data we have gathered – primary (our own qualitative interviews) and secondary (mostly official statistics) – point in this direction.

One can interpret the macro-economic data as either telling us that the trend was hardly dented by the 'SARS effect', as the GDP growth rate, officially at least, touched 9 per cent in 2003. On the other hand, we may decide it may have accentuated key micro-economic imperfections noted above, even if only relatively.

Many policymakers had thought that the expansion of service-industries employment, such as in the hotel industry or any other, would create a positive and stable employment equilibrium and compensate for structural reform. However, the authorities may have to reconsider their strategy and continually be on their guard against unforeseen circumstances. Erosion of secondary as well as primary sector employment may sometimes be compensated for by counter-strategies to create jobs in services; these may not always be as deep-rooted as policymakers believe to be the case.

# 7  Singapore

## A case study

## 7.1  Introduction

The SARS epidemic was soon to spread well beyond East Asia into South-East Asia: there were 'Great fears of Sickenesse ... God preserve us all' (Pepys, ([1660–1669]1993: 486).

This chapter begins with a brief background account of the imported cases of SARS to the city-state of Singapore and then goes on to analyse the impact on the Singapore economy, its labour market and one particularly vulnerable part of its now pre-eminent service sector (Khatri, 2004: 221–2), namely hotels (and hospitality). We will find a very distinctive approach to disease-control exemplified in this case.

## 7.2  SARS in Singapore: origins

The chain of SARS contacts turns out to be fascinating in its detail. Of the six persons who imported the virus to Singapore, all were residents of Singapore and had visited Hong Kong (plus Guangdong Province in two cases and Beijing in another ) (see Table 7.1).

Cases A and B travelled together to Hong Kong at the end of February 2003, and stayed on the 9th floor of the Metropole Hotel (Wilder-Smith *et al.*, 2003) as we have pointed out in Chapters 3 and 5. They were likely to have been infected by the Chinese doctor we mentioned more than once, as he was the vital link in the chain of diffusion. He came from Guangdong Province, a SARS patient who had stayed on the same floor of the same Metropole Hotel on 21 and 22 February, most probably passing the virus through contact in the elevator, but details of this are uncertain. Upon their return to Singapore on 25 February, they developed a fever, and a few days later a dry cough, being subsequently admitted on 1 March to two different hospitals in Singapore and isolated six days later. The first case in Singapore admitted to Tan Tock Seng Hospital infected 20 close contacts (11 health care workers, and 9 relatives or friends). These, in their turn, passed it on to 71 people (all health care workers, patients and relatives), who then contributed to the emerging epidemic in Singapore. Few infectious

*Table 7.1* Imported cases of SARS to Singapore, 25 February–31 May 2003

| Duration of SARS symptoms in the community (days) | Interval between admission and isolation (days) | Imported cases (Age, gender, ethnicity) | Imported from | Secondary cases | Outcome |
| --- | --- | --- | --- | --- | --- |
| 4 | 6 | 23, female, Chinese | Hong Kong, the *Metropole Hotel* | 20 | Recovered |
| 4 | 6 | 22, female, Chinese | Hong Kong, the *Metropole Hotel* | 0 | Recovered |
| 7 | 1 | 33, female, Chinese | Hong Kong, the *Metropole Hotel* | 0 | Recovered |
| 1 | 0 | 42, female, Chinese Indonesian (resident in Singapore) | Guangdong, Hong Kong | 0 | Recovered |
| 2 | 0 | 18, male, Indonesian (resident in Singapore) | Guangdong, Hong Kong | 0 | Recovered |
| 0 | 0 | 29, female, Chinese | Hong Kong, Beijing | 0 | Died |

Source: Wilder-Smith, Annelies, Goh, Kee Tai, Paton, Nicholas I, 2003, 'Experience of Severe Acute Respiratory Syndrome in Singapore: Importation of Cases, and Defense Strategies at the Airport' *Journal of Travel Medicine*, 10: 5, 259–262.

diseases are so selective for health care workers. Most of the 'nosocomial' SARS infections have occurred in individuals looking after undiagnosed patients before the widespread use of complete respiratory and contact precautions (Tambyah, 2002). Isolation and infection control for these patients was instituted on 6 March hospital-wide infection control was enforced on 14 March and Tan Tock Seng Hospital became the SARS-designated hospital on 22 March.

Case C, rather different from the other two, was unrelated to the first cases but had been a guest at the same hotel in Kowloon noted above during the same period, and returned on 25 February. She developed a fever on 27 February, was admitted to Tan Tock Seng Hospital on 5 March, and was isolated the next day. Cases D and E were a mother (42 years) and son (18 years) who had returned on 23 March from visiting relatives in Guangdong Province and Hong Kong. They developed symptoms within two days after arrival in Singapore, and were admitted to hospital and placed in isolation on 25 and 27 March respectively. The father and the other son who had travelled with them were not infected.

We should note here that case F was a 29-year-old designer who had been on a business trip to Hong Kong and Beijing and developed a high fever and a cough while in the latter city. She consulted two doctors in Beijing, but the diagnosis of SARS was not made at that time. She became very unwell and breathless on her return flight from the capital to Singapore on 26 March, but no precautions were taken on the aeroplane, as her diagnosis was not known. Immediately after arrival, her mother took her in a taxi to Tan Tock Seng Hospital, where she was isolated in the Intensive Care Unit. She developed acute respiratory distress syndrome and multi-organ failure, and died ten days later. Both the mother and the taxi driver were quarantined, but neither developed SARS. The Ministry of Health was able to contact 46 of the 47 passengers, as well as all the nine crew members and they were put under home quarantine order and active surveillance for ten days; none of these became SARS patients.

It turns out that three of the six imported cases developed symptoms of SARS only after arrival in Singapore, whereas three had symptoms on the return flight to Singapore (cases A and B had fever only, case F had fever, cough and shortness of breath). The first two were admitted to a hospital at an average of four days after onset of symptoms, and placed in isolation six days later. Cases C to F had symptoms of SARS in Singapore for an average of 2.5 days, and all were immediately placed in isolation after hospital admission (except case C: after one day). Cases A and B were therefore without infection-control measures for ten days, and cases C to F for an average of 3.6 days. Only case A resulted in secondary transmission. No health care workers and no other contacts were infected by cases B to F.

## 7.3 Economic impact of SARS

A model of economic stimulus for many years, Singapore's rate of growth in the service sector turned sharply negative in the second quarter of 2003, falling to −4.2 per cent from positive growth of 1.7 per cent in the first quarter of 2003 (Ministry of Trade and Industry, 2004). Uncertainties associated with the war in Iraq, notwithstanding the SARS outbreak, also caused the growth momentum (on an annualized quarter-on-quarter basis) to dip sharply by 11 per cent, after an increase of 1.4 per cent in the previous quarter (see Table 7.2).

Services are vital for the city-state's prosperity. Since the service sector accounts for about 65.7 per cent of Singapore's GDP (see Table 7.3) and the SARS crisis had a hugely damaging impact in terms of both the 'demand shock' as well as the 'supply shock', it led to a 3.9 per cent fall in GDP in the second quarter of 2003 (see Figure 7.1).

*Table 7.2* GDP of services producing industries, 2003 (Unit: million S$)

|  | First quarter | Second quarter | Third quarter | Fourth quarter |
|---|---|---|---|---|
| Total | 25,019.0 | 23,699.3 | 25,331.3 | 26,016.4 |
| Wholesale and retail trade | 4,849.0 | 5,052.1 | 5,100.9 | 5,684.0 |
| Hotels and restaurants | 832.9 | 613.6 | 740.2 | 811.5 |
| Transport and communications | 4,378.0 | 3,705.0 | 4,611.0 | 4,877.3 |
| Financial services | 4,355.2 | 4,797.8 | 4,950.2 | 4,254.5 |
| Business services | 5,322.5 | 5,181.7 | 5,246.4 | 5,274.9 |
| Other services industries | 5,281.4 | 4,349.1 | 4,682.6 | 5,114.2 |

Source: *Economic Survey of Singapore 2003*, Singapore Department of Statistics website.

*Table 7.3* GDP by industry, 1999–2003 (Unit: million S$)

| Industry | 1999 | 2000 | 2001 | 2002 | 2003 |
|---|---|---|---|---|---|
| Goods producing industries | 46,165 | 54,573 | 49,137 | 52,470 | 52,221 |
| Manufacturing | 32,521 | 42,078 | 36,548 | 41,080 | 41,601 |
| Construction | 11,125 | 9,966 | 9,444 | 8,530 | 7,834 |
| Utilities | 2,319 | 2,339 | 2,967 | 2,694 | 2,622 |
| Other goods industries | 200 | 189 | 178 | 166 | 164 |
| Services producing industries | 89,594 | 97,364 | 99,563 | 101,079 | 100,066 |
| Wholesale and retail trade | 18,008 | 20,003 | 19,079 | 19,511 | 20,686 |
| Hotels and restaurants | 3,272 | 3,545 | 3,628 | 3,503 | 2,998 |
| Transport and communications | 16,634 | 18,236 | 17,403 | 18,223 | 17,571 |
| Financial services | 17,503 | 17,755 | 19,075 | 18,921 | 18,358 |
| Business services | 19,637 | 21,518 | 22,214 | 21,641 | 21,026 |
| Other services industries | 14,540 | 16,307 | 18,164 | 19,280 | 19,427 |

Source: *Economic Survey of Singapore First Quarter 2004*, Singapore Department of Statistics website.

The pronounced psychological impact of SARS may arguably be a principal source of the 'demand shock', particularly in impacting on consumption, as argued in Chapter 4. In specific locations with a high incidence of SARS, physical movement of people was restricted, either voluntarily or involuntarily, thus potentially reducing consumer spending. For instance, a 24-hour vegetable wholesale market in Singapore was ordered to shut down for ten days, as three workers there were diagnosed with SARS and where one of these had died. The Singapore government closed all schools temporarily on 26 March to prevent the spread of SARS, and the vast majority of Singapore's inhabitants – about one-quarter of whom are foreigners – had confined themselves to their homes for fear of catching the disease (*Business Week Online*, 4 March 2003). People had opted to stay at home to reduce the probability of infection. With schools closed, their offspring were at home all day, yet the parents were afraid to

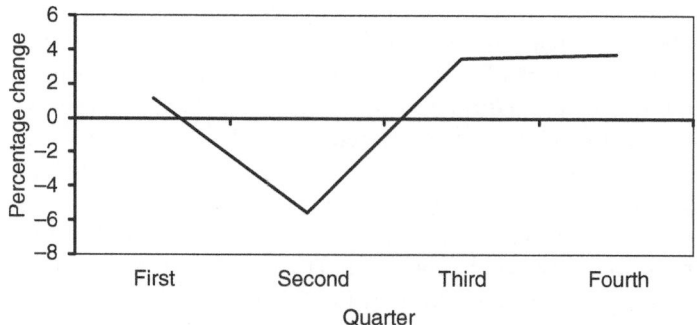

*Figure 7.1* Percentage change of GDP over corresponding period of previous year, 2003 (Unit: percentage).

Source: *Economic Survey of Singapore 2003*, Singapore Department of Statistics website.

take them out for fear of exposing them to SARS. Playgrounds and swimming pools in many private housing estates were deserted – and at some complexes, the companies that manage them had even declared the areas off-limits (*Business Week Online*, 4 March 2003). Attendance at Singapore's exotic animal parks soon plummeted. The playground at Singapore's zoological garden was closed for 'renovations'. The Roman Catholic Church in Singapore even suspended confessions, allowing priests to forgive all churchgoers for their sins instead (Crampton, 2003). Even the hospitals were nearly deserted; outpatients were missing appointments with their physicians for fear they would catch SARS by entering the facility. All this marked a major lifestyle-shift for Singapore residents (Interviews, late Summer 2003).

SARS, we may thus surmise, initially affects the economy by mainly reducing demand, as we have suggested in Chapter 4. Consumer confidence did in fact dramatically decline in a number of economies, one large, and one much smaller, namely Hong Kong and the PRC, as seen in the previous two Chapters, 5 and 6, leading to a significant reduction in private consumption spending. Much of the impact stemmed from the great degree of uncertainty and fear generated by SARS. Three foreign CEOs returned from a conference in Hong Kong, where SARS was spreading even more rapidly than in Singapore, only to be told by their local colleagues to work from home in case they had come in contact with the virus (Interviews, late Summer 2003). Companies that manage office complexes all over Singapore studied contingency plans to shut down if SARS was detected in their buildings. They had warned tenants to procure personal computers for their employees at home to ensure that they were productive (Interviews, late Summer 2003).

Singapore Airlines (SIA) accounts for over 5 per cent of service exports by value, in particular; most of service exports earnings of the city-state are tourism-related, as noted earlier, and these were to prove most vulnerable.

Investment was affected by reduced overall demand, heightened uncertainties and increased risks. An executive of a US multinational with its regional headquarters in Singapore noted that 'between the [Iraq] war and SARS, every buyer in the world has an excuse not to make a commitment, especially for big projects' (*Business Week*, 28 April 2003). The possible fall in the demand for labour when related to goods and services that people would not be buying would therefore, from the specific focus of our study, have to be taken into account (Interviews, late 2003).

The few Singapore residents who left the country, whether in panic or for other reasons, found that an airport official inserted a small brown card into their passports warning immigration officials at the destination that they 'may have been exposed to SARS' (*Business Week Online*, 3 April 2003). At the airport in Manila, passengers disembarking from SIA flights were met by a Filipino nurse, who collected 'accomplished health' forms in which they swore that they were not suffering from a high fever, breathing difficulty or other SARS symptoms (*Business Week Online*, 3 April 2003). Philippine officials manning the immigration counters wore surgical masks to protect themselves from inhaling the virus. In Thailand, travellers from stricken areas were also required to wear masks and stay in their hotels, or undergo a medical check every three days of their stay. Offenders could be punished by up to six months in jail or a maximum fine of US$235 and 'SARS-control officers' were said to be 'operating undercover' to ensure compliance (*TTG Daily News*, 2003).

International cooperation was judged to be crucial and bilateral meetings were arranged between the Association of South East Asian Nations (ASEAN) health ministers and their counterparts from China, Japan and South Korea. There was a 'united front' on steps such as pre-departure screening of travellers and the exchange of information to assist in tracing and quarantining contacts of SARS patients (Henderson, 2003). Another forum standardized health declaration cards for departing passengers and implemented mandatory temperature tests at international airports (Henderson, 2003). People across Asia opted to stay at home to reduce the probability of infection.

Singapore-based business executives, traders and the like were especially unnerved by a government decree on 10 April that all expatriates who left Singapore and re-entered from a SARS-afflicted country, including Canada, must be quarantined for 10 days (Henderson, 2003).[1] That step made frequent business travel highly impractical. The service sector shrank by 3.1 per cent, mainly reflecting the impact of the SARS outbreak on tourism and transport related industries (Ministry of Trade and Industry, 2004). It was thus very likely that there would be closely linked implications in terms of human resources and labour-markets.

Asian economies, as we have noted earlier, are heavily dependent on tourism: these sectors are very labour-intensive (Interviews, late Summer 2003) (see Table 7.4).

*Table 7.4* Number of employees by industry, 1998–2002 (Unit: thousand persons)

| Industry | 1998 | 1999 | 2000 | 2001 | 2002 |
|---|---|---|---|---|---|
| Manufacturing | 404.4 | 395.6 | 434.9 | 384.0 | 367.6 |
| Construction | 131.3 | 130.7 | 274.0 | 124.9 | 119.1 |
| Wholesale and retail trade | 281.2 | 278.9 | 286.8 | 303.6 | 304.4 |
| Hotels and restaurants | 118.9 | 121.2 | 114.5 | 128.3 | 125.3 |
| Transport, storage and communications | 206.4 | 203.7 | 196.5 | 228.2 | 218.8 |
| Financial intermediation | 108.5 | 104.6 | 96.3 | 108.7 | 107.9 |
| Real estate, renting and business activities | 184.3 | 196.8 | 226.2 | 243.1 | 237.4 |
| Community, social and personal services | 418.0 | 436.3 | 452.7 | 506.2 | 518.7 |
| Others | 16.8 | 18.0 | 12.9 | 19.7 | 18.4 |

Source: Department of Statistics, *Yearbook of Statistics Singapore 2003*, Singapore: Department of Statistics, 2003, p. 45.

Airline passenger numbers to Asia dropped by up to 70 per cent, and overall reservations in Asia were down 30–40 per cent in 2003, according to the World Tourism Organization (*USA Today*, 20 June 2003). According to official statistics in April 2003, passenger rates had fallen by 60 per cent in Hong Kong, as compared to 40 per cent in Singapore and South Korea; 37 per cent in Bangkok, 36 per cent in Kuala Lumpur (*Ming Pao*, 7 May 2003). The decline in tourist arrivals shocked Singapore – the figures were 61.6 per cent lower over the previous year in April 2003, and contracted to 70.7 per cent lower in May (Singapore Tourism Board, 2003). Passenger traffic at Changi Airport was halved in April. Dragged down by the dismal performance of the air transport and the communications segments, the sector shrank by 10 per cent in the second quarter of 2003, compared with 1 per cent growth in the first three months of the year (Ministry of Trade and Industry, 2003). Air passengers and cargo handled fell by 50 per cent and 6.7 per cent respectively in the second quarter (Ministry of Trade and Industry, 2003).

Hotel occupancy rates had slumped significantly in China and Hong Kong, as well as in Singapore, as visitor arrivals had plummeted. The hotels and restaurants sector in the latter shrank sharply in the second quarter by 33 per cent, after sliding 5.1 per cent in the first quarter of 2003 (Ministry of Trade and Industry, 2003). Visitor arrivals plunged by 62 per cent in the second quarter, while hotel occupancy rates fell to an average of 20–30 per cent, compared to normal levels of 70 per cent or above (Ministry of Trade and Industry, 2003). Revenues at some restaurants had halved. Attendance at main attractions, such as Tiger Balm Gardens, Sentosa and the like, was at least 50 per cent down, and retail sales dropped by 10–50 per cent (Henderson, 2003). The future of many travel agents, most of which are small scale, was threatened, and the industry overall was estimated to be sustaining weekly losses of S$23 million (US$13.1 million) (*Straits Times*, 5 April 2003).

### 7.4   Human resources consequences

Joblessness in Singapore rose to a 17-year high of 4.7 per cent in 2003 (see Table 7.5). The resident unemployment rate jumped to 6.0 per cent in the second quarter although this was less than the Hong Kong jobless total over the period.

In absolute numbers, according to the Ministry of Manpower (MOM) of Singapore, overall employment diminished by 25,963 in the second quarter of 2003 – not only higher than the total number of jobs lost in 2002 – but also the largest quarterly decline since the mid-1980s recession (*Xinhua*, 24 September 2003). The Ministry attributed the heavy losses in jobs – 47 per cent in the service sector, 28 per cent in construction and 25 per cent in manufacturing – to the weak economic conditions and, in particular, to the adverse impact of SARS. Another estimated job-loss total was 33,160 posts, directly or indirectly (World Travel and Tourism Council, 2003). In order to cut costs and sharpen competitiveness, big corporations like SIA and PSA Corporation (one of the world's leading port operators) where retrenchment had never been heard of for more than two decades, started to lay off employees (ibid.). SIA's subsidiary, SilkAir (flying mainly regional routes), suspended 35 weekly flights, about 25 per cent of its capacity, and terminated the contracts of eight expatriate pilots (Henderson, 2003). The restructuring and privatization of the Housing Development Board (HDB) brought on the loss of another 2,600 jobs. About 9,500 workers were laid off in the first six months of 2003 (*Xinhua*, 24 September 2003).

*Table 7.5* Number of unemployed residents and unemployment rate, 1993–2003

| Year | Unemployed residents (thousand persons) | Resident unemployment rate (%) | Unemployment rate (%) |
|------|------|------|------|
| 1993 | 29 | 2.1 | 1.9 |
| 1994 | 31 | 2.2 | 2.0 |
| 1995 | 32 | 2.2 | 2.0 |
| 1996 | 33 | 2.2 | 2.0 |
| 1997 | 30 | 2.0 | 1.8 |
| 1998 | 54 | 3.5 | 3.2 |
| 1999 | 61 | 3.8 | 3.5 |
| 2000 | 60 | 3.7 | 3.1 |
| 2001 | 63 | 3.8 | 3.3 |
| 2002 | 82 | 4.9 | 4.4 |
| 2003 | 92 | 5.3 | 4.7 |

Source: *Manpower Research and Statistics*, Singapore Ministry of Manpower website, <http://www.mom.gov.sg/publish/momportal/en/communities/others/mrsd/statistics/Unemployment.html>

Unlike previous retrenchments that only affected blue-collar workers, white-collar employees were also affected by the SARS crisis. The resident unemployment rate increased to 5.3 per cent, mostly reflecting the adverse impact of the spread of SARS since mid-March 2003, compounded by structural unemployment because high value-added investments are capital-intensive, not labour-intensive, and because factory jobs continued to relocate to China and other cheaper manufacturing destination (*The Asian Wall Street Journal*, 3 November 2003). Disentangling these multiple economic factors, is of course, very difficult, but it is clear that SARS seriously aggravated both cyclical and structural factors already operative (Interviews, late Summer 2003).

## 7.5  Discussion

We now turn to a discussion and evaluation of the economic and human resources impact of SARS on Singapore, specifically focusing on its service-sector.

We will try to assess the evidence we have collected in terms of the set of hypotheses we adumbrated earlier. Taking each hypothesis in turn, to recapitulate, we posited that

1   the greater the adverse impact of SARS on the Asian economies, the greater will be the negative impact on the service sector and specifically on the hotel industry.

Figure 7.2 shows the impact of SARS on the output of services in Singapore. The imported cases of SARS in Singapore started in late February and March 2003, and the WHO global alert was issued on 12 March 2003. These incidents led to a fall in the percentage change of the GDP in the service sector over the corresponding period in 2002 (see Figure 7.2).

As seen in Figure 7.3, the number of tourist arrivals drastically declined since the travel advice was issued by the WHO (WHO press release, 12 March 2003). The number of visitor arrivals, from the first quarter of 2003 to the second quarter dropped significantly from 1,815,100 to 698,000 (see Table 7.6). Hong Kong also experienced a broadly comparable decline in tourist numbers.

There had already been a marked slowdown in the growth rate of international tourism by the 1990s, affected by the Asian financial crisis at the end of the decade and the 11 September 2001 terrorist attacks in the United States. Despite the bombings on Indonesian island of Bali in 2002, which raised questions about security throughout Southeast Asia, recovery seemed under way as there were more than 7.5 million visitors. The uncertainties relating both to Middle East tensions and SARS, dominated expectations and over time these were made worse by the onset of the epidemic being totally unexpected (see Table 7.7).

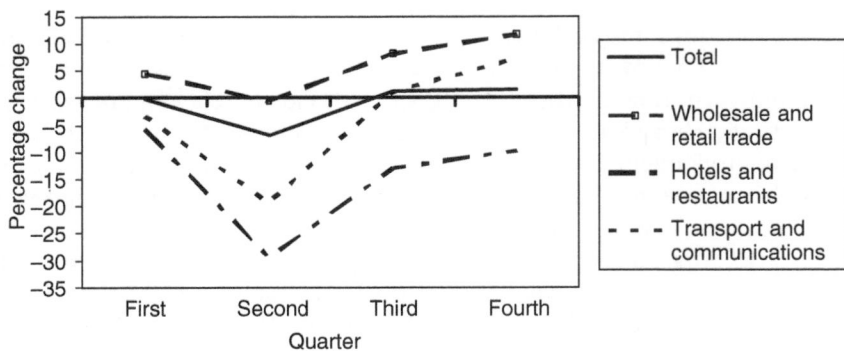

*Figure 7.2* Percentage change of GDP of services producing industries over corresponding period of previous year, 2003 (Unit: percentage).

Source: *Economic Survey of Singapore 2003*, Singapore Department of Statistics website.

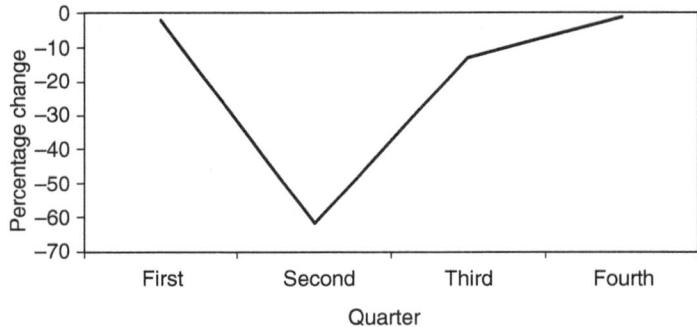

*Figure 7.3* Percentage change of total visitor arrivals over corresponding period of previous year, 2003 (Unit: percentage).

Source: Research and Statistics Information, Singapore Tourism Board website, <http://app.stb.com.sg/asp/tou/tou02.asp#VS>

*Table 7.6* Visitor arrivals, 2003 (Unit: thousand persons)

| Quarter | Total | Asia | Oceania | Europe | America | Africa | Others |
|---------|-------|------|---------|--------|---------|--------|--------|
| First | 1,815.1 | 1,264.6 | 130.3 | 300.7 | 102.1 | 17.3 | 0.2 |
| Second | 698.0 | 494.4 | 58.4 | 106.7 | 32.2 | 6.1 | 0.2 |
| Third | 1,700.0 | 1,243.7 | 143.1 | 212.0 | 84.3 | 16.8 | 0.1 |
| Fourth | 1,913.5 | 1,397.8 | 143.8 | 257.6 | 96.1 | 18.1 | 0.1 |

Source: *Research and Statistical Information*, Singapore Tourism Board website, <http://app.stb.com.sg/asp/tou/tou02.asp#VS>

*Table 7.7* Visitor arrivals, 1998–2003 (Unit: thousand persons)

| Year | Total | Asia | Oceania | Europe | America | Africa | Others |
|------|-------|------|---------|--------|---------|--------|--------|
| 1998 | 6,242.2 | 4,223.8 | 519.8 | 982.7 | 425.4 | 79.1 | 11.3 |
| 1999 | 6,958.2 | 4,797.3 | 564.5 | 1,050.0 | 444.3 | 90.2 | 12.0 |
| 2000 | 7,691.4 | 5,320.8 | 616.6 | 1,127.9 | 483.0 | 99.5 | 43.7 |
| 2001 | 7,522.2 | 5,224.1 | 656.5 | 1,114.6 | 433.6 | 88.0 | 5.4 |
| 2002 | 7,567.1 | 5,326.7 | 644.1 | 1,101.9 | 416.4 | 72.8 | 5.2 |
| 2003 | 6,126.6 | 4,400.5 | 475.5 | 877.3 | 314.7 | 58.3 | 0.2 |

Source: Research and Statistical Information, Singapore Tourism Board website, <http://app.stb.com.sg/asp/tou/tou02.asp#VS>

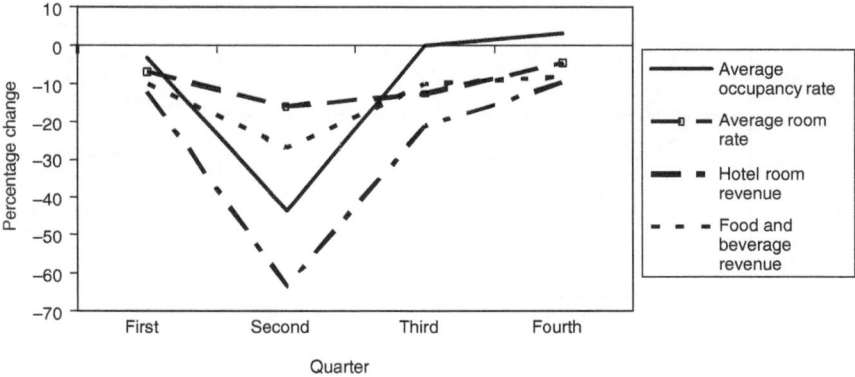

*Figure 7.4* Percentage change of hotel statistics over corresponding period of previous year, 2003 (Unit: percentage).

Source: *Economic Survey of Singapore 2003*, Singapore Department of Statistics website.

The average hotel occupancy rates, average room rates, hotel room revenue and food and beverage revenue recorded dramatic falls, when compared to 2002 (see Figure 7.4). The hotel occupancy rate plummeted from 72 per cent to 42 per cent within a quarter (see Table 7.8). The *volatility*, as well as *vulnerability*, of such indices speaks for itself.

2 The greater the adverse impact of SARS on consumer demand in the Asian hotels and hospitality industry, the greater will be the negative impact on the related demand for labour in terms of hotel employees in specific hotel groups in the industry.

To survive in such turbulent environments, hotels in Singapore resorted to various HRM measures to cut costs. This step led to a falling demand for labour. Figure 7.5 shows the steep plunge in the number of employment in the service sector, in the second quarter in particular.

*Table 7.8* Hotel statistics, first–fourth quarter 2003

| Quarter | Average occupancy rate (%) | Average room rate (S$) | Hotel room revenue (million S$) | Food and beverage revenue (million S$) |
|---------|---------------------------|------------------------|--------------------------------|-----------------------------------------|
| First   | 72.0 | 121.5 | 221.7 | 374.3 |
| Second  | 42.1 | 106.7 | 92.6  | 284.8 |
| Third   | 73.6 | 107.3 | 191.8 | 357.7 |
| Fourth  | 76.9 | 117.4 | 220.2 | 399.6 |

Source: *Economic Survey of Singapore 2003*, Singapore Department of Statistics website.

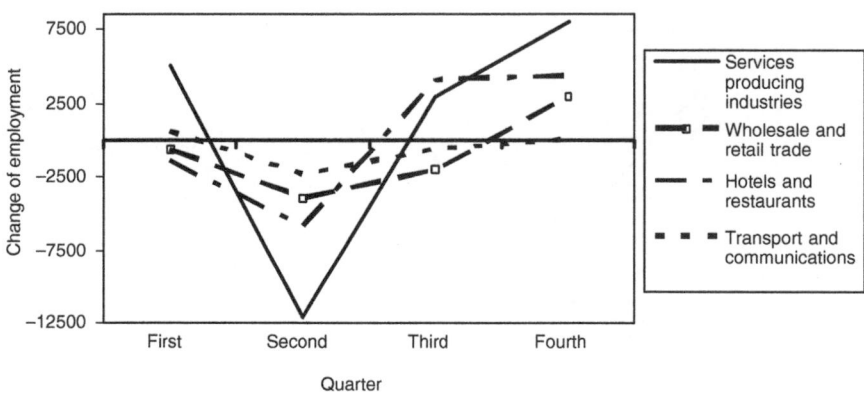

*Figure 7.5* Change of employment in services producing industries over the previous period, 2003 (Unit: person).

Source: *Economic Survey of Singapore 2003*, Singapore Department of Statistics website.

Table 7.9 shows a fall in the number of employees working in the industry. There was a decline of 12,100 in employment, with hotels and restaurants suffering the biggest cut of 5,800 employees.

3    The greater the adverse impact on the demand for labour in the Asian hotel industry, the greater will be the negative impact on the labour-market in terms of lay-offs and redundancy among hotel employees in specific hotel groups in the industry.

Between March and June 2003, many business sectors in Singapore had been adversely affected. Starting from the outbreak of SARS and the issue of global advisory warning by the World Health Organization on Singapore, businesses related to tourism – including airlines, hotels, retail and restaurants – had seen a fall in demand. With regard to air transport, SIA cancelled approximately 30 per cent of its weekly timetable

*Table 7.9* Changes of employment over the previous period, 2003 (Unit: persons)

| Industry | First quarter | Second quarter | Third quarter | Fourth quarter |
|---|---|---|---|---|
| Total | −4,100 | −26,000 | 900 | 16,200 |
| Goods producing industries | −9,200 | −13,800 | −2,100 | 4,300 |
| Manufacturing | −2,600 | −6,400 | 0 | 4,100 |
| Construction | −6,500 | −7,100 | −1,900 | −2,000 |
| Others | −200 | −200 | −200 | 2,100 |
| Services producing industries | 5,100 | −12,100 | 3,000 | 12,000 |
| Wholesale and retail trade | −600 | −3,900 | −2,000 | 4,200 |
| Hotels and restaurants | −1,400 | −5,800 | 4,100 | 5,100 |
| Transport and communications | 600 | −2,300 | −600 | 900 |
| Financial services | 800 | 700 | −100 | 900 |
| Business services | 0 | 1,400 | 700 | −1,600 |
| Other services industries | 5,700 | −2,100 | 1,000 | 2,500 |

Source: *Economic Survey of Singapore First Quarter 2004*, Singapore Department of Statistics website.

(Henderson, 2003). Tourists from all over the world had postponed or cancelled their visits to Singapore.

We now go on to discuss the HRM implications of the changing labour demand and labour supply consequences noted above (see Figure 7.6).

In order to cut costs and sharpen competitiveness, the HRM departments of big corporations like those of SIA and PSA Corporation, one of the world's leading port-operators, where retrenchment had not been heard of for more than two decades, started to lay off employees. Notably, SIA suffered from a deficit of over US$200 million as at June 2003, and decided to lay off 414 employees, of which 129 were ground staff (*Wen Wei Pao*, 20 June 2003). The HDB cut another 2,600 jobs. About 9,500 workers were laid off in the first six months of 2003, bringing the total number of jobless to some 102,000 (*China Daily*, 24 September 2003). Among them, around 25,000 had remained unemployed for at least six months. Unlike previous retrenchments, not only blue-collar workers' jobs had been affected, but also those of white-collar employees (Interviews, 2003). The Singapore government embarked on a series of initiatives to help laid-off workers, including retraining. The government launched the new WDA and gave a second phase of cash injection of S$280 million (US$160 million) to a Skills Redevelopment Programme to help co-fund the retraining of workers (Interviews, 2003).

At the organizational level, the HRM consequences were severe, as our on-site field interviews revealed. Hotels froze recruitment and overtime, dismissed casual workers and cut pay at every level (Henderson, 2003). A HR manager from a logistics firm, who declined to be named, said that the sectors likely to face wage-cuts were likely to be hotels, as well as recreation and travel (Interviews, 2003). The cuts were expected to range from 2 to 15 per cent. According to a survey of 272 companies polled in

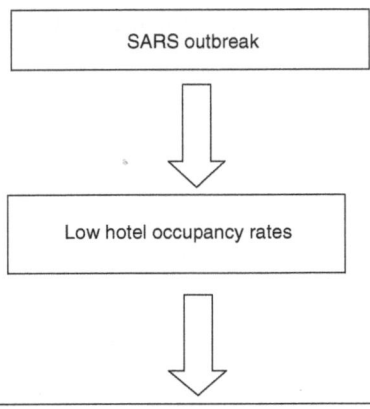

*Figure 7.6* Cost-cutting HRM measures adopted by the Singapore hotel
    industry.

May 2003 by the Singapore Human Resource Institute and Remuneration
Data Specialists, variable bonuses, excluding the annual wage supplement,
would dip from 1.4 months a year before to 1.3 months (*Straits Times*,
2 May 2003). The survey also found that 8 in 10 firms supported the National
Wages Council guidelines that SARS-hit companies cut wages, and urged
wage reforms to more flexible pay systems.[2] With regard to air transport,
SIA's cabin crew employees were instructed to take several days' unpaid
leave every two months until 2004, and over 200 trainees were released.
A similar arrangement for cockpit crew became an issue for negotiation,
after resistance from the pilots' union. Senior management took salary cuts
of 22.2–27.5 per cent (Interviews, late 2003).

Even government ministers, whose monthly pay was reduced by 10 per cent
in November 2001, had their wages frozen further for another year until
December 2003. The then Deputy Prime Minister and Finance Minister,
Lee Hsien Long, told the Parliament in his May Day Rally speech that
'when all have to take bitter medicine, we must start at the top' (*Business
Times*, 2 May 2003).

The implications for training were also evident, as our interviewing made clear. Staff were asked to go on unpaid leave, retrained and redeployed where appropriate. The SARS Relief Tourism Training Assistance grant scheme, which was part of the government's S$230 million relief package, trained nearly 1,000 workers in the tourism sector in just three weeks in May 2003 (*Straits Times*, 10 June 2003). There were 104 approved courses for the scheme, ranging from making sauces, to hotel law and security. Most of the retrainees were rank and file workers like chambermaids, tour guides and event organizers; most of these were schooled up to the secondary school level and had limited skills at best. According to the deputy director of the MOM's labour market development division, resistance to training had been a 'big issue' in the tourism sector for many years.[3] A café hostess, aged 48 who had worked at the Grand Hyatt Hotel for 31 years, remarked after taking a two-week refresher course on the food and beverage industry that 'this is the first time I've been able to train for two weeks at a stretch, because we now have so few guests' (*Straits Times*, 14 May 2003). A restaurant manager of the Raffles Hotel was trained for a totally different job – as a concierge, but he said that 'it will help me a lot as I have patrons who ask me for recommendations on entertainment or places of interest here.' Under the new grant scheme, the government paid an employer S$6.90 an hour for every worker aged 40 or older sent for training; it also paid the course fees. For a younger worker, the government would pay his employer S$6.50 an hour and 90 per cent of the course fees. Such arrangements resulted from negotiations among the MOM, the Singapore Tourism Board, the National Trades Union Congress and other stakeholders in April 14 May 2003. The chairman of the Association of Singapore Attractions informed that they had 'set aside S$30,000 to pay the remaining ten per cent of course fees not subsidized by the grant' as their members' main problem was cash-flow (Interviews, 2003).

At the height of the outbreak, the Shangri-La Rasa Sentosa resort had its sales staff double as banquet waiters, so as to cut down on its part-time labour costs (*Wall Street Journal*, 5 June 2003). To boost the morale of staff who sat idle for much of the day, the hotel organized inter-departmental volleyball games every afternoon on the beach (*Wall Street Journal*, 5 June 2003).

A few hotels offered steep discounts to encourage consumer spending (and boost employment) when SARS was at its worst. Raffles International offered two nights for the price of one at its Singapore properties – the Plaza, Swissotel and Merchant Court – in April and May to Singaporeans. Other packages included lessons in dancing, financial management and cookery in the hotel kitchens. In order to stimulate interest, one hotel opened all its rooms for a free night's stay to locals prepared to queue for 24 hours (*Straits Times*, 14 May 2003).

Some hotels offered low rates through packages put together with airlines. For example, SIA passengers got 50 per cent discounts at a number of the Raffles Group hotels in Singapore; and SIA offered a US$579 'Singapore Plus' package that included airfare to Singapore from New York, San Francisco or Los Angeles and three nights at a five-star lodging with transfers, breakfast and some tours (*USA Today*, 20 June 2003).

## 7.6   Conclusions

It is clear that the impact of SARS on the Singapore economy and specifically the hotel industry may be seen as relatively negative in the time-period in question. Both the quantitative, as well as the qualitative, data we have gathered, point in this direction, although we must be cautious to over-generalize. The HRM implications from the supply-side 'shock', as set out in our hypotheses from Chapter 4, were confirmed, both in a conceptual as well as in an empirical framework, as both immediate and direct, as can be seen from our findings.

As the economy revived by mid-2003, it was thought that recovery in service-sector jobs above all, in industries such as hotels, both in low- as well as high-valued added products and services would compensate for earlier job losses. The SARS epidemic of early and mid-2003 has no doubt been a sharp reminder to both Hong Kong and Singapore, both of which are Overseas Chinese (*Nanyang*) city-state economies, of their economic vulnerability. The Chinese mainland case was somewhat different, given the lower weighting of the service-sector in that economy. Today, there is less of a major 'crisis of confidence', but spirits remain low as the economy slowly recovers and the labour-market still remains fragile.

The Singapore economy, given its market-oriented flexibility (see Hampden-Turner, 2003: 173–6) fortunately recovered fairly quickly. The stock-market index jumped to around half as much again it had been at the beginning of the year (see Figure 7.7).

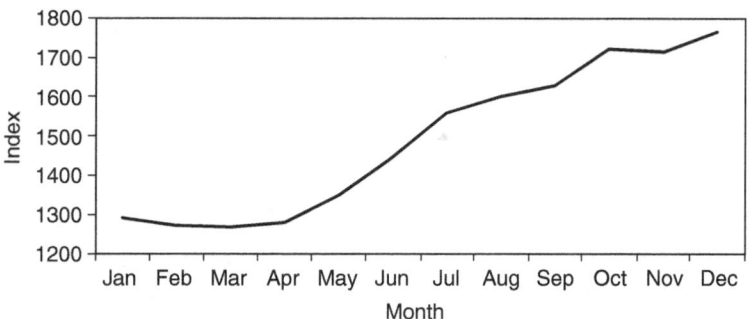

*Figure 7.7  Straits Times* index, January 2003–December 2003.

Source: Monetary Authority of Singapore website, <https://secure.mas.gov.sg/frames/msb/msbIndexpage.html>

Growth of the Singapore economy rose by 12.5 per cent in the second quarter of 2004. During the quarter, growth of external demand rose by 26.3 per cent – exports of both goods and services rose significantly – reflecting the impact of increased visitor arrivals on receipts from travel and transportation services (Ministry of Trade and Industry, 2004). Tourism helped the economy to recover in the second half of 2003. The hotel sector ultimately recovered as the year unfolded.

The hotels and restaurants sector registered a 37.6 per cent gain in output during the second quarter of 2004, compared to 3.1 per cent in the first quarter of 2004 (Ministry of Trade and Industry, 2004). This boost mainly reflected the impact of SARS on activity in 2003. However a number of concerns remained, among them structural problems. Compared to the second quarter of 2002, the sector showed a decline of 3.0 per cent. Although the average hotel occupancy rate remained well supported by strong visitor arrivals, which grew by 9.2 per cent when compared to the second quarter of 2002, lower room rates depressed hotel room revenue in the quarter (Ministry of Trade and Industry, 2004). Even though total employment rose by 10,400 in the second quarter of 2004, it was smaller than the 13,700 gained in the previous quarter. The decline reflected the lower increase of 6,700 jobs in the service sector, compared with 11,400 in the first quarter of 2004. During the quarter, a smaller number of redundancies of 1,900, compared with 2,962 in the first quarter of 2004, contributed to higher total employment. Despite the increase in total employment, the seasonally adjusted unemployment rate remained stable at 4.5 per cent, unchanged since December 2003 (Ministry of Trade and Industry, 2004).

We can nonetheless posit that the SARS effect had a relatively negative impact on the economy and human resources, with both employment and psychological consequences that may have medium- even long-term implications, as in the case of Hong Kong. If it was thought that the expansion of service-employment, such as in the hotel sector or any other, would create a positive and stable employment equilibrium and compensate for the earlier loss of manufacturing jobs, the Singapore, like the Hong Kong, authorities may have to re-consider their long-term economic strategy and continually be on their guard against unforeseen circumstances. In today's globalized economy, *exogenous* shocks may affect labour-demand and supply within weeks, and the HRM implications may be felt almost as rapidly and no one can accurately predict the co-efficient of vulnerability. We now turn to the experience of another *Nanyang* economy, Taiwan, in the next chapter.

# 8 Taiwan

## A case study

## 8.1 Introduction

As Defoe observes of the Great Plague 'the Apprehensions of the People, were ... strangely increased by the Error of the Times' ([1720]2003: 22). Rumour followed rumour: public concern reached a new high-point.

Because of global links, no country in the region seemed to be a safe haven. Vulnerability to epidemics would most likely come through international air travel. Like Hong Kong, Taiwan has one of the busiest airports in Asia, and has numerous arrivals each day from countries in the region that may often be affected by public health risks. Therefore, the nation was, and still is, potentially vulnerable to the importation of SARS that could in turn initiate new cases. This chapter begins with a brief background account of the imported cases of SARS to Taiwan and then goes on to analyse the impact on the Taiwan economy, its labour market, human resources as well as employment and unemployment, in one particularly vulnerable sub-sector of its now pre-eminent service sector, namely hotels (and hospitality). Thus, as will be apparent in our analysis, epidemics, mortality and urbanization are now arguably increasingly interlinked, and mass air travel has become a potentially critical transmission belt in the contemporary, globalized world.

## 8.2 SARS in Taiwan: origins

SARS struck Taiwan sharply and seriously. As of 22 May 2003, a total of 483 probable cases had been reported. All probable SARS patients were hospitalized; 84 (17 per cent) had been discharged, and 60 (12 per cent) had died (Lee *et al.*, 2003). Three hundred and forty-one (71 per cent) cases were from Taipei City and Taipei County, the largest metropolitan region of Taiwan.

The first case in Taiwan was the result of a visit to Taiwan by a resident of Amoy Gardens in Hong Kong, the apartment complex that produced many SARS cases in Hong Kong (Lee and Warner, 2005a) as reported in Chapter 5. The man, surnamed Tseng, flew to Taiwan on 26 March, took a train to Taichung to see his brother the following day – to carry out the traditional 'sweeping of the graves' – and flew back to Hong Kong the day after (Eyton, 2003). His brother was infected with the virus, admitted to hospital on 3 April and had the dubious distinction of becoming Taiwan's first SARS-related fatality.

Up until 21 April, Taiwan reported 28 probable SARS cases. During this period, SARS was characterized by sporadic cases among business travellers who were cared for primarily at large academic hospitals; the secondary spread was limited to identified contacts. Initial actions by the Taiwan Department of Health included the formation of a SARS advisory committee, infection-control training, contact tracing and quarantine, and airport and border surveillance. Because of Taiwan's apparent success with SARS control, in early April, WHO changed Taiwan's designation from an 'affected area' to an 'area with limited local transmission' (Eyton, 2003). Taiwan, interestingly enough, hosted an international conference on SARS on 20–21 April to showcase its 'achievements'.

However, worse was to come when Taiwan's relative complacency over SARS was destroyed on 22 April, when Taiwan's Department of Health was notified of seven cases of SARS among health-care workers (HCWs) at a large municipal hospital in Taipei, the Taipei Municipal Ho-ping Hospital (Hospital A). Since then, SARS cases in Taiwan had increased and had been associated primarily with health care settings. The 'index patient' for the first outbreak of SARS through local transmission in Taiwan was a female fellow traveller on the train Tseng (the first SARS-related fatality in Taiwan) took to Taichung. Feeling ill, she went to Hospital A, where she was thought to have passed the virus on to several medical staff and a laundry worker. They had had multiple exposures with patients, visitors and HCWs who were not protected adequately in order to prevent the acquisition of SARS. The number of potentially exposed persons was estimated at around 10,000 patients and visitors and 930 staff.

On 24 April, Hospital A was contained, and all patients, visitors and staff were quarantined within the building. All 930 staff and 240 inpatients were to be confined for fourteen days. Any staff not in the hospital when the quarantine order was issued was to return to the hospital immediately to start their isolation. Inside the hospital, all recognized SARS patients were concentrated on two floors. Personal protective equipment and disinfection materials were distributed, and active surveillance was enforced for all HCWs. However, incidents of SARS cases in Hospital A continued to increase. The result of the quarantine order had seen several displays of personal selfishness and lack of concern about the public good that had kept newspaper opinion pages and radio phone-in shows busy for a week (Eyton, 2003). 25 April saw a demonstration at the hospital that involved bottle-throwing by staff angry about being quarantined. Meanwhile, some 32 of the staff who were out of the hospital when the order was imposed refused to return and went into hiding. A nurse, hiding from the quarantine order, wrote to a newspaper complaining that 'no punishment can exceed the terror cast by the shadow of SARS' and claiming that quarantine was a death-sentence. While the public was still wondering about the professional ethics of a nurse who was afraid of catching an infectious disease, it was presented with the less than edifying behaviour of an ear, nose and throat specialist at Hospital A, who not only dodged the quarantine but continued to work in his private clinic treating patients. Only when threatened with arrest by the police did he return to the hospital.

From 22 April to 1 May, the number of probable cases in Taiwan more than tripled, from 28 to 89. Subsequent HCW clusters at eight hospitals had been associated with exposures at Hospital A. Many of these clusters occurred when pre-symptomatic patients or patients with SARS symptoms attributed to other causes were discharged or transferred to other health-care facilities. SARS then extended to multiple cities, and regions of Taiwan, including several university and private hospitals. On 3 May, WHO put Taiwan in the same risk category as Beijing and Hong Kong, the epicentres of SARS (Rigger, 2004).

Six days after the earlier mentioned conference on 'SARS achievements' wound up, a seriously panicking Taiwan enacted draconian measures, placing all visitors from Hong Kong, mainland China, Singapore and the Canadian city of Toronto in compulsory 10-day quarantine, as well as imposing extensive quarantine measures locally. Home quarantine was also mandated for discharged patients and visitors who had been at Hospital A since 9 April. As of 22 May, a total of 137 probable cases were associated with exposures at Hospital A, including 45 (33 per cent) cases among HCWs; 26 (19 per cent) persons died. We now turn to the economic costs of the phenomenon.

## 8.3   Economic impact of SARS

We first set out economic background based on our data-base, as well as the HRM data collected at first-hand by ourselves, albeit with the limitations acknowledged earlier, followed, by a discussion of their implications and last, our conclusions.

SARS, we believe, initially affects the economy by mainly reducing demand, as we have argued in Chapter 4. Consumer confidence did in fact dramatically decline in a number of economies, being the 'demand shock' we postulated earlier, leading to a significant reduction in private consumption spending. Much of the impact stemmed from the great degree of uncertainty and apprehension generated by SARS. The Asia Times depicted the city as a place where people wore masks, and taxi drivers drove with all their windows open (Eyton, 2003). Taxi drivers had virtually no business. A self-employed taxi owner-cum-driver informant tried her luck at the National Palace Museum, a popular tourist attraction, two times a day but there were no visitors at all (Interviews, May 2005). The taxi driver informed us that the plight of those drivers who had to pay rent for their taxis was even worse.

Nightlife was virtually non-existent. Nobody, unless very sick indeed, would visit a hospital. The city government doled out bleach to every household in Taipei to encourage what it called a 'mass sterilization of communities' (Eyton, 2003). The government also required all passengers on the Rapid Transit railway system to wear masks, or else there would be a penalty of NT$3,000! (just a little less than US$100) (Interviews, May 2005).[1] Furthermore, the Taiwan government imposed a mandatory 14-day quarantine on all incoming travellers from nearby China, Hong Kong, Singapore, Macau and even from as far away as Canada. It later relaxed this to let passengers who had only transited in Hong Kong avoid the quarantine, very much an essential measure since so many of Taiwan's connections with the outside world were routed through Hong Kong. Taiwan residents had to go home and stay there for two weeks; non-residents were put up at Taipei's Chiang Kai-shek Airport Hotel, while an army-camp was also being prepared for detainees near the airport. Some lawmakers had even suggested that the government declare a state of emergency over the SARS outbreak. This did not materialize because the principal concern of the government, apart from containing SARS, was the potential economic impact of the disease (Interviews, late Spring 2005).

Investment was affected by reduced overall demand, heightened uncertainties and increased risks. SARS highlighted Taiwan's economic interdependence with China, the birthplace of the virus that had spread across Taiwan (Lee and Warner, 2005b). Attempting to accurately assess the impact of SARS on Taiwan's economy would require knowledge of how bad the outbreak had become in China, particularly the Shanghai/ Yangtze River Delta area, and Fujian and Guangdong provinces, which in recent years have become manufacturing centres – and increasingly, development centres as well – for Taiwanese companies. Unfortunately, accurate information on mainland China was not forthcoming at that time. Although Taiwan's key technology sector reported no interruptions in their supply-chains across the Taiwan Strait, many did note that downstream customers in the United States and Europe had requested that they stock up on inventories to prepare for possible SARS-related interruptions (Taylor, 2003). Additionally, some had even been asked to move their manufacturing bases to southeast Asia, which seemed to have contained outbreaks of SARS, or to Latin America (Interviews, May 2005). Wang Yung-ching, chairman of the massive Formosa Group, the core businesses of which revolve around basic materials such as plastics and rubber, and which are heavily invested in hard-hit southern China, said that he expected 'a severe blow' to his companies in terms of weakened orders from overseas clients who were fearful that the spread of the disease might impact Formosa's ability to fulfil the orders in a business environment that required minimal inventory to remain competitive. Furthermore, unlike the majority of foreign-invested firms operating in the PRC, the Taiwanese were not only focused on manufacturing for export, but also on internal Chinese demand.

In Taiwan, the major impact of SARS had centred on the hospitality, travel and tourism industries. In large part, this was due to a dearth of business travel after foreign companies had postponed or cancelled plans for employee travel to Taiwan and other SARS-affected nations as standard corporate policy. Meanwhile, the normal flood of tourists from Japan, by far Taiwan's main source of incoming tourism, failed to materialize during the recent weeklong series of Japanese holidays. Despite cut-rate deals on luxury hotels, occupancy rates in Taipei and elsewhere were at or near rock-bottom. Meanwhile, domestic tourism, which accounted for the bulk of the industry, had melted away as Taiwanese avoid public transit and air travel. The indefinite postponement of Computex, Taiwan's most important industry convention and the third largest IT show in the world after CeBIT in Hanover and Comdex in Las Vegas, struck a further blow to the hotel industry (*BBC News*, 23 May 2003). Originally scheduled for early June 2003 as it had been over the years, the show's organizers postponed it, citing the unwillingness of registered exhibitors to attend. It was thus very likely that there would be closely linked implications in terms of human resources and labour markets, particularly when governments had actively encouraged tourism in their policies to create jobs. Table 8.1 shows the labour intensity of the service sector in Taiwan.

The decline in tourist arrivals shocked Taiwan, as in the case of Hong Kong and Singapore. Passenger arrivals totalled 866,498 in the first four months of 2003, down by 8.39 per cent from the level registered in the same period in 2002, but the gap widened to 49.46 per cent during the period between 19 March and 18 May following the SARS outbreak. Some airlines, such as Singapore Airlines and United Airways, had cancelled direct and indirect flights to Taiwan. A historical low of passengers was recorded for the Taipei airport in its 24 years of operation (*The Taiwan Economic News*, 15 April 2003).

At the same time, the number of outbound departures fell to 1.86 million for the January to April period, a 23.41 per cent decline as compared to 2002. About 90 per cent of the tours to China were cancelled in March 2003; virtually 100 per cent of individual booking of air tickets to Hong Kong were cancelled (*The Taiwan Economic News*, 15 April 2003). The number of outbound departures suffered a 60.94 per cent decline during the 19 March–18 May period (*BBC*, 23 May 2003). Around 80 per cent of the outbound tours had been cancelled in April and May 2003; the number of visitors had dropped to less than 6,000 a day in mid-May 2003. Over 80 per cent of the 100,000-strong employees of the travel industry received half or even none of their salaries. The potentially deadly disease also had taken a heavy toll on domestic travel (Interviews, May 2005). Occupancy rates at tourist hotels across Taiwan averaged 37.44 per cent

*Table 8.1* Number of employees by industry, 1981–2004
(Unit: thousand persons)

| Year | Agriculture | Industries | Services |
|------|-------------|------------|----------|
| 1981 | 1,257 | 2,828 | 2,587 |
| 1982 | 1,284 | 2,813 | 2,7143 |
| 1983 | 1,317 | 2,909 | 2,844 |
| 1984 | 1,286 | 3,089 | 2,934 |
| 1985 | 1,297 | 3,088 | 3,044 |
| 1986 | 1,317 | 3,215 | 3,201 |
| 1987 | 1,226 | 3,431 | 3,366 |
| 1988 | 1,113 | 3,443 | 3,551 |
| 1989 | 1,066 | 3,476 | 3,717 |
| 1990 | 1,064 | 3,382 | 3,837 |
| 1991 | 1,093 | 3,370 | 3,977 |
| 1992 | 1,065 | 3,419 | 4,148 |
| 1993 | 1,005 | 3,418 | 4,323 |
| 1994 | 976 | 3,506 | 4,456 |
| 1995 | 954 | 3,504 | 4,587 |
| 1996 | 918 | 3,399 | 4,751 |
| 1997 | 878 | 3,502 | 4,795 |
| 1998 | 822 | 3,523 | 4,944 |
| 1999 | 774 | 3,492 | 5,118 |
| 2000 | 738 | 3,534 | 5,220 |
| 2001 | 706 | 3,377 | 5,299 |
| 2002 | 709 | 3,332 | 5,413 |
| 2003 | 696 | 3,334 | 5,543 |
| 2004 | 642 | 3,446 | 5,698 |

Source: National Statistics, R. O. C. (Taiwan), *Annual Report on Manpower Survey 2004,* <http://www.stat.gov.tw/public/Attachment/53910445671.xls>

in April 2003, as compared to a normal April occupancy rate of over 80 per cent when Japanese tourists usually flocked to Taiwan, with those in northern Taipei, Taoyuan, Hsinchu and Miaoli regions being the most affected. Since the mass outbreak of SARS in April 2003, visitor arrival numbers to privately run recreational parks had dropped from a 80 per cent to 60 per cent reduction. Taking into account similar establishments on outlying islands, a total of 277 tourist resorts across Taiwan recorded an average contraction of 15.26 per cent, with large indoor facilities suffering the largest impact. Taiwan had lost at least US$350 million in tourism revenue in May and June 2003 because of the SARS outbreak (*BBC News*, 23 May 2003).

## 8.4   Human resources consequences

Stores, restaurants, hotels and travel agencies temporarily reduced staff, halted hiring and forced workers to take unpaid leave as the SARS epidemic

*Table 8.2* Number of unemployed persons and
unemployment rate, 1987–2004

| Year | Unemployed persons (thousand persons) | Unemployment rate (%) |
|---|---|---|
| 1987 | 161 | 1.97 |
| 1988 | 139 | 1.69 |
| 1989 | 132 | 1.57 |
| 1990 | 140 | 1.67 |
| 1991 | 130 | 1.51 |
| 1992 | 132 | 1.51 |
| 1993 | 128 | 1.45 |
| 1994 | 142 | 1.56 |
| 1995 | 165 | 1.79 |
| 1996 | 242 | 2.60 |
| 1997 | 256 | 2.72 |
| 1998 | 257 | 2.69 |
| 1999 | 283 | 2.92 |
| 2000 | 293 | 2.99 |
| 2001 | 450 | 4.57 |
| 2002 | 515 | 5.17 |
| 2003 | 503 | 4.99 |
| 2004 | 454 | 4.44 |

Sources: National Statistics, R. O. C. (Taiwan), *Annual
Report on Manpower Survey 2004*: <http://www.stat.gov.
tw/public/Attachment/53910461771xls>; and <http://
www.stat.gov.tw/public/Attach ment/53910463571.xls>

kept residents at home and tourists away. The official unemployment total in
Taiwan lingered at 4.99 per cent (as the short-term human resources impact
appears not to have led those adversely affected to register as officially
jobless, as most people were not fired once and for all) compared with
Taiwan's all-time high of 5.17 per cent recorded in 2002 (see Table 8.2).

Most HR managers empathized with the income loss suffered by their
employees but they opined that employees expressed a sense of helplessness
and some were able to understand and accept the consequences that were
brought about by the decline of business as they actually saw the gloomy
situation. As one HR manager, who declined to be named had succinctly put
it, 'No guests, no business and no income. The only way to survive, both for
the hotel and the employee, was to cut down the expenses .... It was no good
to complain, as everyone knew the situation' (Interviews, May 2005).

Part-time workers were the usual vulnerable group as most hotels
temporarily laid-off all or part of their part-time workers when SARS hit
the hotel business. At the height of the outbreak, one hotel (Hotel F in
Table 8.3) where one group of tourists from Hong Kong was kept for 10 days'
quarantine because a six-year-old child had a fever, had actually closed
down for several months, and all employees were on 'no-pay' leave.

In order to cut costs and sharpen competitiveness, job-sharing was common in the businesses affected. An employee of a travel agency informed us that even though employees were on duty on a rotational basis, not many of his colleagues thought of changing jobs because they were confident that the crisis would someday be over (Interviews, May 2005); some younger colleagues made use of the opportunity to upgrade themselves by taking professional examinations. On the other hand, an accountant of a travel agency contemplated looking for a part-time job at a convenient store as a monthly salary of NT$15,000 (around US$500) that resulted from her half-salaried employment was inadequate. To help relieve the pain, the Taiwan government embarked on a series of retraining initiatives in tourism, hotel and leisure management. The employer received a possible subsidy for the training costs to a maximum of 80 per cent, capped at NT$500,000 (*Taiwan Ribao*, 28 April 2003).

## 8.5 Discussion

We now turn to a discussion and evaluation of the economic and HRM impact of SARS on Taiwan, specifically focusing on its service sector, specifically in terms of tourism and hotels. We now turn to the hypotheses we set out in Chapter 4, as follows:

1   The greater the adverse impact of SARS on the Asian economies, the greater will be the negative impact on the service sector and specifically on the hotel industry.

The first imported cases started in late March and April 2003, and the WHO global alert was issued on 12 March 2003. These led to a fall in the percentage change of the GDP generated in the service sector vis-à-vis via the corresponding period in 2002.

As seen in Figure 8.1, the number of tourist arrivals drastically declined since the travel advice was issued by WHO on 12 March 2003. The number of visitor arrivals from the first quarter of 2003 to the second quarter plunged from 258,128 in February to 40,256 in May 2003. Hong Kong and Singapore also experienced a broadly comparable decline in tourist numbers.

Taiwan's airline industry also reported heavy losses due to flight cancellations. The cancellation rate for flights to Hong Kong, Macau, Singapore and Vietnam from 17 March to 11 April amounted to 16.2 per cent. From late March to end of April, local airlines had cancelled 796 flights, or 22.95 per cent of their usual total (*South China Morning Post*, 1 May 2003). The number of passengers from Hong Kong had dropped by 10,000 daily while the number of passengers from Macau had dropped by 3,200 per day. Most tour guides had not received any work assignment for periods of months; one we interviewed had no income for three months (Interviews, May 2003).

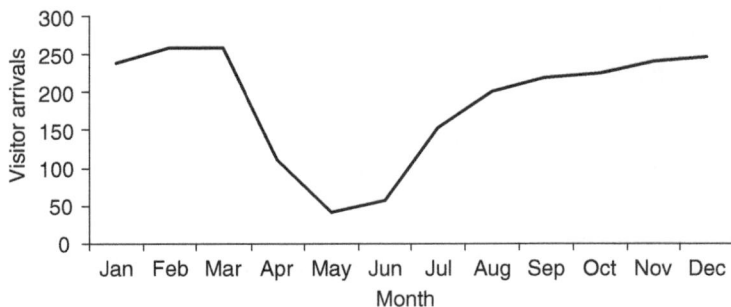

*Figure 8.1* Visitor arrivals, January–December 2003 (Unit: thousand persons).

Source: National Statistics, R. O. C. (Taiwan), *Monthly Bulletin of Statistics, April 2004*, <http://www.stat.gov.tw/bs2/bulletin/xls/k-3.xls.>

A coach-driver interviewed had no income for six months (from March to August 2003). Yet, according to the driver, (who had 30 years of experience), there were very few complaints as employees were said to be understanding of the fact that the employer had no business and hence no revenue to pay its employees (Interviews, May 2005).

The Director of Human Resources of a five-star hotel in Taipei informed that the room occupancy rate fell from a normal 85 per cent to 20 per cent in March 2003 when SARS hit Taiwan (Interviews, May 2005). As the hotel association in Taiwan had not discussed the situation and did not operate in a 'cartel' system, individual hotels had to think of ways to survive. The Westin Taipei was the first hotel to target the local market and introduced free twin-bed accommodation for the purchase of breakfast and dinner buffet combinations at NT$2,900 (Interviews, May 2005). Such marketing efforts proved to be very attractive to the local Taiwanese population. The Personnel Manager of a five-star hotel informed that 15,000 room nights had been sold in five months from the end of March to August 2003 (Interviews, May 2005).

By April and May 2003, virtually all hotels offered steep discounts to encourage consumer spending (and boost employment) when SARS was at its worst (*Minsheng bao*, 26 April 2003). The Howard Plaza Hotel offered a night's stay for single at around NT$3,000 (around US$100) including breakfast and afternoon tea (NT$1,400 for two excluding breakfast); the Grand Hyatt Taipei offered a night of twin accommodation at NT$3,300 (original price at NT$9,100). Other five-star hotels used gimmicks to attract customers: the Grand Formosa Regent Taipei offered a night's stay at the super deluxe room for two at NT$4,000, including buffet breakfast, free Chinese herbal tea and Germany-imported music to enhance self-defence metabolisms against SARS; and the Evergreen Laurel Hotel offered meals and spa treatment for two at NT$9,999 (about 65 per cent discount over the original price of NT$30,000).

Some hotels offered 'cut-throat' bargains as a result of the downturn. For example, the Gloria Prince Hotel offered local Taiwanese a night's stay at a super deluxe room for two at NT$3,999, plus a transferable coupon for one night's free accommodation; the Caesar Park Taipei offered a night's accommodation at NT$2,500 (containing NT$2,000 worth of vouchers for meals in the hotel, purchase of souvenirs and worldwide web service); and the Landis Ritz Hotel offered a two-bedroom apartment for four at NT$4,888 (original price of which was NT$21,450), including breakfast and every night's extension of stay at NT$1,000 per person. Hotel groups that have operations in different cities offered twin-cities packages to lure customers: the Caesar Park Taipei and Caesar Park Hotel Kenting (in the north and south of Taiwan, respectively) collectively offered promotional packages that ranged from NT$999 to NT$29,999 (including airfare, presidential suite, all meals, day trips and ecotours).

Some hotels offered low rates through packages put together with airlines (Interviews, May 2005). For example, the Grand Hotel at Taipei cooperated with a local airline to offer Taiwanese attractive hotel plus airfare packages that ranged from NT$3,088 to NT$4,900; while the Grand Hotel Kaohsiung in the South offered similar packages for four people at a price of around NT$10,000. The Executive Yuan of Taipei called an emergency meeting on 7 April to discuss methods for helping Taiwan's tourism sector to tide over financial difficulties triggered by the outbreak of SARS (*BBC News*, 7 April 2003). The emergency meeting, presided over by the Minister of Transport and Communications – attended by officials from the Tourism Bureau, as well as officials from other cabinet-level agencies, including the Council for Economic Planning and Development, the Ministry of Finance and the Council of Labour Affairs – was aimed at working out expedient and contingency measures to render a helping hand to the domestic tourism industry, particularly travel agencies, at the time when SARS was scaring tourists away from mainland China, which have been a major source of business for Taiwan travel agencies over the past few years. A rescue plan was announced on 1 May to bail out its faltering airline and travel industries. A tax cut or exemption was being considered for some industries (*Zhongguo shibao*, 15 April 2003). The vice-chairwoman of the Council for Economic Planning and Development remarked that the Taiwan government had already reduced fees for local airlines and that would 'cost the government almost NT$2 billion in lost revenue'. The finance committee of the Legislative Yuan also approved a proposal to stop local banks from cutting loans for industries in need of short-term financing during the SARS outbreak.

Turning now to our second hypothesis,

2   The greater the adverse impact of SARS on consumer demand in the Asian hotels and hospitality industry, the greater will be the negative impact on the related demand for labour in terms of hotel employees in specific hotel groups in the industry.

The CEO of an Internet employment agency reflected that SARS impacted hardest on the tourism industry, the aviation industry and the wholesale and retail businesses (in that order). Labour demand for the tourism industry in the short term was worst hit: the number of vacancies they recorded fell from 8.63 per cent in February to 6.32 per cent in late March when SARS broke out, to a further 5.82 per cent in mid April – a 30 per cent drop in one and a half month's time (*Pacific News Taiwan*, 25 April 2003). Yet, the aviation industry and the wholesale and retail sector, which are more capital-intensive, could endure the temporary economic setback and avoided massive retrenchment. This fact could have accounted for the moderate fall in the overall demand for labour in the service-sector's industries, with the biggest drop in the number of employees in the hotel and hospitality industry. It was natural that all hotels in Taiwan resorted to the tactic of frozen recruitment during the period of SARS. One Personnel Manager remarked that even the interns[2] were sent back to the universities; part-time workers, like chefs and service staff, normally recruited for big functions such as wedding banquets, were no longer required (Interviews, May 2005).

We now turn to the third hypothesis.

3    The greater the adverse impact on the demand for labour in the Asian hotel industry, the greater will be the negative impact on the labour-market in terms of lay-offs and redundancy among hotel employees in specific hotel groups in the industry.

To survive in such turbulent environments, hotels in Taiwan resorted to various HRM measures to cut costs. We now go on to discuss these HRM implications, of potential changing labour 'demand shock' and labour 'supply shock' consequences, as we put forward in Chapter 4 as significant causal factors (see Figure 8.2). Compared with our earlier Chapters 5, 6 and 7 on the same focus, Taiwan shares a labour market known for its flexibility with Hong Kong, as well as a paternalistic organizational culture. Singapore's labour market, on the other hand, was more directly affected by government intervention.

At the organizational level, the HRM consequences were noteworthy although not unduly dire, as our questionnaires and on-site interviews revealed (see Table 8.3).

Most hotel employees were required to take an average of two to four days' 'no-pay' leave for up to four months in April to August 2003 (Interviews, April 2005). With certain exceptions, which we shall shortly see, it seemed that the smaller the hotel in Taipei (the worst affected city in Taiwan) in terms of the number of employees, the more drastic the human resources measures. For example, employees of the biggest hotel in our sample (Hotel A that had 744 employees) took no other action other than organizing training courses; in other bigger hotels in our survey (Hotels B and D that

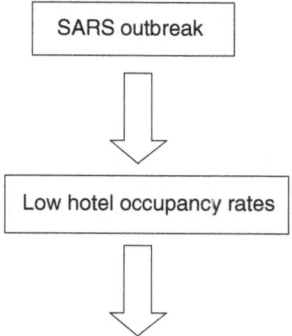

*Figure 8.2* Cost-cutting HRM measures adopted by the Taiwan hotel industry.

had 700 and 333 employees respectively) employees were required to take about 12 and 8 days' 'no-pay' leave, while a 228-employee hotel (Hotel E) made them take 4 to 10 days of 'no-pay' leave *per month* from April to July, peaking in June 2003. In other parts of Taiwan, a relatively small hotel of 110 employees in Yilan (Hotel I) made its staff take 'no-pay' leave of four days *a week* for two months. Another 200-employee hotel (Hotel G) introduced a 10 per cent pay cut on top of the 'no-pay' leave scheme of one day *per week*. Training on the nature of SARS and its preventive measures were held in few hotels as one HR Manager expressed that 'people were too afraid of SARS to hold public meetings' (Interviews, May 2005).

Yet, there were exceptions. Fifty per cent of the employees in Hotel I in Yilan protested against the policy of four days' 'no-pay' leave per week for two months, and resigned (Interviews, April 2005). On the other hand, the Customer Services Manager of a relatively small 41-employee Spring Resort (Hotel H) informed us that their employees were not requested to take 'no-pay' leave or a pay cut, even though other hotel operators of the district had come together to discuss collective measures to be taken, because their CEO was benevolent. Their hotel operator was of the view that the SARS crisis would not last and saw the decision of not introducing pay cuts as some kind of employment benefits. Thus, according to this respondent, employees in the resort did not suffer any loss of income because all the

*Table 8.3* Human resources responses of major hotels in Taiwan

| | |
|---|---|
| Hotel A in Taipei | All 744 staff received training. |
| Hotel B in Taipei | All 700 employees took involuntary no-pay leave of 12 days; all staff received training on the wearing of masks to prevent SARS. |
| Hotel C in Taipei | Annual leaves were cleared; 120 out of 450 staff were re-deployed; One out of 8 restaurants was closed. |
| Hotel D in Taipei | All part-time employees were laid off for 3 months; other 333 staff took 2 days no-pay leave per month for 4 months; all staff received training on the nature of SARS and its prevention. |
| Hotel E in Taipei | All 228 employees took involuntary no-pay leave that ranged from 4 days to 10 days from April to July 2003 (4 days in April, 6 days in May, 10 days in June, 6 days in July). |
| Hotel F in Taipei | Hotel was closed for 3 months; all 200 staff were on no-pay leave. |
| Hotel G in Taichung | All 200 employees were required to take 1 day no-pay leave per week, and 10% pay cut. |
| Hotel H in Yilan | 10% of part-time workers were laid off for 2 months; all other hotel operators in Yilan met to discuss pay cuts, but their operator did not cut staff's salary. |
| Hotel I in Yilan | All 110 staff were on no-pay leave of 4 days a week for 2 months; 50% of staff had resigned. |
| Hotel J in Kaohsiung | All 325 employees took involuntary no-pay leave of 3 days a month from May to August 2003. |
| Hotel K in Hualien | All 120 employees were on no-pay leave for 2 to 3 days a month for 3 months. |
| Hotel L in Hualien | All 228 employees were on 2 days no-pay leave in May. |

Source: Self-administered questionnaires and field Interviews, 2005.

shock was absorbed by the boss (Field survey, April 2005). Income was drastically reduced but expenditure was not lessened by the mere 10 per cent layoffs of the part-time employees for two months.

There were also rare cases of no redundancies, no 'no-pay' leave and no pay cuts in five-star hotels (Hotel A and Hotel C). With access to Hotel C, we focus our discussion on the coping strategies adopted by this particular five-star hotel. According to the Director of Human Resources, the hotel took several measures to cope with the situation as the room occupancy rate fell drastically from the normal 85 per cent to 20 per cent (Interviews, May 2005). First, at the beginning of SARS, staff were required to clear their annual leave; about 2,000 days of annual leave were taken; second, one Cantonese restaurant was closed. The redundant staff, 22 altogether, were absorbed by the remaining nine restaurants. The HR Director confided that such a tactic of redeployment was not very effective in cutting cost as labour costs amounted to 25–30 per cent of total hotel revenue. The 'no retrenchment' policy reflected, to a certain extent, the influence of national culture. The hotel, though a franchise of a US-based international hotel group, was managed by a Korean General Manager of the group, a 'family person' as described by the HR Director. This General Manager was well aware of the fact that each 'associate' (often typically US terminology for 'employee') had a family to support and any retrenchment decision would adversely affect a large number of families.

Hence the hotel came up with a promotional package in collaboration with a credit card company. About one-third of its work force received two days' training before being re-deployed to the selling of a hotel credit card package. Every new card applicant would get some benefits on dining at the hotel. The hotel could receive a commission of NT$2,500, equivalent of a night's room revenue, from each new credit card issued by the credit card company. The 126-strong sales force was drawn from various departments including the front office, house keeping and reservations. In this way, all employees could keep their monthly payroll.

As the promotional packages aiming at local Taiwanese became very popular, the room occupancy rate rocketed from 20 per cent to 95 per cent in the first two months of its introduction (Interviews, May 2005). With one-third of its regular employees redeployed to selling credit cards, the senior management staff from various departments such as finance, human resources and engineering had to help with the increase in demand for service staff. The senior managerial staff was required, on top of their normal duties, to collect used dishes from tables at the buffet restaurant, starting from 7 o'clock in the morning until the busy breakfast hours were over; as well as during lunch and dinner time. These senior staff could only leave the hotel at around 8 or 9 o'clock in the evenings. Even the General Manager and the Director of Human Resources served at the reservation desk so that the hotel could 'survive as a team' (Interviews, May 2005). Thus, it seems that the senior staff was victimized as they worked for longer hours, had a heavier and more menial workload, but got only regular salaries.

According to the HR Director, there were many pros and cons in the arrangements. On the one hand, it provided excellent training to the other 'associates' as they were 'inspired' by the effective managerial skills, and became 'closer' to the senior staff (Interviews, May 2005). On the other hand, it sowed the seeds for complaints from managerial staff, and serious complaints were raised when the hotel contemplated introducing involuntary 'no-pay' leave (three days a month for managers, five days for directors, and seven days for the general managers) in July and August 2003 when the number of local visitors dwindled as a result of the cut-throat competition created by different hotel packages, seeing no end to the SARS episode.

To make matters worse, complaints were also raised by many 'associates' who had been re-employed to the sales work force selling credit cards (Interviews, May 2005). Hotel management was puzzled by the complaint as they perceived that the sales staff actually had a higher salary because they received a commission of NT$500 per new credit card application, and less workload when compared to their long hours helping in the buffet restaurant. The HR Director informed that most sales staff could reach the monthly target of 25 credit card applications early in the month as some could sell up to five credit card applications per day. However, the redeployed staff found it a 'condescending' experience meeting strangers and 'begging' for credit card applications (Interviews, May 2005). The difference in perception suggested a breakdown in communication between staff and management. What seemed to be a 'win-win' approach had a price to pay. Some staff actually complained to the Labour Bureau (Interviews, May 2005)[3] which, according to the HR Director, was very 'protective' of the workers. The Labour Bureau issued a memo to the hotel and held a meeting with the hotel management to ask for evidence of communication and employee consent to redeployment.

As a matter of fact, as we were informed by the HR Director, heads of different departments had been asked to draw up a list of staff suitable for marketing. It was later discovered that the list was drawn up by involving 'associates' who had gone on leave, and they were then asked to report duty at the marketing department upon resumption of work. Although the redeployed staff had signed forms of consent and did not express contempt during the two-day training, they found the job very 'condescending' when they were in actual operation on the streets, and wanted to resume their normal duties, but failed. In the end, the case was closed by the Labour Bureau, but was referred to the Labour Inspection Unit for monitoring of the hotel for another month. The HR Director reflected upon the experience and lamented that better communication with the 'associates' was essential, as instances and rumours of pay cuts and 'no-pay' leave prevalent in the hotel industry led to a 'breach of trust' in labour relations (Interviews, May 2005).

## 8.6   Conclusions

Although we regard our findings as tentative, we can conclude that the impact of SARS on the Taiwan economy and specifically on human resources in the service sector may be seen as a matter of concern in the time-period in question, as in Chapters 5, 6 and 7. Both the *quantitative*, as well as the *qualitative*, data we have gathered, point in this direction, although we must be cautious to over-generalize. We have placed many caveats regarding our study in the body of the chapter and we are aware of the limitations of our investigation.

But the Taiwanese economy was highly resilient and soon able to come up with new promotions. Learning that Taiwan was removed from the WHO travel advisory list on 17 June, the Tourism Bureau organized a three-day festival to kick-start an international campaign to lure back foreign visitors (*The China Post*, 18 June 2003).[4] The Taiwanese economy, given its market-oriented flexibility fortunately recovered fairly quickly. The aviation and tourism sectors did in fact soon see a tangible rebound in the wake of the SARS impact.

As the economy revived by mid-2003 (*Taipei Times*, 13 July 2003),[5] it was thought that recovery in service-sector jobs above all, in industries like hotels and hospitality, both in low- as well as high-value added products and services would compensate for earlier job losses. The SARS epidemic of early and mid-2003 has no doubt been a sharp reminder to Hong Kong, Singapore and Taiwan, all *Nanyang* city-state economies, of their economic vulnerability and their reliance on tourism both to generate revenue and jobs. The Tourism Bureau Director remarked that Taiwan had 'lost at least US$350 million in tourism revenue' in May and June 2003 because of the SARS outbreak (*South China Morning Post*, 7 July 2003). The Chinese mainland case was somewhat different, given the lower weighting of the service sector in that economy. Today, there is less of a major 'crisis of confidence' but spirits remain low as the economy recovers, with the labour market still remaining 'fragile'.

Economic growth rates of the Taiwan economy surged by 71.5 per cent from 3.33 per cent in 2003 to 5.71 per cent in 2004, while GDP per capita rose from US$12,715 in 2003 to US$13,529 in 2004 (Directorate-General of Budget, Accounting and Statistics, 29 March 2005). Tourism helped the economy recover; total number of visitor arrivals jumped from 2.24 million in 2003 to 2.95 million in 2004. Total officially registered employment rose by 22,000, from 957,000 in 2003 to 979,000 in 2004; total officially registered unemployment dropped from 503,000 in 2003 to 454,000 in 2004; the

*Table 8.4* Economic and social indicators comparing 2003 and 2004

| Indicators | 2003 | 2004 |
| --- | --- | --- |
| Economic growth rate (%) | 3.33 | 5.71 |
| GDP (100 million, US$) | 2,860 | 3,054 |
| Per capita GDP | | |
| US$ | 12,715 | 13,529 |
| NT$ | 437.638 | 452.168 |
| Employed persons (thousand persons) | 957 | 979 |
| Unemployed persons (thousand persons) | 503 | 454 |
| Unemployment rate (%) | 4.99 | 4.44 |
| Annual rate of inbound departure of nationals (%) | −24.5 | 31.2 |
| Annual rate of outbound departure of nationals (%) | −19.9 | 31.4 |
| Annual rate of visitors to the principal scenic spots (%) | 15.7 | 15.1 |
| Annual change of tax revenue (%) | 2.2 | 10.5 |
| Tax revenue/GDP (%) | 12.7 | 13.6 |
| Stock price index (average) | 5,162 | 6,034 |

Source: Directorate-General of Budget, Accounting and Statistics, Executive Yuan, Republic of China, March 29, 2005. <http://eng.dgbas.gov.tw/public/Data/54416455371.xls.>

government's jobless rate also fell from 4.99 per cent to 4.44 per cent from 2003 to 2004 (see Table 8.4) (Directorate-General of Budget, Accounting and Statistics, 29 March 2005). The average stock market index jumped from 5,162 in 2003 to 6,034 in 2004; the annual changes of tax revenue also surged from 2.2 per cent in 2003 to 10.5 per cent 2004.

Yet a note of caution must be signalled here: it is clear that if the crisis brought about relatively discernable economic losses at the time, there were also, for example, clearly relatively negative direct consequences for many employees, particularly part-time workers, in the wide range of firms affected at the time. It is also clear that there was observable damage to 'trust' in labour-management relations, as had been seen in both the Hong Kong and Singapore experiences of SARS, some of it very visible but in some other cases less so and more subtle in its impact. As can be seen from the examples presented, the HRM evidence is mixed. Many employees in our Taiwan study, for example, thought that they had been made to lose 'face'. Even managers in some instances said they felt that their treatment had been 'cynical'. Perceptions such as the above may have indirect consequences in terms of human resource management implications that in their turn do not help to reinforce a positive workplace climate and their ultimate impact may be hard to predict. We now turn to the 'lessons' that might be learnt from coping with the SARS epidemic, in the next chapter.

# Part III

# Broader implications for human resources

So week in, week out, the prisoners of the plague struggled along as best as they could

Albert Camus ([1947]2002: 129)

# 9 Lessons to be learnt?

## 9.1 Introduction

Thucydides (1954: 2,47,1) suggests that more was needed than offerings to the gods to deal with the great plague that had struck Athens: 'Supplications in the temples, divinations, and so forth were found equally futile, till the overwhelming nature of the disaster at last put a stop to them altogether.'

As we stand back and regard the SARS epidemic of 2003 with some distance, we can try to ask: what are the lessons to be learnt once the scale of disaster had been realized? In this chapter, we begin with an overview of the themes that we have covered in the preceding ones. We hope to encompass the experiences of Hong Kong, China, Singapore and Taiwan, as noted in Chapters 5, 6, 7 and 8, to refresh the reader's memory concerning the key experiences of the epidemic we reported earlier in the respective chapters dealing with each location, and then attempt to both compare and contrast the measures and policies undertaken by the respective governments in combating SARS, their political will and decisiveness, the economic implications and the consequences for human resources. Then, we will ask what lessons can be learnt from the above, seeking guidance from the *World Health Report 2003 – Shaping the Future* (WHO, 2003d) published by the World Health Organization. Last, we offer a note of caution on the apparent successful containment of the epidemic and the discernable, not insubstantial albeit limited damage it did to economies and human resources.

## 9.2 Hong Kong

We saw in Chapter 5 that huge numbers of travellers cross the frontier by land, sea and air, into the Special Administrative Region every day and an equally sizeable head count goes in the opposite direction into the Mainland. One of these was to be the fatal link in the chain. The onset of SARS in Hong Kong was a result of transmission of the virus from Guangzhou by a doctor attending a wedding and staying at the Metropole Hotel in Kowloon in late February 2003. There, he infected a number of guests who then spread the virus to the rest of Hong Kong, Vietnam and even on to Canada.

Hong Kong is tiny compared with China itself but it has considerable economic importance. In terms of population, it is small in absolute size, compared with its neighbour. Yet its population density is one of the highest in the world and this makes it very vulnerable to cross-infection. It is also a 'window' to the outside global environment through its manifold transport links. On the other hand, its health care systems are superior to those on the Mainland; its citizens have a much higher GDP per capita; are better fed and nurtured; and thus might, it could be argued, have more robust immune systems.

The onset of SARS was to put severe strains on its health infrastructure. On 11 March, more than 20 health care workers on ward 8A of the PWH were showing symptoms of atypical pneumonia. Within the next few days, nearly a third of the medical staff in the Department of Medicine also showed symptoms (Lee and Yun, 2006: 136–7). The infection continued to spread. Fears grew. Fearful that the virus might be contracted in confined spaces, the staff of the 11-storey PWH ceased using the elevators, and the stairways of the building was crowded with panic-stricken health-care workers. To improve the ventilation, most staff kept their windows opened.

> Before long, many departments in the hospital and medical school decided to divide their staff into 'dirty' and 'clean' teams .... There was an unspoken sense that the clean team would be entrusted with 'carrying on' or 'ensuring the future' of the hospital should the dirty team perish. There was a genuine fear of dying; and indeed affected medical staff were extremely ill, some on respirators, and some would die.
>
> (Lee and Yun, 2006: 136–7)

Around the same time, the infection was also spreading to the community. One of the most severely affected paces was the Amoy Gardens, a residential complex which housed thousands. Block E was particularly hard hit, as we saw in Chapter 5. By 31 March, 107 of the 200 residents of the block were affected by SARS. Until the Amoy Gardens outbreak, most Hong Kong citizens believed that they could avoid SARS by not leaving their homes. But the home itself could become a dangerous site. In response, most families in Hong Kong started the ritual of cleaning the furniture and floor daily with diluted bleach solution. Another ritual that had become common was the 'undressing procedure' on returning home.

The news of the epidemic spread very quickly. Mobile calls, texts and emails accelerated the usual 'word of mouth' diffusion of bad news. The Special Administrative Region had ground to a halt. Public services, like nurseries, schools and colleges, were closed down; movement around the city was discouraged; consumers shopped only for necessities, if indeed they dared to do so.

The economy was immediately hit with the service sector taking the brunt. The SARS epidemic could not have come at a worse time for Hong Kong, whose economy was already facing a serious recession, with negative equity, rising unemployment and low growth. Unemployment was at a high of 7.8 per cent in 2002, while economic growth was only 2.3 per cent in the same year. According to WHO, the Hong Kong authorities actually bargained with WHO on the issuing of a travel advisory, asking WHO to 'wait overnight while [Hong Kong] drew up the most comprehensive assessment possible of the situation' (Omi, 2006). Yet, WHO concluded that the information received 'was not sufficiently persuasive and that the data available on the newly reported cases suggested that travel to the area could contribute to the international spread of SARS', and the advisory was issued on 2 April.

Hong Kong's economic woes were further exacerbated. In the second quarter of 2003, real GDP contracted by 0.5 per cent, down from an increase of 4.5 per cent in the first quarter (Wong *et al.*, 2004: 34).

As on the Mainland, the privately owned service sector with its component parts such as hospitality, retail, tourism and the like were the first economic victims. Since it was a hub for airline traffic, Hong Kong was gravely affected by the decline in air travel, particularly, as we have seen in Chapter 5. Among the Greater China economies, Hong Kong's tourism-related services including airlines, hotels, restaurants, entertainment and retail trade, was the worst hit by SARS since tourism receipts account for 5.1 per cent of its GDP. The 'demand shock' as adumbrated in Chapter 4 was soon evident.

As the economy recovered by the early 2000s, it was thought that service-sector jobs above all, in sectors like the hotel industry, both in low as well as high-value-added products and services would compensate for job losses. The SARS epidemic of early and mid-2003 has been a grim reminder of the HKSAR's economic vulnerability.

## 9.3 People's Republic of China

The experience of the epidemic in the PRC clearly had a highly significant impact on this vast country and especially its cities. We have observed that there was probably the first case of SARS in Guangdong Province in mid-November, 2002. At first, it was thought to be a variety of influenza; this was not the first time a new respiratory infection had emerged from southern China, as we have seen in Chapter 6. In 1957, a new strain of influenza appeared in Hunan, China, which spread throughout the world and led to the Asian flu pandemic of that year (Murray, 2006: 17). That strain persisted until 1968, when it was supplanted by yet another influenza strain that emerged from southern China and rapidly moved to Hong Kong before disseminating around the globe. Since then, several new variants of flu have arisen from the same region, most recently, an avian strain of influenza A that emerged in 1997, killing large numbers of poultry – before it spread to humans and that resulted in at least six deaths among the 18 cases reported (Murray, 2006: 17). Given this history, the Chinese authorities immediately suspected that a new strain was the most likely culprit responsible for the mysterious respiratory infection spreading in Guangdong Province. However, tests for influenza quickly came back negative. The term 'SARS', we may note, was not aired until early 2003, when WHO used it for the first time. It employs the term 'severe acute respiratory syndrome' (coined by WHO specialist the late Dr Carlo Urbani who treated the first SARS patient in Vietnam and died shortly afterwards). He had worked in public health programmes in Cambodia, Laos and Vietnam; he was 46 years old.

A global alert on the epidemic was issued by WHO on 12 March 2003. The initial response of the Chinese authorities was initially not impressive. In retrospect, we may even see it as rather depressing. The fact that China was undergoing a major leadership transition that started formally in November 2002 at the Sixteenth Party Congress – and only ended in March 2003 with the Tenth National People's Congress – did not help matters and meant that 'leaders were not only preoccupied with political jockeying but also that no one wanted to be the bearer of bad tidings' (Saich, 2006: 73). Additionally, leadership obsession with social stability and economic development meant that there was no incentive to release information about the disease. The government, ever cautious, was fearful that the economy would suffer, that consumption would fall, employment would be jeopardized and that foreign investment would be discouraged. Employment in large cities, we may note, is now heavily dependent on the service sector, which is potentially vulnerable to downturns in consumer spending, hospitality, retail, tourism and the like, a point now well reinforced by the experience of Spring 2003.

But later, quite quickly, the Chinese government got to grips with the problem, as the 'digital revolution' generated vast numbers of mobile-phone calls and texts and the 'internet' sent emails bouncing around the country and beyond. The news spread with almost instant speed, public apprehension burgeoned and the official media could not contain it. When an outraged doctor from a Beijing military hospital reported to the media that there were over 120 cases at the Number 301 PLA Hospital and two other military hospitals in Beijing, as opposed to the official announcement of only 22 cases with four deaths, the Chinese government fired the Minister of Health, Zhang Wenkang, and the Deputy Mayor of *Beijing*, Meng Xuenong, on 20 April. The government faced with both growing national and international ire dramatically changed course, instituting a rarely seen transparency and honesty in reporting, and allocated two billion yuan in emergency funding for national SARS control (Kaufman, 2006: 56). Following the sacking on 20 April of Zhang and Meng, the government revised the capital's SARS case number to 339, 10 times that reported one week earlier. Ultimately, China bore the brunt of SARS, and over 6 in 10 of the deaths incurred were Chinese. Out of the almost 10,000 cases worldwide, a sub-total of

5,327 was in China of which 349 or 6.55 per cent proved fatal. Although a tiny percentage of the population, it was to have a disproportionately high, perhaps unprecedented, impact on public awareness.

Since the economy of the PRC was so large, it was ultimately able to absorb the material impact of the epidemic but at a cost. As Rawski (2006: 118) points out it was a 'brief but sharp setback' to China's economic advance. Calculations by Ren Ruoen indicate that 'seriously affected regions, including Guangdong Province, Beijing and provinces adjacent to the capital, accounted for 22.7 per cent of China's 2001 gross domestic product (GDP)' (Rawski, 2006: 108–9). Peripheral regions accounting for 3.9 per cent of GDP felt little effect from SARS. The remaining provinces, accounting for 73.4 per cent of GDP suffered only modest effects from the outbreak (Rawski, 2006: 108–9). It is observable that the effect on employment in the service sector in general and in the hotels industry in particular was, as we have seen in Chapter 6, relatively negative in the short-term, at least at the time. SARS particularly hit China's service sector and related parts of it, such as hospitality, restaurants, retail and so on. Beijing is uniquely dependent today 'upon this mainly privately-owned service contribution, which contributed 61.3 per cent of the city's GDP in 2002, 10 percentage points higher than any other jurisdiction and 27 percentage points above the national average' (Rawski, 2006: 111). The fact that Beijing was among one of the first places where a travel advisory notice was issued by WHO, but the last place to have it lifted, hit the greatest blow (see Table 9.1).

Shigeru Omi, Director of the WHO Western Pacific Region, acknowledged that 'the possible impact of travel advisories on the economies of affected areas and on the morale of people living there was one of the most difficult issues of the SARS experience' (Omi, 2006). Public service activity also was heavily curtailed, although wages and salaries were here mostly unaffected.

*Table 9.1* Dates and places where travel advisory notices were issued and lifted by the WHO (2003)

|  | Issued | Lifted |
| --- | --- | --- |
| Hong Kong Guangdong, PRC | 2 April | 23 May |
| Beijing, PRC | 23 April | 24 June |
| Shanxi, PRC |  | 13 June |
| Toronto, Canada |  | 29 April |
| Tianjin and Inner Mongolia, PRC | 8 May | 13 June |
| Taipei, Taiwan |  | 17 June |
| Hubei, PRC | 17 May | 13 June |
| All of Taiwan | 21 May | 17 June |

Source: Adapted from World Health Organization (2006) *SARS: How a Global Epidemic was Stopped*. Manila: World Health Organization.

However, public service outputs were adversely affected at the time and extra costs were clearly incurred. Damage was not confined to the regions with the largest concentration of disease victims. The hard-hit sectors accounted for approximately one-tenth of China's total output in 2001 (Omi, 2006).

Many policy makers had thought that the expansion of service-industry employment, particularly in privately owned enterprises, would create a positive and stable employment equilibrium and compensate for structural reform, downsizing of SOEs and the like. However, the authorities may have to reconsider their strategy and continually be on their guard against unforeseen circumstances. Erosion of secondary as well as primary sector employment may sometimes be compensated for by counter-strategies to create jobs in services; these may not always be as deep-rooted as policy makers believe to be the case.

## 9.4   Singapore

We had also noted that Singapore had reported the third largest number of SARS cases. As at 7 April, a total of 106 people with SARS were reported to the Ministry of Health, with six deaths. The cases in Singapore are traceable to the three people who travelled to Hong Kong and contracted SARS, as we reported in Chapter 7.

Singapore is often called the 'Switzerland of Asia': a well-organized society. It had one of most severe control-regimes in Asia during the SARS epidemic. Some regard it as a model for coordinating disease control. Singapore was the first country in Asia to take immediate, decisive action to tackle this public health threat. The Ministry of Education and Ministry of Health decided to close all kindergartens, primary schools, secondary schools, junior colleges and centralized institutes from 27 March to as late as 16 April (Leung and Ooi, 2003: 49). Rawski (2006: 120) claims that apart from the later PRC response, Singapore controlled the spread of the epidemic more effectively than Hong Kong and Taiwan, because they did not shirk from introducing very stringent quarantine regimes as soon as they could. The government invoked the Infectious Disease Act, under which all people who have come into contact with infected victims have to be quarantined. Hefty fines were imposed on those who break the 10-day quarantine. SARS patients who were discharged from the Tan Tock Seng Hospital (TTSH) were followed up in accordance with the guidelines from WHO. Upon discharge, SARS patients were given medical leave for two weeks and were required to stay at home. They were reviewed by the doctors at TTSH before they return to work or school. During their two weeks' medical leave at home, their condition was monitored by staff from TTSH through daily phone-calls (Rawski, 2006: 120). A commercial security firm was hired by the government to serve Home Quarantine Orders and to install 'electronic picture cameras' in homes to ensure compliance (Whaley and Mansoor, 2006).

A 50-year-old man who disobeyed home quarantine orders was the first person to be publicly named and charged under the Infectious Disease Act on 4 May (Whaley and Mansoor, 2006).

The private sector also had elaborate crisis preparations. An internationally known bank segregated employees into three groups: the first group worked in the central office in Singapore's central banking district; the second moved to a remote site some miles away; and the third worked from home. Senior managers made it a practice not to meet together in the same room at the same time. Most significantly, visits to clients abroad ceased entirely, given that each trip required a 10-day quarantine at the entry port (Watson, 2006: 201).

The economic impact of the SARS epidemic in Singapore was immediate. Singapore's rate of growth in the service sector, turned sharply negative in the second quarter of 2003, falling to minus 4.2 per cent from positive growth of 1.7 per cent in the first quarter of 2003 (Ministry of Trade and Industry, 2004). Uncertainties associated with the war in Iraq, notwithstanding the SARS outbreak, also caused the growth momentum (on an annualized quarter-on-quarter basis) to dip sharply by 11 per cent, after an increase of 1.4 per cent in the previous quarter. Since the service sector accounts for about 65.7 per cent of Singapore's GDP and the SARS crisis had a hugely damaging impact, it led to a 3.9 per cent fall in GDP in the second quarter of 2003.

## 9.5 Taiwan

The majority of Taiwan's SARS cases, we saw earlier, can be traced to a single patient, a resident of the Amoy Gardens in Hong Kong, who visited Taiwan for the traditional 'sweeping of the graves' and infected his brother there, as we saw in Chapter 8. Taiwan tightened measures to prevent a SARS epidemic by declaring a city-wide alert in Taipei. As of 7 April, 21 people were affected, after five employees of a major engineering company who developed SARS symptoms after returning from China. The city government tracked more than 1,000 people, including 200 or so who had boarded the same plane with the five affected employees (Leung and Ooi, 2003: 54). The Health Department officially declared SARS a communicable disease. Anyone who defied a local health office's order to stay at home in compliance with quarantine rule would be fined up to NT$300,000. Doctors or medical institutes who failed to report any suspected cases to the Health Department, or who refused to treat suspected patients would be fined NT$1 million (Leung and Ooi, 2003: 54). Public transport companies, such as subways, buses and taxis, had also started disinfecting their facilities. Jittery residents were also rushing to buy masks, thereby driving up their price.

Taiwan's economy was already slowing down before SARS due to the recession in the United States and global slump in electronics exports. The economic loss during the SARS outbreak was estimated at US$820 million to US$1,300 million (Maloney *et al.*, 2006). The SARS-induced downturn, a short, sharp 'demand shock', however proved to be temporary for Taiwan's economy and most of the return to growth was cyclical. Wong *et al.* (2004: 26–8) referenced a report by the Cabinet's Council of Economic Planning and Development that 'the economy continued to grow at a rate of 3.5 per cent in the first quarter of 2003, but contracted by 0.1 per cent in the second quarter due to the outbreak of SARS, though grew 4.2 per cent year-on-year in the third quarter.' The initial impact of SARS was felt in the service sector, as in China, Hong Kong and Singapore. Tourist arrivals to Taiwan in April fell by 56–60 per cent compared to the same period the previous year and hotel occupancy dropped by more than 30 per cent. Domestic tourism fell by as much as 70 per cent in May as people avoided travelling, due to fear of catching SARS. As governments and companies imposed travel restrictions to SARS-affected areas, and tourists cancelled holiday booking, passenger volume to Taiwan 'declined by as much as 80 per cent in the first week of May while airline carriers grounded up to 24 per cent of the flights' (ibid.). However, Taiwan's tourism-related services were the least hit by SARS compared to Hong Kong and China since tourism receipts accounts for only 1.4 per cent of its GDP.

Unemployment in Taiwan rose from 4.9 per cent in April to 5.1 per cent in June, partly due to the SARS outbreak and partly as a result of rising first-time job seekers. Wong *et al.* (2004: 31) quote the Directorate-General of Budget, Accounting and Statistics that 'the slump in the economic activity caused by SARS contributed to a rise in the number of people made unemployed, owing to the closure or downsizing of businesses, the "supply shock" side, from 429,000 in April to 433,000 in May; the non-seasonally adjusted unemployment rate continued to hover above 5 per cent in June.'

## 9.6   Comparing

SARS was potentially a major threat to the Asian economies and especially the Chinese economy but the epidemic was controlled quickly enough, according to Rawski (2006), to minimize what could have been much greater damage. Traditional basic disease-control strategies of surveillance, quarantine, isolation and infection control proved to be adequate to stop transmission (Schnur, 2006: 41).

The battle against SARS took place on two fronts in all the countries it affected: on the one hand, doctors, scientists and researchers worked frantically to treat infected patients and analyse the disease; on the other, government officials formulated and implemented emergency policies to control the outbreak (Leung and Ooi, 2003: 65–8). As the rate of infection was alarmingly high, the authorities in every country adopted strict precautionary measures, sometimes seemingly excessive ones, to combat the disease.

The general strategy that governments adopted was to identify, to isolate and to contain. One of the top priorities of any responsible government is to identify all cases of infection and suspected cases, and then isolate them so as to prevent them from spreading to the rest of the population. The recent activities of infected patients were traced, so as to identify the people who had come into close contact with them. In all our case-studies, the people who came into close contact with infected cases were quarantined or monitored closely. In China, all those who worked or lived in the same building were required to quarantine themselves for twelve days even if they did not have direct contact with the suspected case (Kaufman, 2006: 61).

Infected patients and suspected cases were moved to specific hospitals, with exclusive teams of medical staff to tend to them. A SARS hospital, Xiaotangshan, was constructed in a rural county outside Beijing. National infection-control guidelines for health care workers were developed and proper medical waste disposal was instituted. In Singapore, all SARS patients were treated in TTSH; a fleet of ambulances was specially set aside for the transportation of SARS patients to hospitals. All medical staff took preventive measures such as wearing protective gear and their health was closely monitored for symptoms of infection. These hospitals, or specific wards within these hospitals, were made out-of-bounds to non-SARS related patients or staff; strict restrictions were also implemented on visitors. In Hong Kong, the residents of Block E in Amoy Gardens where about large numbers of cases, were found, as we have seen earlier, were quarantined in countryside vacation camps.

As it has been established that the disease spread globally by air travel, many airlines and airports implemented screening procedures. Both authors of this book saw these implemented at first hand. Aircrews were instructed to look out for SARS symptoms among passengers, and to single them out for medical examination. Plane-loads of passengers were also quarantined whenever an infected case was detected on board. In fact, very few air crew were infected with SARS. Airports also adopted proactive measures like distributing flyers to passengers to inform them about the disease, taking body temperatures of passenger arrivals by infrared sensors, and stationing medical teams who are trained to handle suspected cases near passenger arrival halls. One of the authors of this monograph was briefly detained (for a few, tense hours) by the medical authorities while transiting through Hong Kong airport even a year later, as he had caught a chill from the airconditioning and was running 'a temperature'.

Schools and the work place are places where large numbers of people congregate, and hence, are potential centres for mass infection. Hence, the respective governments had taken a drastic but prudent step of closing schools until the SARS outbreak was controlled – to minimize the risk of further outbreak (see Table 9.2).

Some companies also suspended their operations when their employees were found to be infected with SARS. For example, Hewlett-Packard shut

*Table 9.2* Dates of school closures (2003)

| Singapore | 27 March–6 April (all schools) |
|---|---|
| Hong Kong | 29 March–22 April (senior secondary)/28 April (junior secondary)/19 May (primary, other special schools) |
| Beijing, PRC | 23 April–22 May (primary and secondary) |

Source: Adapted from World Health Organization (2006) SARS: *How a Global Epidemic was Stopped.* Manila: World Health Organization.

down its five-storey office in Hong Kong when one worker was infected by SARS; Motorola suspended an entire shift from its factory when one of its workers got infected (Leung and Ooi, 2003: 73–4); The Chinese government even cancelled the week-long May Day holiday to prevent hordes of travellers from moving around.

The level of public and personal hygiene was raised.

> Governments and property management companies took extra care to clean and disinfect public areas such as lift lobbies and lift buttons. Transport companies also disinfected their trains, buses and taxis thoroughly. Individuals became more conscious about washing their hands with soap regularly and refrained from touching the eyes, noses and lips with hands. Governments had also launched intensive public education and awareness campaigns via the media such as newspapers, television and radio. The public was informed of the symptoms of SARS and to seek treatment at appropriate designated treatment centres. Multiple-user text messages were sent out in Hong Kong on a regular basis. Proper education of the public on the disease could certainly allay fear, squelch fallacious rumours and prevent public panic, and help foster better understanding of the disease.
>
> (Leung and Ooi, 2003: 68)

## 9.7   Contrasting

An issue that became salient due to the outbreak of SARS is governmental transparency and the authority's ability to act decisively when faced with a crisis. China, the place where the SARS epidemic was suspected to originate, has been most widely criticized for its lack of transparency in dealing with the SARS outbreak. 'Much of this was rightly blamed on the Chinese government, which at the early stages of the epidemic withheld information, controlled the media, and discouraged international access to SARS victims' (see Saich, 2006: 71–104).

However, as international criticism mounted and a Chinese doctor blew the whistle, the Chinese government relented and took decisive actions.

A national SARS headquarters was set up in Beijing under the direction of Wu Yi, acting Minister of Health and a Vice Premier. SARS was classified as an infectious disease, subject to the reporting requirements specified under the Law on Prevention and Control of Contagious Disease, and additional legislation in the form of regulations dealing with SARS prevention and control was enacted, which required daily reporting and control measures (Kaufman, 2006: 61). 'Mass mobilization' and 'mass campaigns', which had been used by China to fight SARS, proved to be a very effective approach to combating the communicable disease. The China case demonstrated how political will and national mobilization are required for tackling serious threats to public health. For instance, Xiaotanshan, the 1,000-bed quarantine facility was completed in less than a week, with work continuing 24 hours a day.

To a lesser extent, the authorities of Hong Kong were also accused of dragging their feet. Hong Kong started off underestimating the danger of the disease, and hence, acted too slowly. The Hong Kong government had initially chosen to play down the outbreak. On 14 March, the Secretary of Health, Welfare and Food E.K. Yeoh assured the public that there was no outbreak in the community. On 17 March, Dr Yeoh accused WHO of causing panic over SARS and asserted again that there was no outbreak in the community. On the same day, Professor Sydney Chung of the Chinese University of Hong Kong revealed to the press that there were signs that SARS was spreading in the community, contradicting Yeoh's earlier comment. The next day, Dr Yeoh admitted that there were SARS cases outside of the health care workers and families. However, when the seriousness of the outbreak was realized, the government took quick and decisive actions.

Elsewhere, governments in Singapore and Taiwan adopted an open and transparent attitude in dealing with the health crisis; and coordinated with WHO. There were regular public updates as well as a relatively free flow of information from the authorities. It was hoped that such an approach would raise public awareness and help curb the SARS outbreak more effectively. An 'open approach' also allows better cooperation between the government and the public, as well as better coordination between different countries hit by the same disease.

## 9.8 Possible lessons

The SARS outbreak showed that communicable diseases remain a grave threat to humans and the stability of their societies and constitute a potential 'catastrophe' as suggested in Chapter 2. Although much about SARS – including its potential to reoccur – remains to be learnt through systematic analysis of existing data, and focused research activities in China, WHO (2003d) pointed out that several important lessons are already apparent. We summarize them below and comment on them *en passant*:

The first and most compelling lesson WHO proposes relates to the need to report, promptly and openly, cases of any epidemic with the high potential for global spread, as has been seen from the various WHO reports we have noted earlier. Attempts to cover up cases of an infectious disease, for fear of social and economic implications, must be recognized as a short-term stop-gap measure that carries a costly price: the potential for serious levels of human suffering and death; a substantial loss of credibility in the eyes of the international community; escalating negative domestic economic impact; damage to the health and economies of neighbouring countries; and a very real risk that outbreaks within the nation's own territory will spiral out of control.

The second WHO-led lesson is closely related to the first: for instance, timely global alerts, particularly when widely supported by a responsible press and wisely diffused by electronic communications, worked well to boost awareness and vigilance to levels that can prevent imported cases of an emerging and transmissible infection from causing significant outbreaks. The global alerts issued by WHO on 12 and 15 March offer a clear line of demarcation between regions with severe SARS outbreaks and those with none or only a few secondary cases. After the SARS alerts, all the areas that experienced imported cases, with the exception of the PRC and Taiwan, either prevented any further transmission or kept the number of locally transmitted cases very low.

The third WHO lesson is that 'travel recommendations', encompassing screening measures at airports, do seem to be effective in helping to contain the international spread of an emerging infection. Analyses of data on in-flight transmission of SARS has implicated four flights in the exposure of 27 probable cases, of which 22 occurred on a single flight from Hong Kong to Beijing, China, on 15 March. A number of these cases may also have been exposed elsewhere because of being in the same tour group. Following the recommendation of airport screening measures on 27 March, no cases associated with in-flight exposure were reported; and initial information reveals that two probable SARS cases were identified by screening procedures at airport monitors in Hong Kong and immediately hospitalized.

The fourth lesson from WHO focuses on international collaboration: the world's scientists, clinicians and public health experts were willing to set aside academic competition and work together for the good of the public health as and when the situation so requires. International collaboration greatly boosted understanding of the science of SARS. Within a month after the laboratory network was established, participating scientists collectively announced conclusive identification of the SARS virus; complete sequencing of its RNA followed shortly afterwards. The global network of clinical experts offered a platform for comparison of patient management strategies to indicate to the world which treatments and strategies were effective. In addition, the epidemiology network confirmed the modes of transmission of SARS and began the long-term collaboration needed to understand clearly the clinical spectrum of disease, including its case-fatality ratio, while also ensuring the information needed to regularly reassess and adjust the case definition.

Lesson five from WHO is that weaknesses in health systems can encourage emerging infections to amplify and spread, and can greatly compromise patient care. The strengthening of health systems thus deserves the highest priority. The population at greatest risk for SARS were health workers who either became infected by close face-to-face contact with patients or by procedures that brought them into contact with respiratory secretions. The surge of SARS patients infected placed a huge burden on health services, showing the need for facilities for isolation, long periods of intensive and expensive care, and the use of very demanding and highly socially disruptive steps such as mass-screening, contact-tracing, active surveillance of contacts and – at some outbreak sites – the strongest measure, enforced quarantine. Even in areas with highly developed social services, the load of coping with SARS, including the large number of hospitals with patients and the high number of health workers who had became infected, often required the closure of some hospitals and sections of others. As a result of SARS, many long-standing and apparently intractable problems that have traditionally weakened health systems are now being corrected in fundamental and often permanent ways. New surveillance and reporting systems, methods of data-management, protocols for collaborative research, hospital policies, procedures for infection control and channels for educating the public, are part of the positive legacy of SARS that will shape the capacity of WHO and those in its sphere of influence to respond to future outbreaks of new or re-emerging infections.

Lesson six from WHO is that in the absence of a curative drug and a preventive vaccine, existing interventions, geared to the epidemiological data and backed by political commitment and public concern, can be used positively to contain an outbreak. Some countries introduced effective observation of suspected contacts using surveillance cameras or military personnel. Others were based on self-surveillance by contacts who voluntarily isolated themselves in their houses and flats and regularly checked for fever. Measures introduced at airports stretched from passive screening of travellers, involving optional completion of questionnaires, to the use of interviews conducted by health workers and sophisticated infrared equipment to screen all passengers for fever and signs of possible exposure. In addition to maximizing the effectiveness of surveillance and screening, these measures were also seen by governments to be reassuring for its citizens as well as international travellers.

The seventh WHO lesson highlights one of the major obstacles faced during the containment activities for SARS: risk communication about emerging infectious diseases is a great challenge. SARS will not be the last new epidemic to take advantage of modern global needs. Globalization, with its increased trade and travel, meant that outbreaks even in a small prefectural city can quickly become international in scope and threat.[1] 'If the SARS outbreak has taught us anything', notes Ilona S. Kickbusch of the Yale School of Public Health, 'it is how interconnected the world is .... This isn't just an issue for developing countries' (quoted in Kleinman and Watson, 2006: 5). In the last two decades of the twentieth century, new diseases emerged at the rate of one per year, and this trend is certain to continue (WHO, 2003d).

## 9.9   Conclusions

The rapid containment of SARS, thus, constitutes a success in public health terms, but is also a warning. It is nonetheless proof of the power of international collaboration supported at the highest political level. At the same time, containment of SARS was aided by 'good fortune'. The most severely affected areas in the SARS outbreak had well-developed health care systems. Had SARS established a foothold in countries where health systems are less well developed cases might still be occurring, with global containment much more difficult, if not impossible. The lessons for a possible Avian Flu pandemic[2] are self-evident. The ultimate damage to the regional and national economies was contained but was not insubstantial; the employment and human resources consequences were temporary but hard-felt for those who were laid off or on half-pay. Vigilance remains our first line of defence.

In the next and last chapter, we will attempt to draw the various themes we have sketched out thus far and try to set out some conclusions.

# 10 Conclusions

## 10.1 Introduction

The SARS epidemic of 2003 was a voyage into the unknown. Here was a new virus, with no known remedy. In Albert Camus' novel, *The Plague* (*La Peste*), to which we earlier referred, we see that the disease spreads very quickly indeed: 'I have the figures,' says the Prefect, 'they certainly are disturbing' – 'They are more than disturbing, they are unequivocal' replies the Doctor ([1947]/2002: 49). But in the case of the plague in the novel, at least there was a serum at hand, if in short supply.

As Weinstein (2004: 1) notes in the *New England Journal of Medicine*,

> In terms of sheer drama, the emergence of the severe acute respiratory syndrome (SARS) rivaled the most exotic Michael Crichton thriller. A novel viral strain spread in 'wet markets' from an obscure animal to food handlers; through a rural province in southern China; to Hong Kong, by way of an ill Chinese physician who had traveled to attend a wedding; and in one night at a Hong Kong hotel, from that man to at least 12 other people. These 12 returned to their five home countries and created multiple chains of transmission.
>
> (2004: 2332)

This chain of events, now familiar to anyone who has studied the epidemiology of SARS, and to the reader of this study from previous chapters, was to prove to be the main route to a potential catastrophe.

It is therefore appropriate to review our conclusions in terms of the taxonomy of catastrophic events we sketched out earlier (see Chapter 2, Figure 2.3). We had proposed using three dimensions, *length* (temporal), *breadth* (geographic) and *depth* (human impact). We looked at four categories across the horizontal span, namely *natural catastrophes*, *epidemics*, *wars* and *slumps*. The first two are often said to be 'Acts of God'; the second pair are most likely to be 'man made'. We noted the main variation in each and gave some examples in terms of the dimensions arranged vertically.

Epi- and pandemics, we concluded, varied a great deal on their dimensions but pandemics are, of course, by definition, epidemics writ large. They may be short or long; local or wider in scope; minimal or maximal in effect. The impact may range from a thousand dead in the SARS case, to tens of millions, as in the worst historical occurrences like the Black Death or Spanish Flu. Under epidemics (see Chapter 2, Figure 2.4), we noted that SARS was, however, for example, *short in duration* rather than lengthy, *regional* rather than global (in its most severe actual consequences) and *minimal* (vis-à-vis pandemics) in human impact *ex post facto*. Under the pandemics heading, Spanish Flu would have been *long*, *global* and *maximal*, by comparison.

Thus, historically speaking, the SARS epidemic although severe in its impact, did not devastate populations and generations – as did the past pestilences of the late and post-medieval periods (see Cohn, 2002) or at the end of the First World War (Beveridge, 1977). Nor can SARS be compared numerically in terms of its mortality – vis-à-vis contemporary killers such as malaria or HIV/AIDs, we have seen earlier.

The public's response to the SARS outbreak could have arguably been seen as disproportionate to the event's eventual clinical severity or lethality, as is often the case when catastrophic epidemics strike, on the dimensions we set out above. However, it was not clear during the outbreak that the response was in reality disproportional because there was a vast amount of uncertainty about the epidemic's severity, as we saw in Chapter 3. The origins of the outbreak were obscure but news spread very fast, given the role of the 24/7 global media, electronic rumour by mobile phone and text, internet and so on.[1] Social and economic life came to a virtual standstill; officialdom was baffled; politicians struggled to respond. The medical infrastructure was severely challenged and was almost overwhelmed.[2] The economic consequences of the reaction to the SARS epidemic were very soon evident but clearly on a lesser scale than a global sum, as we noted earlier (see Chapter 4, Figure 4.5).

We attempt now to sum up below, the ultimate burden of SARS to the Asian economies and societies we have covered in this book.

## 10.2   Impact of SARS

Figure 10.1 gives an overview of the intensity of impact of SARS – in summary form – on the Asian countries most affected by SARS, epidemically, economically and on human resources.

The immediate impact of the SARS epidemic was a surge in demand for medical services throughout the region as we have seen in Chapters 5, 6, 7 and 8 in the national case-studies in Hong Kong, PRC, Singapore and Taiwan that we have explored. It is no exaggeration to say that there was near-panic evident once the full scale of the epidemic became known. Health care workers being exposed to the disease, resulted in further strains on the health care system's capacity, as some workers became sick (33 medical doctors and students fell sick in the Prince of Wales Hospital when the virus first hit Hong Kong); and others stayed home to care for

|  | EPIDEMICS | ECONOMICS | HRM |
|---|---|---|---|
| CHINA | + + + + + + | + + + | + + |
| HONG KONG | + + + + + | + + + + + | + + + + |
| SINGAPORE | + + + | + + + + | + + |
| TAIWAN | + + | + + | + + + |

*Figure 10.1* Overview: intensity of impact [high–low].
Key: + + + + + = high, + = low.

family members or to avoid becoming ill (32 staff of Taiwan's Taipei Municipal Ho-ping Hospital who were out of the hospital refused to return and went into hiding).

As the SARS epidemic progressed, individuals changed their behaviour by for example, reducing air travel in order to avoid infection in the enclosed space of a plane, avoiding travel to infected destinations and reducing consumption of services such as restaurant dining, tourism, mass transport and non-essential retail shopping. Even though domestic and international air travel did not cease completely, Hong Kong airline passenger arrivals had declined by 75 per cent at the peak of the SARS outbreak in April 2003, and there was an average decline of 50–60 per cent during the four-month period the outbreak was active (Siu and Wong, 2004). Retail sales in Hong Kong, as we saw, declined by 15 per cent at the peak, and by about 9 per cent over the four month period (Siu and Wong, 2004).

It soon became a consensus prediction that the SARS outbreak was to have a potentially significant impact on the political economy of the Asian region, with the labour-intensive service sector hardest hit, as we initially posited in previous chapters. As Hanna and Huang (2004) surmised,

> Without a workable diagnostic test and a treatment for the illness, surveillance and quarantine were the key weapons against SARS last year. In general, risks are greater in countries with poor public health care, poor sanitation systems, high mobility, or high population density. During the height of the SARS outbreak, we estimated that the total costs of the epidemic would be about 1.5 per cent of GDP for China. Better-than-expected containment of the virus reduced the impact to only about 0.5 per cent of GDP. The experiences of the SARS outbreak point to the strong need to improve both the public health system and the governance structure in Asia.

> (2004: 102)

Economic signals soon indicated a major exogenous 'shock'. Consumer demand went into a tail-spin. It is clear that the impact of SARS specifically on the service sector at the organizational level was to be a matter of serious

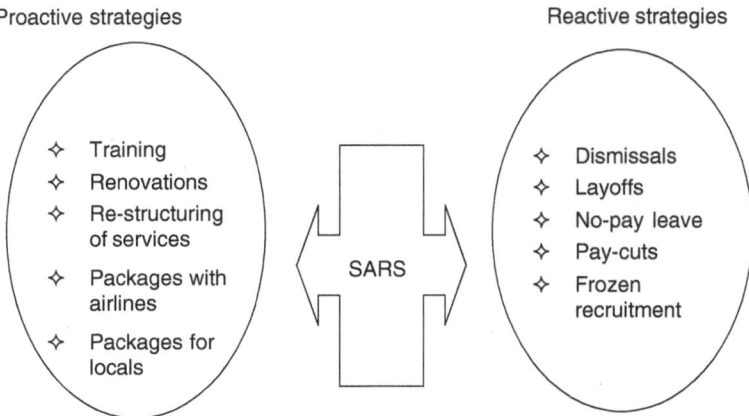

Proactive strategies                                    Reactive strategies

| Proactive | | Reactive |
|---|---|---|
| ✧ Training | | ✧ Dismissals |
| ✧ Renovations | | ✧ Layoffs |
| ✧ Re-structuring of services | SARS | ✧ No-pay leave |
| ✧ Packages with airlines | | ✧ Pay-cuts |
| ✧ Packages for locals | | ✧ Frozen recruitment |

*Figure 10.2*  Hotel proactive versus reactive strategies to SARS.

concern. The three hypotheses regarding economies, labour markets and jobs that we originally generated in Chapter 4, we may conclude, were aptly exemplified in the case-studies of Hong Kong, China, Singapore and Taiwan in the specific ways we showed in Chapters 5, 6, 7 and 8. The 'devil' is always 'in the detail'. *Ex post facto*, as we saw earlier, the damage was less than anticipated but still involving both hardship and loss.

The HRM implications, as we expected, were both widespread in their scale and serious in their consequences, if in varying degrees of severity. To survive, businesses had to take drastic action. Figure 10.2 summarizes the hotel strategies vis-à-vis SARS at the organizational level in the economies we studied.

The strategies adopted by organizations and enterprises to cope with the 'shock' in their environments were varied. They may broadly be divided into *proactive* strategies and *reactive* organizational strategies. *Proactive* managerial strategies in the case of hotels include staff training; restaurant renovations; restructuring of services; designing attractive packages with airlines to attract international visitors, or packages for locals to boost the occupancy rates and revenues. Staff training and renovations of hotel facilities had been considered a luxury at times when the much sought-after hotels in Hong Kong and Singapore were too busy. *Reactive* managerial strategies, including frozen employment; unpaid leave; pay-cuts; lay-offs; and dismissals, did have adverse impact on employees. Although mass lay-offs and redundancies were not rife among permanent employees, part-timers (mostly migrant workers in the case of China) were the group most adversely affected.

As people quarantined themselves and their families by staying at home, non-essential activities that required social contact was sharply cut, which led to significant declines in retail trade. People avoided public places, such as shopping malls, public transport and recreation parks; attendance at theatres and restaurants also declined, as we noted earlier. The actions of governments also influenced the effects of the epidemic on the economy. The quarantine policies, such as a mandatory 10-day quarantine for all expatriates who left Singapore and re-entered from a SARS-afflicted country, amplified the reductions in trade, travel and tourism. The large-scale closing of schools for weeks when SARS was at its peak in China, as well as in Hong Kong and Singapore, though necessary and desirable, could have led to a spike in workplace absences, part of the 'supply shock' we spoke of in Chapter 4, because parents would have to stay at home to care for their children even if they were not sick.

Economic activity clearly slowed down, but it would not halt completely. Experience with such catastrophes may help HR managers to learn from adversity and find ways by which they may better to cope with and adapt to extremely difficult environmental circumstances. As Figure 10.3 shows, HRM strategies could range from *minimal* to *maximal*, starting with minimising exposure, to changing what people do, to escalating actions and finally, taking large-scale action (see Mercer Human Resource Consulting, 2005). The Mercer SARS findings are both qualitative and quantitatively derived and are based on 455 organizations studied in mid-April 2003;[3] the research concluded that there were three principal components determining

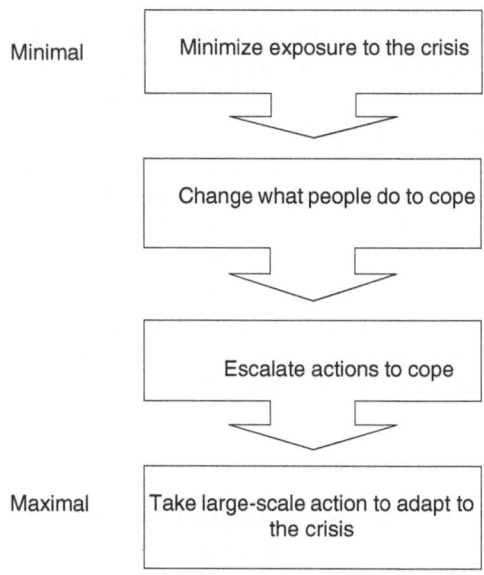

*Figure 10.3* Spectrum of HRM strategies.

Source: Adapted from Mercer Human Resource Consulting, 22 February 2005, <http://www.ceoforum.com.au>

a business' preparedness: the prevalence of SARS as an issue on the minds of people in their organization, the likely length of time that the impact of SARS will be felt, and the likely impact it will have for their business.

We could see in the last chapter that in order to minimize the risk of infecting SARS and thus jeopardizing the running of the business, senior managers of an internationally known bank in Singapore made it a practice *not* to meet together in the same room at the same time. Moreover, the advances in technology of recent years allowed many companies, especially those in the supporting functions, to conduct business via electronic communications, which would permit their employees to work from home. Online purchases might also offset some of the decline in retail trade.

As *The Economist* suggested at the time,

> Despite the gloom, some analysts reckon that the public is overreacting to the threat of SARS – after all, 36,000 people a year die of flu in America alone. They believe that there is a big pent-up demand for travel, and that the business market will rebound. Firms are switching to cheaper ways to communicate, from video-conferencing to e-mail. But such technologies are still inferior to face-to-face meetings. Until they improve, it will take more than SARS to kill off business travel.
>
> (3 April 2003: 62)

As the economy revived by mid-2003, it was thought that recovery in service-sector jobs above all, in industries like the hotel business, both in low- as well as high-value-added products and services would compensate for earlier job losses. The SARS epidemic of early and mid-2003 has no doubt been a sharp reminder to both Hong Kong and Singapore, both overseas Chinese (*Nanyang*) city-state economies, of their economic vulnerability. The Chinese mainland case and the Taiwan case were somewhat different, given the lower weighting of the service sector in those economies.

Many policy makers had thought that the expansion of service-industry employment, such as in the hotel industry or any other, would create a positive and stable employment equilibrium and compensate for structural reform. Erosion of secondary as well as primary sector employment may sometimes be compensated by counter-strategies to create jobs in services; these may not always be as stable as policy makers believe to be the case.

## 10.3   Conclusions

Where do we go from here? What threats exist right now, which are to come and what can we do about them? Current dangers lurk in the form of HIV/AIDS, malaria, TB and so on. There are many threats on the horizon, most importantly the prospect of an Avian Flu pandemic. There is widespread concern among policy makers and public health experts about the possibility of a worldwide epidemic with this flu-variant (H5N1), a strain that has caused repeated epidemics with high mortality among poultry in Asia, has spread from Southeast Asia to flocks in Central Asia and Europe, and has made the jump from birds to humans, causing deaths of only hundreds of people to date. Moreover, viruses of the H5 subtype are not known to have circulated among the human population, which means that, as in the SARS epidemic, there would be little immunity to it. To date, close contact with infected poultry is thought to be required for human infection, but the danger exists that the virus will evolve in a way that allows for efficient human-to-human transmission. If the virus does acquire that ability, another worldwide epidemic, or pandemic, could occur (Congress of the United States, 2005).

Burns, Mensbruggle and Timmer of the World Bank envisaged three possible scenarios of a human pandemic and estimated their economic consequences. The first (mild) scenario is modelled on the Hong Kong flu of 1968–1969; the moderate flu has the characteristics of the 1957 Asian flu; and the severe situation is benchmarked on the 1918–1919 Spanish flu. Each of these scenarios 'assumes that efforts by individuals and official agencies to limit the spread of the disease are no more effectual than those observed during previous epidemics and reflects differences in population density, poverty, and the quality of healthcare available' (Burns *et al.*, 2006: 3).

They suggested that 'even a flu with "normal" characteristics in terms of transmissibility and deadliness could have serious consequences for the world economy if the world's population has limited immunity' (Burns *et al.*, 2006: 3). Estimates suggest that such a flu could infect as much as 35 per cent of the world's population, spreading throughout the world in as few as 180 days (WHO, 2006a). As compared with a normal flu season, where some 0.2–1.5 million die (WHO, 2003e), deaths from even a mild flu might include an additional 1.4 million people worldwide (Burns *et al.*, 2006). A more virulent form, such as the 1918–1919 flu, which was more deadly for healthy adults than a normal flu, could have much more serious consequences, killing as many as 1 in 40 infected individuals (Barry, 2005) or some 71 million, with some authors suggesting that as many as 180–260 million could die in a worst case scenario (Osterholm, 2005). For the world as a whole, 'a mild pandemic would reduce output by less than 1 per cent of GDP, a moderate outbreak by more than 2 per cent, and a severe pandemic by almost 5 per cent, constituting a major global recession' (Burns *et al.*, 2006: 3). Given the tremendous uncertainties surrounding the possibility and eventual nature of a pandemic inflation, these experts have cautioned that 'these simulations must be viewed as purely illustrative. They provide a sense of the overall magnitude of potential costs' (Burns *et al.*, 2006: 5). Actual costs, both in terms of human lives and economic losses, are likely to be very different. That said, 'these simulations serve to underlie the importance of mobilizing global efforts to meet potential crises. Because a pandemic, as in the case of SARS, would spread very quickly, substantial efforts need to be put into place to develop effective strategies and contingency plans that could be enacted at short notice' (Burns *et al.*, 2006: 6).[4] There is a desperate consensus that time is running out and we are still not adequately prepared for an impending pandemic (or indeed potential Climate Change). Global health as a priority remains on the G8 agenda, for better or worse (see editorial, *Nature*, 20 July 2006: 223).

As WHO has pointed out, one of the main lessons of SARS is to prepare both populations and health-care systems, on a national as well as an international scale. 'Epidemics and pandemics can place sudden and intense demands on health systems. They expose existing weaknesses in these systems and, in addition to their morbidity and mortality, can disrupt economic activity and development. The world requires a global system that can rapidly identify and contain public health emergencies and reduce unneeded panic and disruption of trade, travel and society in general in order to avoid future catastrophes (see Mileti, 1980; Perrow, 1984, 2007; Beck, 1992). The revised International Health Regulations, IHR (2005) provide a global framework to address these needs through a collective approach to the prevention, detection and timely response to any public health emergency of international concern' (WHO, 2006b).

Let us hope that this global framework, necessary though it is, is also sufficient to safeguard our collective well-being and survival in the face of a future pandemic! But we can never be wholly sure and we can only take what we think are the most feasible precautions. There may always be the highly improbable event, the 'Black Swan', round the corner (see Taleb, 2007). Albert Camus ([1947]2002: 237) concludes his novel, *The Plague/La Peste*, with his Dr Rieux's warning against complacency: 'that perhaps the day will come when, for the instruction or misfortune of mankind, the plague will rouse its rats and send them to die in some well-contented city.'

# Notes

## 1 Introduction

1 The number of deaths could well have been much higher. These are only the reported cases passed on to WHO. The lack of transparency in the Chinese case suggests many cases slipped through the net. The WHO figures for both cases and fatalities have been generally accepted but both could have been underestimated.
2 Greater detail on this occurrence in the PRC can be observed in Chapter 6.
3 There was, as the number of deaths reported grew, a fear of major recession hitting the Asia-Pacific region, perhaps having repercussions for world markets. There was indeed a severe downturn in the months affected. These are discussed further in Chapters 5–8.
4 There is, for example, minimal welfare-state protection in Hong Kong, except for unemployment insurance of a very limited kind in Mainland China (see Lee and Warner, 2002; 2005a).

## 2 Catastrophes, epidemics and history

1 The level of unemployment caused by the Wall Street Crash was probably unprecedented in modern economic history; by 1933, unemployment in the United States had risen to officially almost 25 per cent of the workforce.
2 On the prospective economic costs of Climate Change, see the Stern Report to the British Government (October, 2006) http://www.direct.gov.uk/Nl1/Newsroom/NewsroomArticles/fs/en?CONTENT_ID=10040030&chk=ahNChy (accessed on 20 November, 2006).
3 See Duncan (2003), Phillips and Killingray (2003) for some possible reasons.
4 We are indebted to the eminent virologist, Professor John S. Oxford for his help in elucidating this possible causal connection in the First World War.
5 On the challenge of emerging and re-emerging infectious disease, see Morens *et al.*, 2004.
6 The Hong Kong government took the unprecedented step of intervening in the stock-market, the second largest in Asia and the eighth largest in the world, to underpin a bottom-stop level. It created a Special Fund which bought up shares when they were cheap and profited handsomely when stock prices recovered.
7 See Lee and McKibbin (2003) on the impact of SARS compared with other ongoing epidemics.

## 3 The SARS epidemic of 2003: a timeline

1 Large numbers of residents at Amoy Gardens in Hong Kong were infected with SARS. Within one month, 329 residents had infected SARS, with

42 subsequent deaths; many lived in the same wing of the building. The reasons for the Amoy Gardens outbreak were unclear, with baffled investigators blaming everything from the sewage system to rats. Initial studies by the Hong Kong Government and WHO concluded that the problem probably lay in the plumbing system and the inflow of droplets of infected sewage into apartments when bathroom fans were running. The source of the Amoy Gardens disaster has been attributed to a patient with renal failure receiving haemodialysis at the PWH who stayed with his brother at Amoy Gardens. He had diarrhoea, and infection may have spread to other residents by a leaking sewage-drain, allowing an aerosol of virus-containing material to escape into the narrow light-well between the buildings and spread in rising air-currents (Tomlinson and Cockram, 2003). Sewage also back-flowed into bathroom floor drains in some apartments. Infection also spread to people in nearby building, probably by person-to-person contact and by contamination of public installations. However, the exact cause of the outbreak is still unknown. See Stephen Ng (2004) for a detailed study.

2   The first known case of SARS in Hong Kong became a 'super-spreader' through the contaminated hotel elevator buttons.

3   See note 7 in Chapter 2.

4   On 1 February 2003, Fan, a 57-year-old ambulance driver in the southern Chinese city of Guangzhou, was told to transfer a critically ill patient to the Third Affiliated Hospital a few kilometres away (Abraham, 2004). He was warned that the patient was extremely infectious and given a triple-layer surgical mask and gloves to wear. Three days later, Fan began to feel feverish while at work. He was kept in the hospital for observation. The next day, Fan was so weak that he could not walk to the toilet unaided. He needed help even drinking a glass of water. The ambulance driver's condition deteriorated, and X-rays showed patches on his lungs that were growing at an alarming rate. The doctors treated him with antibiotics, but his lungs became increasingly inflamed and filled with fluid. After battling to stay alive for 20 days, Fan died on 24 February.

5   The case fatality rate for normal strains of influenza, for example, is around 1 per cent, and this is mostly among the elderly and infirm (Abraham, 2004).

6   As the ambulance driver, Fan (see note 4), lay critically ill, panic was spreading through the Hospital. The day he was admitted, other hospital workers were falling sick with the same symptoms. At first, doctors and nurses on the twelfth floor respiratory illness ward fell ill. Then patients on the ward caught the disease. Next it travelled to the thirteenth and fifteenth floors. The disease spread relentlessly; within two weeks, 93 hospital staff, patients and relatives had fallen ill (Abraham, 2004).

7   On 9 September 2003, the Singapore Government announced that a medical researcher was confirmed as a SARS case. While this was regarded as a 'single isolated case', it provided a timely reminder that SARS is still lurking (*South China Morning Post*, 10 September 2003).

8   In late May 2003, WHO reported that researchers in Hong Kong and Shenzhen, China announced that they had detected several viruses closely related genetically to the SARS virus in two wild animal species, the masked palm civet and the raccoon-dog, animals 'traditionally considered delicacies and are sold for human consumption in markets throughout southern China' (WHO, 2003c).

## 4  Impact on economies, labour markets and human resources in East Asia

1   SARS had the biggest impact on China, where the disease originated and caused the largest number of deaths – 349. Jane Duckett, an expert on Chinese

health policy at Glasgow University, said SARS had prompted Beijing to launch a US$1 billion programme to improve the country's readiness for future epidemics (*Financial Times*, 30 July 2005). The programme includes a better reporting system and the founding of a centre for disease control. The impact on the Chinese economy has been discussed by Rawski (2006).

2 Unemployment in Hong Kong rose to 8.7 per cent at the height of the epidemic (see Lee and Warner, 2005a).

3 See Brown (2004) however which makes a commendable attempt for Hong Kong.

## 5 Hong Kong: a case study

1 He was replaced by Donald Tsang in March 2005, due to the unpopularity of the government's policies. Dissatisfaction as to how the SARS crisis was handled may also have been a contributing factor.

2 The background relating to unemployment in Hong Kong is set out in our earlier research (see Lee and Warner, 2001a for example).

3 See Chapter 6 for further details; also see Kleinman and Watson, 2006.

4 Trade unions in Hong Kong 'remained docile at the workplace level' even after the changeover of sovereignty to mainland China (Ng, 1997; Ng and Rowley, 1997).

5 Occupational health and safety has for some time been an area of concern in the catering industry. In the past three years, the number of industrial accidents in the catering industry has been the highest among the other trades in Hong Kong (Labour Department, 2003). To bring about improvement in work safety in the catering trade, the Labour Department and key stakeholders of the industry, namely the Occupational Safety and Health Council, Occupational Deafness Compensation Board, five employers' associations and two trade unions, have been jointly organizing safety award schemes since 1999 with the objectives of heightening good safety and health culture and promoting safe work practices in the industry. The health and safety performance of the catering industry has since gradually improved over the last couple of years (Labour Department, 2003).

6 Lacking an effective power-base anchored upon collective bargaining, the unions were limited in articulating and protecting the employees' interests (see Ng and Ip, 2003).

## 6 People's Republic of China (PRC): a case study

1 Jiang Yanyong, former chief of surgery for the Number 301 military hospital in Beijing and a Communist Party member, made the disclosure in an email to a state-run television station. The *Wall Street Journal* Asian edition reported the disclosure on 9 April 2003. The poor whistle-blower was penalized by the Chinese government and was kept under house arrest for about six months (*Ming Pao*, 23 November 2006).

2 The two officials were Party Secretary of the Ministry of Health, Zhang Wenkang, and Deputy Party Secretary of Beijing, Meng Xuenong.

3 In recent years, income generated by tourism during week-long holidays, such as the Labour Day Holiday and National Day, though as high as 30 billion yuan (US$3.6 billion), accounted for less than 0.3 percent of the total economy.

4 It was noted that the telecommunications and medical industries are in need of labour, as are shopping websites, restaurants with delivery services and express delivery companies. China's economic hub, Shanghai, is capitalizing on the situation, employing 15,000 laid-off workers in the public hygiene and environments fields. Liaoning, northeast China's important industrial base, plans to provide 100,000 jobs for laid-off workers.

5 China's actual FDI surpassed that of the United States for the first time in 2002 and became the world's largest. According to the Ministry of Commerce, it rose 12.51 per cent to US$52.74 billion. Actual FDI in China hit US$13.09 billion in the first quarter of 2003, up 56.7 percent from a year earlier.

6 Jiuzhaigou was listed as a 'world heritage site' by UNESCO in 1992. It joined the international protection network of 'man and biosphere' in 1997. Yellow Dragon joined 'man and biosphere' in 2000.

7 China's employment population reached 737.4 million in 2002, absorbing 7.2 million more employees than the previous year, according to the latest data from the National Bureau of Statistics.

8 In terms of each industry's contribution to the increase of China's employment, the three have been largely the same in 1979. But by 2000, the primary, secondary and tertiary industries have each contributed 37, minus 39 and 105 per cent respectively to the employment increase in the year. Service industry has become the major channel for new labour absorption.

9 South China's Guangdong Province, the first area hit by SARS, publicized tax exemption policies that were expected to trim 900 million yuan from tax revenue. Other areas, such as Shanghai, Beijing, Shanxi Province and Henan Province, have followed suit with similar tax policies.

10 According to Xinhua News Agency, 23 June 2003, 'Title of the News', a total of 2.12 million college students were to graduate that year, 46 per cent more than in 2002, as China begins to increase college enrolment by around 15 per cent in a bid to give more young people access to higher education.

11 Dorothy Solinger (2003) quoted sources to suggest that 'the total of those laid off from state enterprises and the unemployed (both registered and unregistered) combined could have been as high as 60 million as of mid-2001' and that 'those city residents of working age who were not in full-time formal work numbered not less than 60 million, amounting to an unemployment rate of 12–15 per cent.'

12 China had declared its unemployment rate, as of the end of 2002, at 4 per cent. The figure released by the government refers to the registered unemployment rate in cities and towns, and does not include rural labour and rural migrant workers in cities.

13 The above judgement was made in the *Report on China's Population and Job Opportunity* published by Chinese Publishing House for Social Sciences and Documents when dealing with China's entry into the WTO and its influence on the employment situation in China.

14 Avian influenza viruses do not normally infect species other than birds and pigs. The first documented infection of humans with an avian influenza virus occurred in Hong Kong in 1997, when the H5N1 strain caused severe respiratory disease in 18 humans, of whom 6 died. Extensive investigation of that outbreak determined that close contact with live infected poultry was the source of human infection. Studies at the genetic level further determined that the virus had jumped directly from birds to humans. Rapid destruction – within three days – of Hong Kong's entire poultry population, estimated at around 1.5 million birds, reduced opportunities for further direct transmission to humans, and may have averted a pandemic. That event alarmed public health authorities, as it marked the first time that an avian influenza virus was transmitted directly to humans and caused severe illness with high mortality.

## 7 Singapore: a case study

1 The Singapore legislature, known for its swift passing of laws, met quickly to legislate harsher penalties for those who defied the quarantine laws (Ho, 2003).

2 Under the flexible wage system, the income of a worker comprises a fixed income component and a variable component, often referred to as an annual bonus. The main body promoting the flexible wage system is the tripartite National Wages Council comprising representatives from the National Trades Union Congress (NTUC), the Singapore National Employers' Federation (CNEF) and other employers' federations, as well as various government ministries. According to Chew and Chew, 'the sole purpose of implementing the flexible wage system is to allow firms to reduce labour costs during recession' (2005: 90). See Chew and Chew (2005) for a detail discussion of the issues in implementing the flexible wage system in Singapore.

3 It was already noted in the early 1990s that training in the service sector has lagged behind the manufacturing sector. According to Torrington and Tan (1994: 287), a worker in the service sector was given an average of only 12.6 hours of training in 1988, much lower than the 39.2 hours given in the manufacturing sector.

## 8 Taiwan: a case study

1 The price of masks had risen to a few hundred New Taiwan dollars each and became a commodity of speculation.

2 Taiwan hotels have been sponsoring the internship programmes of the hospitality schools of Taiwan universities for over 10 years. The prospective degree-holders will serve two six-month period of internship during their two-year study, earning about HK$4,500 (around US$600) per month, about 65 per cent of the salary of regular staff.

3 Industry-wide hotel unions were not popular among hotel employees, although all but one Taiwan government-owned hotel has a trade union affiliated to the hotel; accordingly, hotel employees resorted to seeking help from the state.

4 Altogether NT$2 million worth of dinner coupons were distributed at the festival, 10,000 cans of beer were provided by the Taiwan Tobacco and Liquor Company, while 200 discounted airline tickets were offered in a raffle draw. The government had spent NT$300 million (around US$8.7 million) on promotional activities targeting visitors from Hong Kong, Japan, Europe, the United States, New Zealand, Australia and other South East Asian countries, including Singapore and Malaysia. The government and private tourist agencies organized a delegation to five major cities in Japan, including Tokyo and Osaka, to exchange views with travel agents on how to promote tourism in Taiwan. The Tourism Bureau had invited 3,000 travel agents from the targeted countries to 'experience safe travel to Taiwan'. Lottery draws were held in Japan to offer 1,000 Japanese the chances to visit Taiwan for free; cheap sightseeing packages were also offered to 5,000 Japanese. A HK$999 (around US$128) three-day, two-night package was offered for Hong Kong people, while cheap tours were also available for Southeast Asians. Starting from July 1, foreign passengers arriving at Taipei were given a half-day city tour free of charge; an overnight stay cost only 49 Euro dollars. The Taipei Food Festival took place from August to September 2003, and the Taiwan Visitors Association sent delegates to a series of meetings abroad to promote travel to Taiwan.

5 The Council for Economic Planning and Development officials said that the aviation industry has shown an obvious rebound, with the cancellation rate on international flights dropping to 20 per cent in the first week of July 2003, compared with a high of 50 per cent in early June. Although the number of passengers on international flights in the first week of July was down 33 per cent compared with the same time last year, it marked an improvement over May, when the figure was down 82 per cent over the same period last year. Although

the number of passengers on domestic flights in May was down 55 per cent compared with the same time last year, it was up 4 per cent in the first week of July over the previous year's figure. Meanwhile, the entertainment and tourism sectors had also seen a rebound. Ticket sales at Taipei theatres in June were up 57 per cent over May, while the average occupancy rate at hotels in the second part of June was 51 per cent as compared to 22 per cent in May. At Taiwan's various scenic spots, the number of tourists decreased by 62 per cent in May, but had shown a growth of 24 per cent in June. The council officials reported that the number of travel agencies had remained steady, while the number of staff had continued to decrease, though the level of decrease had slowed down.

### 9  Lessons to be learnt?

1 Hong Kong's former Director of Health Margaret Chan who became Director-General of the WHO in November 2006 gained international recognition for alerting the world to H5N1 avian flu, which jumped the species barrier in Hong Kong in 1997, killing 6 of 18 people infected. Her decision to 'cull all poultry earned her a WHO citation for stopping a potential pandemic' (*SCMP*, 9 November 2006).
2 Smith *et. al.* (2006) quoted their updated virological and epidemiological findings from market surveillance in southern China to demonstrate that 'H5N1 influenza viruses continued to be panzootic in different types of poultry. Genetic and antigenic analyses revealed the emergence and predominance of a previously uncharacterized H5N1 virus sublineage (Fujian-like) in poultry since late 2005. Viruses from this sublineage gradually replaced those multiple regional distinct sublineages and caused recent human infection in China. These viruses have already transmitted to Hong Kong, Laos, Malaysia and Thailand, resulting in a new transmission and outbreak wave in Southeast Asia. Serological studies suggest that H5N1 seroconversion in market poultry is low and that vaccination may have facilitated the selection of the Fujian-like sublineage. The predominance of this virus over a large geographical region within a short period directly challenges current disease control measures' (Smith *et. al.*, 2006: 16936).

### 10  Conclusions

1 Jokes, for example, regarding SARS spread via the Web and other electronic media (see Zhang, 2006), many verging on political satire. Disasters often generate jokes as a way of turning anxiety into laughter, as a classic 'displacement mechanism'.
2 The experience of the Hong Kong hospital system is a salutory reminder that an entire medical infra-structure could potentially collapse (Reuters report, 'Hong Kong Health System on Brink as SARS Spreads', Thurs 10 April 2003 11: 48 am ET).
3 The sample that the Mercer team based their findings on was one of the largest undertaken regarding the effects of the epidemic, given the difficult crisis circumstances in which they found themselves.
4 A survey conducted by the Hong Kong Institute of Human Resources Management (HKIHRM) found that 81.1 per cent of the Hong Kong companies it surveyed were not prepared for the occurrence of a pandemic flu. About 130 companies from 17 different industries were surveyed by the HKIJHRM on their level of awareness and preparedness, including the stock-up of medical supplies, review of company medical insurance schemes and so on (see *Ming Pao*, 29 November 2006).

# Bibliography

Abraham, T. (2004) *Twenty-first Century Plague: The Story of SARS*, Hong Kong: Hong Kong University Press.

Adams, S. (2003) *The Economic Impact of SARS in Vietnam*, Hanoi: IMF Office.

*Asia Pacific Business Network*, Vol. 7, No. 9, 2003.

*Asia Wall Street Journal (Asian Edition)* (various).

Asian Development Bank (ADB) (2003) *Action Plan to Address Outbreak of Severe Acute Respiratory Syndrome (SARS) in Asia and the Pacific*, May Manila: ADB.

Barry, J. M. (2005) *The Great Influenza: The Epic Story of the Deadliest Plague in History*, London: Penguin Books.

*BBC News* (various).

Beck, U. (1992) *Risk Society: Towards a New Modernity*, London: Sage.

Belau, D. (2003) 'New threats to employment in the travel and tourism industry', *ILO Report*, 14 May, Geneva: ILO.

Bell, C. and Lewis, M. (2005) 'The economic implications of epidemics old and new, center for global development', *Working Paper*, Number 54, February 2005, Oxfordshire: NTC Economic & Financial Publishing.

Benedict, C. (1988) 'Bubonic plague in nineteenth-century China', *Modern China*, 14:2, 107–55.

——(1993) 'Policing the sick: plague and the origins of state medicine in late Imperial China', *Late Imperial China*, 14:2, 60–77.

——(1996a) *Bubonic Plague in Nineteenth-Century China*, Stanford: Stanford University Press.

——(1996b) 'Framing plague in China's past', in Hershatter, Gail, Honig, Emily, Lipman, Jonathan N., Stross Randall (eds) *Remapping China: Fissures in Historical Terrain*, California: Stanford University Press, 27–41.

Beveridge, W. (1977) *Influenza: The Last Great Plague, an Unfinished Story of Discovery*, New York: Prodist.

Bocaccio, G. (1921) *The Decameron*, translated by J. M. Rigg, London: The Navarre Society.

Brahmbatt, M. (2005) *Avian Influenza: Economic and Social Impacts*, Washington: World Bank.

Braudel, F. ([1979]1981–1984) *Civilization and Capitalism, 15th–18th Century*, in 3 volumes, translated by Siân Reynolds, New York: Harper and Row.

Briggs, A. (1961) 'Cholera and society in the nineteenth century', *Past and Present: Journal of Historical Studies*, 19:76–96.

Brown, S. (2004) 'The economic impact of SARS', in Christine Loh and Civic Exchange (eds) *At the Epicentre: Hong Kong and the SARS Outbreak*, Hong Kong: Hong Kong University Press.

Burns, A., Mensbruggle, D. and Timmer, H. (2006) *Evaluating the Economic Consequences of Avian Influenza*, Washington DC: World Bank.

*Business Times* (various).

*Business Week* (various).

*Business Week Online* (various).

Camus, A., ([1947]2002) *The Plague* (*La Peste*), translated by Robin Buss, London: Penguin Books.

Census and Statistics Department, *Report of Weekly Consultations on Effect of SARS on Business*. http://www.info.gov.hk/censtatd/eng/interest/sars/sars_index. html (accessed on 28 November 2003).

Census and Statistics Department website, HKSAR government, http://www.info. gov.hk/censtatd (accessed on 28 November 2003).

Centers for Disease Control and Prevention (2006) *Selected Reports*, Washington DC: Department of Health and Human Services, January.

Chan-Yeung, M. (2004) 'At the frontline: the medical challenge', in Christine Loh and Civic Exchange (eds) *At the Epicentre: Hong Kong and the SARS Outbreak*, Hong Kong: Hong Kong University Press.

Chan-Yeung, M. and Loh, C. (2004) 'The new coronavirus: in search of the culprit', in Christine Loh and Civic Exchange (eds) *At the Epicentre: Hong Kong and the SARS Outbreak*, Hong Kong: Hong Kong University Press.

Chew, R. and Chew, S. B. (2005) 'Wage issues and human resources in Singapore', *The Journal of Comparative Asian Development*, 4:1, 77–104.

*China Daily* (various).

China Securities Regulatory Commission website, http://www.csrc.org.cn/cn/ tongjiku/ehtml/ (accessed on 18 February 2004).

Cipolla, C. M. (1976) *Before the Industrial Revolution; European Society and Economy 1000–1700*, London: Routledge, reprinted 1997.

—— (1981) *Fighting the Plague in Seventeenth Century Italy*, Madison: University of Wisconsin Press.

Cohn, S. K. (2002) *The Black Death Transformed: Disease and Culture in the Early Renaissance*, London: Edward Arnold and Oxford University Press.

Collier, R. (1974) *The Plague of the Spanish Lady: The Influenza Pandemic of 1918–1919*, New York: Atheneum.

Collins, S. and Lehman, J. (1953) *Excess Deaths from Influenza and Pneumonia and from Important Chronic Disease During Epidemic Periods 1918–1951*, Public Health Monographs No. 10. Washington, DC: Public Health Service Publications.

Commissioner for Labour (2002) *Report of the Commissioner for Labour 2002*, HKSAR Government, Hong Kong: Government Printer.

Congress of the United States (2005) *A Potential Influenza Pandemic: Possible Macroeconomic Effects and Policy Issues*, US Congressional Budget Office, Washington DC.

Crampton, T. (2003) 'Asian isolation grows in response to SARS', *International Herald Tribune*, 10 April.

Crosby, A. (1989) *America's Forgotten Pandemic: The Influenza of 1918*, Cambridge: Cambridge University Press.

Davis, D. and Siu, H. F. (2007) (eds) *SARS: Reception and Interpretation in Three Chinese Cities,* London: Routledge.

Defoe, D. ([1720]2003) *A Journal of the Plague Year,* London: Penguin Classics.

Department of Statistics (2003) *Yearbook of Statistics Singapore 2003*, Singapore: Department of Statistics.

Directorate-General of Budget, Accounting and Statistics, Executive Yuan, Republic of China (2005) http://eng.dgbas.gov.tw/public/Data/54416455371.xls (accessed on 29 March, 2005).

*Dow Jones Business News* (2003) 'Hong Kong hotel group: hotel occupancy rates still below pre-SARS levels', 9 September.

Drosten, C., *et al.* (2003) 'Identification of a novel coronavirus in patients with Severe Acute Respiratory Syndrome', *New England Journal of Medicine* 348:20, 1967–76.

Duncan, K. (2003) *Hunting the 1918 Flu: One Scientist's Search for a Killer Virus,* Toronto, Canada and Buffalo, NY: University of Toronto Press.

Eastday.com (various).

*Encyclopaedia Britannica* http://www.britannica.com/eb/article-9032787/epidemic (accessed on 22 November 2003).

Eyton, L. (2003) 'SARS: Taiwan's WHO bid nothing to sneeze at.' *Asia Times,* 3 May.

Fan, E. X. Q. (2003) *SARS: Economic Impacts and Implications, Asian Development Bank,* ERD Policy Brief, 15.

Fidler, D. (2004) *SARS, Governance and the Globalization of Disease,* Basingstoke, Hampshire; New York: Palgrave Macmillan.

*Financial Times* (various).

Floud, R. and McCloskey, D. (1994) *The Economic History of Britain since 1700,* 1:1700–1860. 2nd Edition, reprinted 2000.

Galbraith, J. K. (1992 edition) *The Great Crash 1929,* London: Penguin Books.

Gerberding, J. L. (2003) 'Faster...but fast enough? responding to the epidemic of Severe Acute Respiratory Syndrome', *New England Journal of Medicine,* 348:20, 2030–1.

Gibbs, W. W. and Soares, C. (2005) 'Preparing for a pandemic', *Scientific American,* 293:5, 45–52, 54.

Gilbert, M. (1994) *The First World War: A Complete History,* New York: Henry Holt and Company.

Hampden-Turner, C. (2003) 'Culture and management in Singapore', in Warner, M. (ed.) *Culture and Management in Asia,* London: Routledge Curzon, 171–86.

Hanna, D. and Huang, Y. (2004) 'The Impact of SARS on Asian Economies', *Asian Economic Papers,* 3:1, 102–12.

Health, Welfare and Food Bureau, HKSAR Government, *SARS Bulletin,* 23 June 2003. http://www.info.gov.hk/dh/diseases/ap/eng/bulletin0623e.pdf

Henderson, J. (2003) 'Managing a health-related crisis: SARS in Singapore', *Journal of Vacation Marketing,* 10:1, 67–77.

Herlihy, D. and Cohn, S. K. (1997) (eds) *The Black Death and the Transformation of the West,* Cambridge, MA.: Harvard University Press.

Hildreth, M. L. (1991) 'The Influenza epidemic of 1918–1919 in France: contemporary concepts of aetiology, therapy, and prevention', *Social History of Medicine,* 4:2, 277–94.

Ho, K. L. (2003) 'SARS, policy-making and lesson-drawing', in Koh, T., Plant, A. and Lee, E. H. (eds) *The New Global Threat: Severe Acute Respiratory Syndrome and its Impacts*, Singapore: World Scientific, 195–208.

Hoehling, A. A. (1961) *The Great Epidemic*, Boston: Little Brown and Company.

Hoenig, L. (1985) 'The plague called *"shechin"* in the Bible', *American Journal of Dermatopathology*. 7:6, 547–8.

*Hong Kong Standard* (various).

Hong Kong Tourism Board (26 June 2003) *May Arrivals Figures Hit New Low, But Signs of Recovery Now Starting to Show*. HKSAR, Hong Kong: Hong Kong Tourism Board.

Howard, N. (2005) 'War fever', *Socialist Review*, November: 20–25.

Hsu, L. Y., Lee, Cheng-Chuan, Green, Justin A. Ang, Brenda, Payon, Nicholas I., Lee, Lawrence, Villacian, Jorge S., Lirn, Poh-Lian, Earnest, Arul and Leo, Yee-Sin (2003) 'Severe Acute Respiratory Syndrome (SARS) in Singapore: clinical features of index patient and initial contacts', *Emerging Infectious Disease*, 9:6, 713–7.

Hu, A. G. and Hu, L. L. (2003) 'A review of China's health and development from the perspective of SARS', *Paper* presented at the celebrations of the 20th anniversary of the founding of the China Health Economics Society, 6 November, Beijing.

Huque, A. S. and Lee, G. O. M. (2000) 'Managing public confidence' in Huque, A. S. and Lee, G. O. M., *Managing Public Services: Crises and Lessons From Hong Kong*, Aldershot: Ashgate, 65–84.

ILO Press Release (various).

Information Services Department, Press Release (various).

International Monetary Fund News (various).

JAMA (1918) Editorial, *Journal of the American Medical Association* (28 December 71:2154, 2174–5).

Johnson, N. and Mueller, J. (2002) 'Updating the accounts: global mortality of the 1918–1920 "Spanish" Influenza pandemic', *Bulletin of the History of Medicine*, 76:7, 105–15.

Kahneman, D. and Tversky, A. (1979) 'Prospect theory: an analysis of decision under risk', *Econometrica*, 47:2, 263–92.

Kantarevic, J., Kralj, B. and Weinkauf, D. (2005) *Excess Burden of Infectious Diseases: Evidence from the SARS Outbreak in Ontario, Canada*. Toronto: Ontario Medical Association.

Katz, R. S. (1977) 'Influenza 1918–1919: a further study in mortality', *Bulletin of the History of Medicine*, 51:4, 617–19.

Kaufman, J. (2006) 'SARS and China's health-care response: better to be both red and expert', in Kleinman, A. and Watson, J. (eds) *SARS in China: Prelude to Pandemic?*, Stanford: Stanford University Press, 53–70.

Keith, M. (2003) 'Back to normal after SARS? let's hope not...', Online. Available http://www.hotel-online.com/news/pr2003_2nd/jun03_afterSARS.html (accessed on 21 November 2003).

Keynes, J. M. (1924) *A Tract on Monetary Reform*, London: Macmillan.

Khatri, N. (2004) 'HRM in Singapore', in Budhwar, Pawan S. (ed.) *Managing Human Resources in Asia-Pacific*, London and New York: Routledge, 221–38.

Kleinman, A. and Watson, J. (2006) 'Introduction: SARS in social and historical context', in Kleinman, A. and Watson, J. (eds) *SARS in China: Prelude to Pandemic?*, Stanford: Stanford University Press, 1–16.

Koo, J. and Fu, D. (2003) 'The effects of SARS on East Asian economies', Federal Reserve Bank of Dallas, *Expand Your Insight*, 1 July. http://www.dallasfed.org/eyi/global/0307sars.html

Ksiazek, T. G., *et al.* (2003) 'A novel coronavirus associated with Severe Acute Respiratory Syndrome', *New England Journal of Medicine*, 348:20, 1953–66.

Labour Department (2003) *Catering Industry Safety Award Scheme (2003/2004)*, Online. Available http://www.labour.gov.hk/eng/news/cisas03-04.htm

*Labour Focus* (16 June 2003 to 1 July 2003), Labour Department, HKSAR Government.

Lee, D. and Yun, K. W. (2006) 'Psychological responses to SARS in Hong Kong – report from the front line', in Kleinman, A. and Watson, J. (eds) *SARS in China: Prelude to Pandemic?*, Stanford: Stanford University Press, 133–147.

Lee, G. O. M. and Warner, M. (2001a) 'Human resources, employment and labour-market policies in China: a comparative study of Shanghai and Hong Kong', *Employment Relations Record*, 1:2, 43–64.

—— (2001b) 'Labour-markets in "Communist" China and "Capitalist" Hong Kong: convergence revisited', *Asia Pacific Business Review*, 8:1, 167–91.

—— (2002) 'Labour-market policies in Shanghai and Hong Kong: a study of "one country, two systems" in Greater China' *International Journal of Manpower*, 23:6, 505–26.

—— (2004) 'The Shanghai re-employment model: from local experiment to nationwide labour market policy', *China Quarterly*, 177, 174–89.

—— (2005a) 'Epidemics, labour-markets and unemployment: the impact of SARS on human resources management in the Hong Kong hotel industry', *International Journal of Human Resource Management*, 16:5, 752–71.

—— (2005b) 'The impact of the SARS epidemic in Taiwan: implications for human resources, labour markets and unemployment in the service sector', *Issues and Studies*, 41:3, 81–111.

—— (2006a) 'The impact of SARS on China's economy, labour market and level of employment', *International Journal of Human Resource Management*, 17:5, 860–80.

—— (2006b) 'Epidemics, labour-markets, and unemployment: the impact of SARS on Singapore', *Asia-Pacific Business Review*, 12:4, 507–27.

—— (2007a) 'Active labour-market policies in the Hong Kong Special Administrative Region', in Lee, G. O. M. and Warner, M. (eds) *Unemployment in China: Economy, Human Resources and Labour Markets*, London and New York: Routledge, 166–83.

—— (2007b) (eds) *Unemployment in China: Economy, Human Resources and Labour Markets*, London and New York: Routledge.

Lee, J. W. and McKibbin, Warwick J. (2003) 'Globalization and disease: the case of SARS', Paper presented at the Asian Economic Panel Meeting in Tokyo, May 2003.

Lee, M. L., *et al.* (2003) 'Severe Acute Respiratory Syndrome – Taiwan, 2003' *Morbidity and Mortality Weekly Report* 52:20 (23 May), 461–64.

Lee, N., Hui, D. and Wu, A., *et al.* (2003) 'A major outbreak of Severe Acute Respiratory Syndrome in Hong Kong', *New England Journal of Medicine*, 348:20, 1986–94. .

Leung, G., Hedley, A., Lau, E. and Lam, T. H. (2004) 'The public health viewpoint', in Christine Loh and Civic Exchange (eds) *At the Epicentre: Hong Kong and the SARS Outbreak*, Hong Kong: Hong Kong University Press, 55–80.

Leung, P. C. and Ooi, E. E. (2003) *SARS War: Combating the Disease*. Singapore: World Scientific.

Loeb, L. (2005) 'Beating the Flu: orthodox and commercial responses to Influenza in Britain, 1889–1919', *Social History of Medicine*, 18, 203–24.

Loh, C. and Welker, J. (2004) 'SARS and the Hong Kong community', in Christine Loh and Civic Exchange (eds) *At the Epicentre: Hong Kong and the SARS Outbreak*, Hong Kong: Hong Kong University Press, 215–334.

McNeill, W. (1976) *Plagues and People*, New York: Anchor Books.

Maloney, S., Olowokure, B. and Roth, C. (2006) in World Health Organization (ed.) *SARS: How a Global Epidemic was Stopped*. Manila: World Health Organization.

Malthus, T. R. ([1798]1999) *An Essay on the Principle of Population*, Oxford: OUP.

Mann, T. ([1911]1971) *Death in Venice*, translated by H. T. Lowe-Porter, London: Penguin Books.

Mao Zedong (1976) *Poems*, Peking: Foreign Languages Press.

Marx, K. ([1867]1977) *Das Kapital*, Vol. I, Part VII, Chapter XXV, translated by Ernest Mandel. New York: Vintage.

Mercer Human Resource Consulting (2005) *Spectrum of HRM Strategies*, 22 February. Online. http://www.ceoforum.com.au (accessed on 12 March 2005).

Mileti, D. S. (1980) 'Human adjustment to the risk of environment extremes', *Sociology and Social Research*, 64(3), 327–47.

*Ming Pao* (various).

Ministry of Commerce (2003) *Invest in China* website, http://www.fdi.gov.cn/common/info (accessed 10 July 2003).

Ministry of Labour and Social Security, PRC (2004) Ministry of Labour and Social Security website, http://www.molss.gov.cn/news/2004/0216.htm (accessed 16 February 2004).

Ministry of Trade and Industry (2003) *Performance of the Singapore Economy in Second Quarter 2003 and Outlook for 2003*. Singapore: Ministry of Trade and Industry.

—— (2004) *Performance of the Singapore Economy in Second Quarter 2004 and Outlook for 2004 and 2005*. Singapore: Ministry of Trade and Industry.

*Minsheng bao* (various).

Monetary Authority of Singapore website (2004), http://secure.mas.gov.sg/frames/msb/msbIndexpage.html (accessed 16 February 2004).

Morens, D. M., Folkers, G. K. and Fauci, A. S. (2004) 'The challenge of emerging and re-emerging infectious diseases', *Nature*, 430, 242–49.

Murray, M. (2006) 'The Epidemiology of SARS', in Kleinman, A. and Watson, J. (eds) *SARS in China: Prelude to Pandemic?*, Stanford: Stanford University Press, 17–30.

National Bureau of Statistics (2003) *China Statistical Yearbook 2003*, Beijing: China Statistics Press.

National Bureau of Statistics website (2003) *Statistical Communiqué of the People's Republic of China on the 2003 National Economic and Social Development* (various).

National Bureau of Statistics of China (2005) *China Statistical Yearbook 2005*, http://www.stats.gov.cn/tjsj/ndsj/2005/indexeh.htm

National Statistics, R. O. C. (Taiwan) website, http://www.stat.gov.tw (accessed on 22 December 2003).

Nature (2006) 'WHO's in charge?', *Nature*, 442, 223–223 (20 July) Editorial.

Ng, S. (2004) 'The mystery of Amoy Gardens', in Christine Loh and Civic Exchange (eds) *At the Epicentre: Hong Kong and the SARS Outbreak*, Hong Kong: Hong Kong University Press, 95–115.

Ng, S. H. (1977) 'Reversion to China: implications for labour in Hong Kong', *International Journal of Human Resource Management*, 8:5, 660–70.

Ng, S. H. and Ip O. (2003) 'Phenomenon of union exhaustion: is there a "third way" for trade unionism in Hong Kong?', *The Journal of Industrial Relations*, 45:3, 378–94.

Ng, S. H. and Rowley, C. (1977) 'At the break of dawn? Hong Kong industrial relations and prospects under its political transition', *Asia Pacific Business Review*, 4:1, 83–96.

Omi, S. (2006) 'Overview' in World Health Organization (ed.) *SARS: How a Global Epidemic was Stopped*. Manila: World Health Organization, 1–12.

Osterholm, M. T. (2005) 'Preparing for the next pandemic', *New England Journal of Medicine* 352:18, 1839–42.

Oxford, J. S. (2005). 'Preparing for the first pandemic of the 21st century'. *The Lancet Infectious Diseases*, 5, 129–31.

Oxford, J. S., Bossuyt, S. and Lambkin, R. (2003) 'A new infectious disease challenge: Urbani severe acute respiratory syndrome (SARS) associated coronavirus', *Immunology* 109:3, 326–8.

Oxford, J. S., Lambkin, R., Sefton, A., Daniels, R., Elliot, A., Brown, R. and Gill, D. (2005a) 'A hypothesis: the conjunction of soldiers, gas, pigs, geese and horses in northern France during the Great War provided the conditions for the emergence of the "Spanish" influenza pandemic of 1918–1919', *Vaccine*, 23: 940–5.

Oxford, J. S., Manuguerra, C., Kistner, O., Linde, A., Kunze, M., Lange, W., Schweiger, B., Spala, G., Rebelo de Andrade, H., Perez Brena, P. R., Beytout, J., Brydak, L., Caraffa de Stefano, D., Hungnes, O., Kynel, J., Montomoli, E., Gil de Miguel, A., Vranckx and R. Osterhaus, A. (2005b) 'A new European perspective of influenza pandemic planning with a particular focus on the role of mammalian cell culture vaccines', *Vaccine*, 23, 5440–9.

*Pacific News Taiwan* (various).

*People's Daily* (various).

Pepys, S. ([1660-1669]1993) *The Shorter Pepys*, London: Penguin Classics.

Perrow, C. (1984) *Normal Accidents: Living with High-Risk Technologies*, New York: Basic Books.

—— (2007) *The Next Catastrophe: Reducing Our Vulnerabilities to Natural, Industrial, and Terrorist Disasters*, Princeton: Princeton University Press.

Phillips, H. and Killingray, D. (eds) (2003) *Spanish Influenza Pandemic of 1918–19: New Perspective*, New York: Routledge.

Plant, A. (2003) 'SARS and public health: lesson for future epidemics', in Tommy Koh, A. Plant and Lee, E. H. (eds) *The New Global Threat: Severe Acute Respiratory Syndrome and Its Impacts*. Singapore: World Scientific Publishing Company, xiii–xxiv.

Posner, R. A. (2004) *Catastrophe: Risk and Response*, Oxford: Oxford University Press.

Poutanen, S. M., Low, D. E and Henry, B., *et al.* (2003) 'Identification of Severe Acute Respiratory Syndrome in Canada', *New England Journal of Medicine*, 348:20, 1995–2005.

Pressman, S. (1999) *Fifty Major Economists*, London: Routledge.

Quarantelli, E. L. (2006) 'Catastrophes, are different from disasters: some implications for crisis planning, and managing drawn from Katrina', *Understanding Katrina: Perspectives from the Social Sciences*, SSRC, New York, available at http://understandingkatrina.ssrc.org/Quarantelli (accessed on 20 July 2006).

Rawski, T. G. (2006) 'SARS and China's eonomy', in Kleinman, A. and Watson, J. (eds) *SARS in China: Prelude to Pandemic?*, Stanford: Stanford University Press, 105–21.

Reuters report (2003), 'Hong Kong health system on brink as SARS spreads', April 10, 11:48 am ET.

Rigger, S. (2004) 'Taiwan in 2003: plenty of clouds, few silver linings', *Asian Survey*, 44:1, 182–87.

Saich, T. (2006) 'Is SARS China's Chernobyl or much ado about nothing?', in Kleinman, A. and Watson, J. (eds) *SARS in China: Prelude to Pandemic?*, Stanford: Stanford University Press, 71–104.

SARS Expert Committee (2003) *SARS in Hong Kong: From Experience to Action*, Hong Kong: Government Logistics Department.

Schnur, A. (2006) 'The Role of the World Health Organization in combating SARS, focusing on the efforts in China', in Kleinman, A. and Watson, J. (eds) *SARS in China: Prelude to Pandemic?*, Stanford: Stanford University Press, 31–52.

Seno, A. and Reyes, A. (2004) 'Unmasking the SARS: voices from the epicentre', in Christine Loh and Civic Exchange (eds) *At the Epicentre: Hong Kong and the SARS Outbreak*, Hong Kong: Hong Kong University Press, 1–15.

Shakespeare, W. (2005 edition) *Romeo and Juliet*, Oxford: Oxford University Press.

Shellum, S. (2003) 'Pressure Cooking: A SARS Case Study', 25 June. http://www.hotelresource.com/article6600.html

*Sing Tao Daily* (various).

Singapore Department of Statistics, *Economic Survey of Singapore 2003*, website (accessed on 12 October 2003).

Singapore Ministry of Manpower, *Manpower Research and Statistics*, website (accessed on 12 October 2003).

Singapore Tourism Board, *Research and Statistical Information*, website (accessed on 12 October 2003).

—— (2003) *Weekly fact sheets*, April to May.

Singer, M. (1998) 'Forging a political economy of AIDS' in M. Singer (eds) *The Political Economy of AIDS*, New York: Baywood Publishing Company, 3–31.

Siu, A. and Wong, R. (2004) *Economic Impact of SARS: The Case of Hong Kong*, Hong Kong, Hong Kong Institute of Economics and Business Strategy, Working Paper 1084.

Slovic, P. (1987) 'Perception of risk'. *Science*, 236, 280–5.

Smith, A. ([1776]1904) *An Inquiry into the Nature and Causes of the Wealth of Nations*, Cannan 5th Edition, London: Methuen.

Smith, G. J. D., Fan, X. H., Wang, J., Li, K. S., Qin, K., Zhang, J. X., Vijaykrishna, D., Cheung, C. L., Huang, K., Rayner, J. M., Peiris, J. S. M., Chen, H., Webster, R. G. and Guan, Y. (2006) 'Emergence and predominance of an H5N1 influenza variant in China', *Proceedings of the National Academy of Sciences*, 103:45, 16936–41.

Solinger, D. J. (2003) 'State and society in urban China in the wake of the 16th Party Congress', *China Quarterly*, 173, 943–60.

*South China Morning Post* (various).

State Statistical Bureau (2003) *China Labour Statistical Yearbook 2003*, Beijing: China Statistics Press.

—— (2003) 'China economic cycle monthly report, September 2003', in Hu Angang and Hu Linlin, *A Review of China's Health and Development from the Perspective of SARS*, a paper presented at the celebrations of the twentieth anniversary of the founding of the China Health Economics Society on 6 November, Beijing.

Steinberg, T. (2003) *Acts of God: The unnatural History of Natural Disaster* in America, Oxford: Oxford University Press.

*Straits Times* (various).

Swiss Re (2006) 'Hurricanes hardly happened, so it's a good year for the insurers', 21 December: Corporate Report.

Swiss Re, policy statements, various company websites, www.swissre.com.

*Ta Kung Pao* (various).

*Taipei Times* (various).

*Taiwan Ribao* (various).

Taleb N. N. (2007) *The Black Swan: The Impact of the Highly Improbable*, London: Allen lane penguin.

Tambyah, P. A. (2002) 'The SARS Outbreak: how many reminders do we need?', *Journal of the Singapore Medical Association*, 44:4, 165–204.

Tang F. C. (2003) 'Survey shows SARS impact on China's economy, 6 May 2003', Online. http://www.china.org.cn (accessed on 10 September).

Taylor, M. (2003) 'SARS: Taiwan Thinks the Unthinkable', *Asia Times*, 20 May.

*The Asian Wall Street Journal* (various).

*The China Post* (various).

*The Economist* (various).

*The Taiwan Economic News* (various).

Thucydides (1954 edition) *The History of the Peloponnesian War: Revised Edition*. London: Penguin Classics.

Tomlinson, B. and Cockram, C. (2003) 'SARS: experience at Prince of Wales Hospital, Hong Kong', *The Lancet*, 361:3, 1486–7.

Torrington, D. and Tan, C. H. (1994) *Human Resource Management for Southeast Asia*, Singapore: Prentice Hall.

Tourism Commission, *Tourism Performance*. Online. http://www.info.gov.hk/tc/tourism_per/index.htm (accessed 29 July 2003).

*TTG Daily News*, (2003) 'Taking extra precautions', 7 May.

United Nations International Strategy for Disaster Reduction (2007) *Guidelines for National Platform for Disaster Risk Reduction*, Geneva: UN/ISDR.

US Census Bureau (1920) 'Special tables of mortality from influenza and pneumonial in Indiana, Kansas, and Philidelphia, Pa., September 1 to December 1, 1918'. *US Census Reports*, Washington, DC: US Census Bureau.

*USA Today* (various).

*Wall Street Journal* (various).

Watson, J. L. (2006) 'SARS and the consequences for globalization', in Kleinman, A. and Watson, J. (eds) *SARS in China: Prelude to Pandemic?*, Stanford: Stanford University Press, 196–204.

Watts, S. (1997) *Epidemics and History: Disease, Power and Imperialism*, New Haven and London: Yale University Press.

Weinstein, R. A. (2004) 'Planning for epidemics – the lessons of SARS', *New England Journal of Medicine*, 350:23, 2332–4.

*Wen Wei Po* (various).

Whaley, F. and Mansoor, O. D. (2006) 'SARS chronology', in World Health Organization (eds) *SARS: How a Global Epidemic was Stopped*. Manila: World Health Organization, 3–49.

WHO (2002) 'Influenza: preparedness for the inevitable', *Global Defence Against the Infectious Disease*, 68–73.

—— (2003a) *Summary Table of SARS Cases by Country, 1 November 2002–7 August 2003*, WHO: Geneva. Online. http://www.who.int/csr/sars/country/en/country/2003_08_15.pdf (accessed 15 August 2003).

—— (2003b) Press Release (various).

—— (2003c) *SARS Update 64*, 23 May 2003, WHO: Geneva.

—— (2003d) *The World Health Report: Shaping the Future*, WHO: Geneva. Online. http://www.who.int/whr/2003/chapter5/en/index5.html (accessed 11 September 2006).

—— (2003e) 'Influenza' Fact Sheet, No. 211 http://www.who.int/mediacentre/factsheets/fs211/en/index/html (accessed on 10 August 2003).

—— (2004a) 'China's latest SARS outbreak has been contained, but biosafety concerns remain – update 7'. http://www.who.int/csr/don/2004_05_18a/en/print.html (accessed on 12 June 2004).

—— (2004b) *Unprecedented spread of avian influenza requires broad collaboration*. http://www.who.int/mediacentre/news/releases/2004/pr7/en/ (accessed on 23 Februrary 2004).

—— (2006a) 'Avian influenza ("bird flu") – Fact sheet' https://www.who.int/mediacentre/factsheets/avian_influenza/en/index.html (accessed on 15 June 2006).

—— (2006b) 'Epidemic and pandemic alert and response' http://www.who.int/csr/en/ (accessed on 15 June 2006).

Wilder-Smith, A., Goh, K. T. and Paton, N. I. (2003) 'Experience of Severe Acute Respiratory Syndrome in Singapore: importation of cases, and defence strategies at the airport', *Journal of Travel Medicine*, 10:5, 259–62.

Wong J., Chan, S. and Liang, R. (2004) 'The impact of SARS on Greater China economies', in Wong J. and Zheng Y. (eds) *The SARS Epidemic: Challenges to China's Crisis Management*. Hong Kong: Hong Kong University Press, 11–44.

World Tourism Organization, *China Tourism Statistics*, http://www.cnto.org/chinastats.asp (accessed 1 November 2006).

World Travel and Tourism Council (2003) *Singapore: Special SARS Analysis – Impact on Travel and Tourism*, London, United Kingdom: WTTC.

*Xinhua* (various).

*Xinhua News Agency* (various).

Zhang, H (2006) 'Making light of the dark side' in Kleinman, A. and Watson, J. (eds) *SARS in China: Prelude to Pandemic?*, Stanford: Stanford University Press, 148–70.

*Zhongguo shibao* (various).

Zinsser H. (1935) *Rats, Lice and History*, Boston: Little, Brown & Co.

# Index

eBooks – at www.eBookstore.tandf.co.uk

## A library at your fingertips!

eBooks are electronic versions of printed books. You can store them on your PC/laptop or browse them online.

They have advantages for anyone needing rapid access to a wide variety of published, copyright information.

eBooks can help your research by enabling you to bookmark chapters, annotate text and use instant searches to find specific words or phrases. Several eBook files would fit on even a small laptop or PDA.

**NEW:** Save money by eSubscribing: cheap, online access to any eBook for as long as you need it.

### Annual subscription packages

We now offer special low-cost bulk subscriptions to packages of eBooks in certain subject areas. These are available to libraries or to individuals.

For more information please contact webmaster.ebooks@tandf.co.uk

We're continually developing the eBook concept, so keep up to date by visiting the website.

## www.eBookstore.tandf.co.uk